I0235157

Nordic Mythologies

Interpretations, Intersections, and Institutions

THE WILDCAT CANYON ADVANCED SEMINARS

Publication Series
Occasional Monograph Series
Cultural Studies
Folklore
Mythology
Nordic Studies
Classic Studies Reprints

MYTHOLOGY

Volume 1

Nordic Mythologies

Interpretations, Intersections, and Institutions

Edited by

Timothy R. Tangherlini

NORTH PINEHURST PRESS
BERKELEY • LOS ANGELES

Publisher's Cataloging-in-Publication data

Nordic mythologies : interpretations , intersections , and institutions / edited by Timothy R. Tangherlini .

p. cm.
ISBN 978-0-692-32886-6
Includes bibliographical references and index.
Series : The Wildcat canyon advanced seminars.

1. Mythology, Norse. 2. Mythology, Norse --History and criticism. I. Tangherlini, Timothy R. II. Series.

PT7114.5.L56 .N67 2014
839/.609 --dc23 2014920625

COVER PHOTOGRAPHY BY OLAV SEJERØE AND JØRGEN LARSEN
COVER IDEA BY BRETT LANDENBERGER
COVER DESIGN BY LORAINE VILBARNE

North Pinehurst Press
Berkeley and Los Angeles

Printed on acid-free paper

ISBN: 978-0-692-32886-6
LCCN: 2014920625

Contents

Introduction

Timothy R. Tangherlini

Nordic mythology—with its remarkable stories of gods, giants and the catastrophic end of the world—has captured the imaginations of scholars and the public alike for centuries, keeping the Medieval North front and center in the popular imagination. Hollywood blockbuster films, such as *Thor*, contribute to the popularity of the Nordic mythological world while, at the same time, proliferate myriad misunderstandings about that same world. The goal of this volume, and the conference from which it sprang, is to initiate meaningful dialogue on the Nordic mythological world while recognizing the shifting interpretive and cultural terrain on which current scholarship rests.

The Nordic mythological world is often conceptualized as a homogeneous one, with little change in space and time. This convenient narrative of temporal and geographic homogeneity and predictable structure gained popularity already in the Scandinavian Renaissance, with the important works of writers such as Olaus Magnus and Arngrímur Jónsson, whose engagement with Nordic mythology was intended to counteract the general notion of the Nordic region as barbaric and strange, a view that prevailed in the rest of Europe. Subsequent Scandinavian humanists in the late Renaissance were inspired by this work, and used Nordic mythology to reveal the heroism, intelligence, and bravery of the early Medieval Scandinavians. By the mid eighteenth century, this narrative of a homogeneous mythological world was widely accepted, and enthusiastically embraced not only in the Nordic countries, but also in the rest of continental Europe (to wit Thomas Carlyle's 1840 lectures on "Heroes, Hero-worship and the Heroic in History"). This representation was greatly developed through the nineteenth century, and refined by later scholars such as Georges Dumézil, Jan de Vries, and E. O. Gabriel Turville-Petre in the early and mid twentieth century. Indeed, it has been the dominant narrative thread in the interpretation of Nordic mythology for most of the past century.

This interpretive narrative generally installs a straightforward interpretation of the mythology as one based on a tripartite (and easily recognizable) structure with Óðinn as the magical-religious god, Þórr the warrior god, and Freyr the fertility god. Various institutions including academic, religious, literary, and even cinematic ones, political parties, and governments have deployed this overarching narrative as part of their largely ideological projects. The narrative, however, only tells a small part of the story. It misses the complexity and dynamism of the Nordic region in the middle ages, occludes the shifting roles of the gods and stories about the gods in popular belief and religious practice, selectively considers the archaeological record, downplays the influence of medieval literary texts (vernacular, classical and biblical) on the written mythology, ignores the lively cultural exchange between the Scandinavians and their immediate neighbors—most prominently the Sámi but also populations in Ireland, the Orkneys, Greenland, and Britain—and dismisses the important interplay between the "folkloric" and the "mythic." If one takes these factors into account, the actual narrative of Nordic Mythology that emerges is one of surprising complexity, contradiction and cultural dynamism.

This volume contributes to recent work in mythological studies that seek to explore this complexity, these contradictions, and this overall dynamism. Here we engage Nordic mythologies from the earliest medieval archaeological record through more recent reconfigurations of those mythologies in interpretive texts, folklore, and popular culture. The complexity of the Nordic mythological realm and its resonances throughout Northern Europe is widely attested in the archaeological, textual, folkloric, and cultural record during the past millennium. Indeed, the evidence of this complexity is so overwhelming that we should no longer speak of "Nordic Mythology" *per se* but rather "Nordic Mythologies."

The essays in this volume interrogate the complexities of the Nordic mythological realms from the scholarly perspectives of folkloristics, anthropology, religious studies, cultural history, linguistics, archaeology, philology, film criticism, textual criticism, and the history of ideas. In the essays presented here, we explore how religious and secular institutions have imposed differing narratives of interpretation on this mythological world, and explore the intersections of the Scandinavian realm with the realms of other belief groups and other modes of cultural production.

The volume is organized into three main sections—"Myths, Gods, Giants", "Comparative Historical Focus", "Archaeology and the Cosmos"—with a fourth, more speculative section—"Virtual Mythology"—at the end. These divisions are by no means deterministic, but rather "fuzzy" categories, the boundaries of which are transgressed by the perspectives of the various authors. Because of the theoretical overlap of many of the essays, a fairly extensive index is included to allow for the discovery of intersections across these arbitrary divisions. As noted, the volume is based on a conference, but should not be seen as a simple "conference proceedings" volume, as the essays presented here are substantively more elaborated than the original presentations on which they are based.

The conference, held April 27-28 2012 at the University of California, Los Angeles, included several additional presentations, and a slightly different organization. At the conference, the papers were arranged into six sessions of three to four presentations each, interspersed with a "graduate student roundtable" and preceded by two days of "workshops" targeted at students taking courses in "Old Norse-Icelandic Language and Literature", "Mythology", and "Scandinavian Folklore." Unfortunately, not all of the papers from the conference are included in this volume—several had been promised to other publication venues, while others were of a preliminary nature and deemed by their authors not quite ready for consideration for publication.

A brief overview of the conference provides a taste of the broad reach of these papers; in this overview, the papers that have not been included in the volume receive a bit more attention, as they added significantly to the complexity of the investigations that characterized the conference, and the formal and informal discussions that sprang up around these papers.

The first conference session, entitled, "Myth, Gods, and Giants", included presentations by Margaret Clunies Ross (University of Sydney), John Lindow (University of California, Berkeley), Jens Peter Schjødt (Århus University), and John McKinnell (Durham University). McKinnell, in a presentation entitled "Useless Wisdom: The Paradox of *Alvíssmál* ", proposed that *Alvíssmál* can be read as a parody of the Odinic wisdom contest known from other myths. In his reading, the wisdom that the dwarf Alvíss presents is of little or no value, and the simplistic listing of unimportant knowledge—largely names for natural phenomena—leads to the dwarf's demise. McKinnell extends his analysis proposing that the "race of dwarves" derives power from the dark, and points out that Þórr's victory is based on trickery that gets the dwarf to waste this power until the light of the sun kills him.

The second session, entitled, "Archaeology, Historical Events and Nordic Mythology", included presentations by Rudolf Simek (University of Bonn), Anders Andrén (University of Aberdeen), and Stefan Brink (University of Aberdeen). Simek, in his presentation, "The Sanctuaries in Uppsala and Lejre and Their Literary Antecedents", investigated the literary relationship between Thietmar of Merseburg's and Adam of Bremen's descriptions of the sanctuary in Uppsala and Lejre and teases out possible written resources that these two German clerics may have had at their disposal as they wrote their descriptions. He then couples this to an evaluation of the broader models that existed throughout Europe for this type of work.

The third session of the conference, "Myth, Magic, and Folklore", included presentations by Stephen Mitchell (Harvard University), Terry Gunnell (University of Iceland), and Catherina Raudvere (University of Copenhagen). While only Gunnell's presentation is presented in this volume, the two other presentations also emphasized the complex interaction between mythology on the one hand, and the conceptualization and practice of magic on the other. Mitchell's presentation, entitled "Charming Sex: *Skírnismál*, the Orkneys, and the Faroes", focused on the verb *serða*, and the semantic range attributed that word. Based on evidence from the Orkneys and the Faroes, he suggests that the interpretation of the term be expanded to include magically-induced heterosexual sex. Raudvere, in, "To Meet Hardship, Illness and Malice: Valter W. Forsblom and his Documentation of Healing Practices in Swedish Speaking Finland", offered a long-term perspective on healing practices in Swedish speaking Finland, with a primary focus on Forsblom's extensive recordings of healing practices from the early part of the twentieth century.

The fourth conference session, under the rubric, "Nordic Mythology in Comparative Historical Focus", is the only session presented in its entirety here. For the sake of thematic consistency, however, Judy Quinn's presentation has been moved to the first section of this volume. The fifth session, "Nordic Mythology and Edda", included presentations by Joseph Harris (Harvard University), Gísli Sígurðsson (University of Iceland), and Merrill Kaplan (The Ohio State University). Kaplan, in her presentation, "*Vaxinn vǫllum hæri*: The Mistilteinn in *Vǫluspá*", provided a convincing reading of *Vǫluspá* that makes the problematic description of the mistletoe in the poem far less of a problem. Here, the current form of mistletoe known from nature is argued to be a transformation of the plant subsequent to its fatal deployment in the death of Baldr. This close reading of the poem, in which Kaplan adduces this dynamic transformation of the plant with reference to the motif A2720: Plant Characteristics as Punishment, solves a thorny problem that has confounded scholars for quite some time—how could a simple sprig of mistletoe as we know the plant today be used to fashion a missile that could kill a god?

The sixth conference session, "Nordic Mythology and Contemporary Culture", brought the conversation around to the impact of Nordic mythologies—and mythological thinking in general—to the current age. Presentations in this session included ones by Kendra Willson (University of Helsinki), Jackson Crawford (UCLA), and Ulf Palmenfelt (University College Gotland). Willson, in her presentation, "Views of Myth in Two California Rings", explored the Los Angeles and San Francisco operas' productions of Wagner's "Ring Cycle", both of which were modern departures from Wagner's original production. The Los Angeles ring, deeply introspective and wildly abstract, offers a counterpoint to the more literal San Francisco production. That latter production sets the cycle in the context of the American foundation myth of westward expansion and concludes with the environmental catastrophe of climate change. Willson, in her reading of these two complementary productions, suggests that these radical reimaginings of the Ring Cycle, and the myths on which Wagner based it, emphasize the cultural flexibility of these narratives and their ability to create meaning for modern viewers and listeners. Crawford, in a presentation entitled, "The Language of the Norse Gods (and Their Worshipers) in Popular Culture", explored how pop culture—from film to comics to literature—has represented early Scandinavian languages and runic inscriptions in their diverse media.

Ultimately, this volume is intended to capture some of the energy and dynamism that characterized the conference while opening up debate and new directions for inquiry. The contributors to this volume were challenged to confront orthodoxy and present challenging new interpretations to the material with which they work. Admittedly, a project with as broad a scope as this current one can never be comprehensive. Rather than closing off discussion, this volume is intended to stimulate it.

Producing a volume such as this always requires the collaboration of a great number of people. I would like to thank the conference participants who are either represented in these pages or whose contributions are discussed above. Because of their efforts, the conference was a remarkable success, attracting hundreds of participants and audience members from across southern California and beyond. I would also like to thank the formal discussants, Joseph F. Nagy (UCLA) and Úlfar Bragason (University of Iceland), who guided the discussions and structured the question and answer sessions into vibrant forums. Similarly, I would like to thank Massimo Ciavolella, director of UCLA's Center for Medieval and Renaissance Studies, who acted as the main host of the conference, and David Schaberg, Dean of the Humanities division, who opened the conference and provided unwavering support for this project.

At the Center for Medieval and Renaissance Studies, Karen Burgess, Benay Furtivo, and Brett Landenberger, provided attentive and expert support. Brett Landenberger also deserves credit for designing the program, and assisting with the cover design for this volume. I would like to thank Arne Lunde, chair of the Scandinavian Section at UCLA, for assisting with the organization of the conference, and with help in securing funds for the event. The staff of the Royce Administration Group, including Gina White and Dacia Imakura, deserves thanks for assisting with processing all the reimbursements related to this project. Funding for the project, including the conference, was generously provided by Norden: The Nordic Council of Ministers, The Ahmanson Foundation, UCLA's Center for Medieval and Renaissance Studies, UCLA's Scandinavian Section, and the UCLA Humanities Division.

I would like to thank all the authors whose hard work, attention to detail, patience, and good humor have carried me through this project. I would also like to thank our anonymous reviewers who provided guidance on individual essays, and the volume as a whole. Their unrecognized work has made this volume all the stronger. The editorial board of the Wildcat Canyon Advanced Seminars also deserves recognition. Their vision of bringing the best scholarship in Nordic studies rapidly to publication in affordable volumes is an important corrective to the market-driven publishing industry, which is marred by shrinking opportunities for the publication of scholarship that does not have broad commercial appeal. The staff of North Pinehurst Press has been a great partner, and they deserve kudos for their rapid turnaround on production issues, and their good-natured willingness to entertain even the smallest of questions. With a project as complex as the current one, certain infelicities are bound to have crept into the final manuscript—I take full responsibility for these (and apologize for them). Finally, I would like to thank my wife Margaret, my daughter Isabella, and my son Magnus for their patience, good cheer, constant support, and love.

Myths, Gods, Giants

Mythic Narrative Modes as Exemplified in the Story of Þórr's Journey to Geirrøðr (and His Daughters)

John Lindow

Myths comprise more or less abstract plot structures that are made concrete by variants. In oral cultures these variants are performances, and each is unique. Each could be analyzed in any number of ways, and groups of variants could profitably be compared. The received Old Norse mythology, on the other hand, is a textual tradition, and most myths are instantiated in just one or two variants. Only a few myths show multiple variants, and what I will here call the Geirrøðr material is among those with the largest number. My purpose in this essay is to isolate the narrative modes employed in these variants, which in turn may represent the narrative modes available to those who transmitted Old Norse mythology.

I begin with an episode found in Morkinskinna, Hulda-Hrokkinskinna, and Flateyjarbók and often separately edited as *Sneglu-Halla þáttr*. Although the versions differ somewhat, they agree on the main points (for the Morkinskinna text see the edition of Ármann Jakobsson and Þórður Ingi Guðjónsson (2011: 271); translation by Andersson and Gade 2000: 244-45; for the composite *Sneglu-Halla þáttr* see Þorleifur Jónsson 1904 and Jónas Kristjánsson 1956). King Haraldr harðráði and the poet Þjóðólfr Árnason are walking down the street when they observe a quarrel between a tanner and an ironsmith. The king orders the skald to make verses about the quarrel, letting one man be Þórr and the other Geirrøðr in one, and Sigurðr and Fáfnir in the other. The order of the two stanzas varies in the manuscripts, but that is not significant for the points I wish to make here. First, the juxtaposition of the two subjects suggests something like equal renown for the two monster-slayings, and Sigurðr's dragon-slaying was perhaps the most widely known act within heroic legend, parallel in renown, perhaps, to Þórr's duel with the Midgard serpent. The juxtaposition of the two stanzas thus suggests a certain fame for Þórr's encounter with Geirrøðr. Sigurðr's dragon-slaying could be pictured both with the rest of the story (so the Hylestad portal) and without (so the Ramsundsberg carving). So, I will argue on the basis of the textual tradition, might Þórr's encounter with Geirrøðr.

The stanza pitting Þórr against Geirrøðr runs as follows, in Diana Whaley's edition and translation.

Varp ór þrætu þorpi
Þórr smiðbelgja stórra
hvapteldingum hǫldnum
hafra kjǫts at jǫtni.
Hljóðgreipum tók húða
hrøkkviskafls af afli
glaðr við galdra smiðju
Geirrøðr síu þeiri.

The Þórr <god> of huge forge-bellows [SMITH] flung jaw-lightnings [INSULTS] from his quarrel hamlet [MOUTH] at the proud giant of goats' flesh [TANNER]. The cheerful Geirrøðr <giant> of the curving scraper of hides [TANNER] took in with his sound-grabbers [EARS] that molten substance of the smithy of spells [MOUTH > INSULTS], powerfully. [Whaley ed. and trans 2009: 169]

Þórr's name is the base word of the kenning for the ironsmith (*Þórr smiðbelgja stórra*), and Geirrøðr's name is the baseword of the kenning for the tanner (*húða hrøkkviskafls Geirrøðr*). Þjóðólr fashions the ironsmith's insults as molten metal that Þórr threw at Geirrøðr: *hjapteldingar* "jaw-lightnings" in the first helming and *sía smiðra galdra* "molten substance of the smithy of songs" in the second, and he has Þórr hurl it in the first helming and the giant receive it in the second. Thus the mode of Þórr's killing of Geirrøðr stands out in this variant as a—or the—salient feature of the story.

Haraldr harðráði had ample skaldic interests, and it is not hard to imagine that he might have known the myth of Þórr and

Geirrøðr in the late tenth-century form given it by Eilífr Goðrúnarson in *Þórsdrápa*. *Skáldatal* makes Eilífr a skald of Hákon Sigurðarson jarl of Hlaðir (Heimir Pálsson ed. 2012:110), and Edith Marold has advanced an argument, convincing in my opinion, that the best way to understand the rather strange if copious ethnic kennings for giants in the poem is as part of an encomium to Hákon (Marold 1998; see also Marold 2007). Here, however, I will focus on plot. The following summary agrees with that of Marold (2007), but I omit the stanza numbers while we await Marold's edition in the new skaldic project, which will introduce new numbering.[1] The first three strophes of *Þórsdrápa* indicate that Loki lied to get Þórr on the road to Geirrøðr and that Þjálfi accompanied him. Seven stanzas describe the crossing of the river, made difficult by giantesses. Then come two stanzas in which Þórr and Þjálfi kill giants; then two in which they enter a giant house; Þórr is threatened by giantesses, and he breaks their backs. Now come four stanzas containing the struggle between Þórr and Geirrøðr with the molten metal we have just seen, and Þórr kills Geirrøðr. In the final two stanzas of the summary, Þórr kills additional giants. Here we have the opposite extreme from þjóðólfr's stanza, that is, a full story with motivation and multiple episodes, with a narrative weight, at least as indicated by the number of stanzas devoted to it, on the difficult crossing of the river rather than on the slaying of Geirrøðr.

Þórsdrápa is the oldest and fullest version of the myth. I want to draw attention to two moments in the text, stanzas 12-13 and 20-21 in Marold's new numbering. The first pair occurs, apparently, after Þórr and Þjálfi have crossed the river.[2]

Ok sifuna síðan
sverðs liðhatar gerðu
hlífar borðs við Hǫrða
harðgleipnis dyn *barða,
áðr hylriðar *hæði
hrjóðendr fjǫru þjóðar
við skyld-Breta skytju
skálleik Heðins reikar. (Faulkes ed. 1998, 28)

And then the allied sword's help haters waged shield's hard-fetter-[strap-]board's [shield's] din [battle] against slope-Hords [giants], before the pool-riders [river-crossers, Thor and Thialfi], destroyers of the strand-people [giants], performed Hedin's parting-bowl-[helmet-]game [battle] with the cave's kindred-Briton [Geirrod]. [Faulkes transl. 1995: 84.]

Dreif með dróttar kneyfi
(dólg- Svíðjóðar *kólgu,
sótti -ferð á flótta)
flesdrótt í vá nesja,
þá er funhristis fasta
(flóðrifs Danir) stóðu
(knáttu) Jólnis ættir
(útvés fyrir lúta).
(Faulkes ed. 1998, 28)

The hostile troop [giants] of Sweden of frost [Scythia] scattered before the ness-court [giants] shatterer. The slab-court [giants] took to flight in terror when the kin of Iolnir's [Odin's] blaze-wielder [sword-wielder, warrior] stood firm; the Danes [giants] of the distant flood-rib [rock] sanctuary [Giantland] had to bow before them. (Faulkes transl. 1995, 84-85)

The action in these stanzas follows the crossing of the river (*síðan* in the first helmingr of stanza 12) and precedes the duel with Geirrøðr (*áðr* in the second). Þórr and Þjálfi do battle with giants and kill them (*lúta*) in stanza 13. These stanzas cannot refer to the upcoming encounter with the giantesses, not only because the verbs are in the past tense, but also because the next stanza tells us that our heroes entered the abode of the giants, and that is where the encounter takes place.

The second pair of stanzas (20-21 in Marold's edition) to which I want to draw attention comes after Þórr has slain Geirrøðr.

Glaums niðjum fór gǫrva
gramr með dreyrgum hamri;
of salvanið-Synjar
sigr hlaut *arinbauti.
Komat tvíviðar tývi
tollur karms sá er harmi
brautarliðs of beitti

bekk- fall jǫtuns -rekka.
(Faulkes ed. 1998, 29)

Extremely angry, he destroyed with bloody hammer Glaum's descendants [giants]. The beater [Thor] of the frequenter [giant] of hearth-stone-Syn's [giantess's] dwelling gained victory. No lack of support befell the double-wood-stave [bow-tree, warrior], the god of the wagon, who inflicted grief on the giant's bench-fellows. [Faulkes transl. 1995: 85]

*Herblótinn vá hneitir
hógbrotningi skógar
undirfjálfrs af *afli
álfheims bliku kálfa.
Ne liðfǫstum Lista
látrval-Ryg‹j›ar máttu
aldrminkanda *aldar
Ellu steins of bella. (Faulkes ed. 1998, 30)

Worshipped by multitudes, he who overcomes the calves [giants] of the secret cave of elf-world's shine [in the darkness of mountains] wielded the forest's handy fragment [Grid's pole] mightily]. Nor could the Rugians of falcon-lair-Lister [mountain-giants] stand up to the trusty stone-Ella [giant] people's life-curtailer. (Faulkes transl. 1995, 86)

Once again, Þórr kills giants, outside the main story of the river-crossing and the encounters with the giantesses and Geirrøðr.

In my view a key to understanding the inclusion of these two pairs of stanzas is provided by the two stanzas addressed to Þórr from the late conversion period, probably in Iceland. Snorri cites them in *Skáldskaparmál* and assigns one to Vertrliði Sumarliðason and one to Þorbjǫrn dísarskáld. Indeed, Snorri cites them after explaining Úlfr Uggason's Þórr-kenning *jǫtunn Vimrar-vaðs* ("giant of the Vimur ford"), referring to Þórr's journey to Geirrøðargarðar. I suspect that the reason for including the verses here is that Vetrliði referred to Gjálp, the name of one of the giantesses killed by Þórr on this journey according to Snorri, and that both verses belonged together (and perhaps traveled together in oral tradition?) in their virtually unique use of the second person and listing of the god's victims.

Vetrliði's verse is in *málaháttr* and is free from skaldic ornamentation.

Leggi brauzt þú Leiknar,
*lamðir Þrívalda,
steyptir *Starkeði,
stóttu of Gjálp dauða. (Faulkes ed. 1998, 17)

You broke Leikn's bones, you pounded Thrívaldi, you cast down Starkad, you stood over the dead Gjálp. (Faulkes transl. 1995, 74)

Besides Gjálp, we also know Þrívaldi and Starkaðr.

Þorbjǫrn's stanza is formally *dróttkvætt*, but like Vetrliði's, it uses simple sentence structure and avoids kennings.

Ball í Keilu kolli,
Kjallandi brauzt þú alla,
áðr draptu Lút ok Leiða,
léztu dreyra Búseyru,
*heptir þú Hengjankjǫptu,
Hyrrokkin dó fyrri,
þó vas snemr hin sáma
Svívǫr numin *lífi. (Faulkes ed. 1998, 17)

There was a clang on Keila's crown, you broke Kiallandi completely, before that you slew Lut and Leidi, you made Buseyra bleed, you halted Hengiankiapta, Hyrrokkin died previously, yet was the dusky Svivor's life taken earlier. (Faulkes transl. 1995, 74)

In studying these verses some years ago (Lindow 1988), I stressed the preponderance of female giants on the list of victims and drew attention to the fact that some Þórr myths include slaying of both female and male giants. Here I wish instead to focus initially on what Þórr did to his victims. First Gjálp: he stood over her dead body. *Þórsdrápa* and Snorri agree that the threat the giantesses posed to Þórr came from above, and that he exerted downward pressure to break their backs. Vetrliði places Þórr above Gjálp, but now as an exultant victor, not as someone struggling for his life. Gjálp and Greip were mangled (Saxo gives them tumors to help this idea along), and the late pagan poets who sang praises to Þórr knew of other mangled giant bodies. Þórr broke the bones of Leikn (probably another giantess). He pounded Þrívaldi—that is, he killed him. This must have been a bloody slaying, since in the one other poem using the second person, Bragi addresses Þórr as *sundrkljúfr níu haufða Þrívalda* ("severer of the nine heads of Þrívaldi)." Þorbjǫrn dísarskáld praises similar violence: "There was a clang on Keila's crown [presumably a giantess], you broke Kjallandi completely [possibly a giant] … you made Búseyra bleed [presumably a giantess]." This is close-up, physical combat, dealt out to giantess and giant alike.

Þórsdrápa shares more with these tantalizing fragments, I want to argue, than the physicality of the struggles and the mangling of his victims. If we read the whole poem, once Þórr and Þjálfi get across the river, we have something that is not unlike the catalogue of victims offered up by Vetrliði and Þorbjǫrn. In *Þórsdrápa* Þórr and Þjálfi kill nameless giants; in the direct address fragments, Þórr kills numerous giants and giantesses, most of whom could just as easily, based on the extant textual tradition, have been nameless; in *Þórsdrápa*, Þórr kills giantesses who are—this is important here—never named in the text. Þórr then dispatches Geirrøðr, but after Þórr and Þjálfi kill more nameless giants, and these could be male or female: Glaumr's descendants, Rugians of the mountains, and so forth, could denote beings of either sex. It's not just the mixing of giants and giantesses, or the correspondence of names that are beyond our knowledge with giants who are given no names; it is the back and forth of dead giant or giantess after dead giant or giantess. It seems that alongside stories that would have had a single focus, such as the encounter between Þórr and the Midgard serpent, poets and others familiar with Þórr's dossier could also see him as a kind of serial killer of giants, and they could fashion texts around that idea. I propose to call this an agglutinative mode of mythic narration.

By agglutinating, I mean a textual strategy that focuses more on listing than narrative detail, one that achieves its effect strictly by cumulative means. Cumulation is also behind the numerous Þórr-kennings in *Þórsdrápa* that portray him as "killer of giants," where the giants themselves are famously kenned through the use of ethnic groups as base words. I see this modal variation as captured clearly in the list of Þórr kennings Snorri provides in *Skáldskaparmál*. Many of these rely on his kinship relationships and control of artifacts, but when it comes to giant-slaying, Snorri moved from a single model for serial killer, *dólgr ok bani jǫtna ok trǫllkvinna* ("enemy and killer of giants and troll-women"), with unnamed and unnumbered giants (agglutination) to specific cases, beginning with Hrungnir.

> Hvernig skal kenna Þór? Svá at kalla hann son Óðins ok Jarðar, faðir Magna ok Móða ok Þrúðar, verr Sifjar, stjúpfaðir Ullar, stýrandi ok eigandi Mjǫllnis ok megingjarða, Bilskirnis, verjandi Ásgarðs, Miðgarðs, dólgr ok bani jǫtna ok trǫllkvinna, vegandi Hrungnis, Geirrøðar, Þrívalda, dróttinn Þjálfa ok Rǫsku, dólgr Miðgarðsorms, fóstri Vingnis ok *Hlóru. (Faulkes ed. 1998, 14)

> How shall Thor be referred to? By calling him son of Odin and lord, father of Magni and Modi and Thrud, husband of Sif, stepfather of Ull, ruler and owner of Miollnir and the girdle of might, of Bilskirnir, defender of Asgard, Midgard, enemy and slayer of giants and troll-wives, killer of Hrungnir, Geirrod, Thrivaldi, lord of Thialfi and Roskva, enemy of the Midgard serpent, foster-son of Vingnir and Hlora. (Faulkes transl. 1995, 72)

Alongside this "agglutinative mode," the materials adduced thus far permit postulation of other modes. The stanzas of Vetrliði and Þjóðólfr, and the one in which Bragi addresses Þórr as as *sundrkljúfr níu haufða Þrívalda* ("severer of the nine heads of Þrívaldi") comprise a tiny corpus of second-person praise poetry. Given the state of transmission, we cannot know whether such verses were even conjoined with third-person narrative verse, but what we can state is that the verses of Vetrliði and Þjóðólfr are agglutinative, but Bragi's is not. It runs thus:

> Vel hafið yðrum eykjum

aptr, *Þrívalda,[3] haldit
simbli sumbls of mærum
sundrkljúfr níu haufða.
(Faulkes ed. 1998, 16)

Well have you, cleaver apart of Thrivaldi's nine heads, held back your steeds with notorious giant-feast drinker [Thrym = thunder]. (Faulkes trans. 1995, 73)

The reference is hardly clear, but Bragi praises Þórr not for lopping off Þrívaldi's heads but rather for restraining his transport, perhaps his goats. In any case, there is no sign of agglutinating. Rather, the mythic referent "stands alone," at least as we have the text here.

Þjóðolfr's verse constitutes an extreme version of what we might call a "standalone" mode. Given the natural intertextuality of myth, a "standalone" mode should always be possible, since the various facets of a myth should be latent in any given motif.

My "standalone" and "agglutinative" modes correspond more or less to what Indo-Europeanists have established as hymns (praise of single acts of deities) and "*Aufreihlieder*" ("stringing together poems" or "list poems"); the *Aufreihlieder*, according to F. R. Schröder (1954), briefly refer to a whole group of praiseworthy acts of the deity (see also Schmitt 1967: 52-56, 138-41 and Lindow 1988).[4] Where my "agglutinative" mode differs from Schröder's notion of the *Aufreihlied* is in the lack of specificity of the deeds that are brought together. While Vetrliði's stanza certainly looks like an *Aufreihlied*, with three of the four victims clearly elsewhere in the textual tradition, Þorbjǫrn's stanza has victims mostly unknown from that tradition, and *Þórsdrápa* does not name most of the giants whom Þórr eliminates.

We have *Þórsdrápa* from *Skáldskaparmál*. Snorri cites it after providing his own version of the story (or perhaps summary of the story, so quickly does he tell it). Although the narrative of *Þórsdrápa* accords in general with Snorri's own version of the myth in fundamental ways—the river, the giantesses, the giant, the molten metal—it also show significant differences. These begin at the beginning. Thus Snorri introduces his account of what I've just described as a blood-spattered series of giant-slayings, discriminate and not, as part of a dialogue between Bragi and Ægir.

> Þá mælir Ægir: 'Mikill þótti mér Hrungnir fyrir sér. Vann Þórr meira þrekvirki nokkvot þá er hann átti við trǫll?'
>
> Þá svarar Bragi: 'Mikillar frásagnar er þat vert er Þórr fór til Geirrøðargarða....' [Faulkes ed. 1998: 24]
>
> Then Ægir said: 'Hrungnir seems to me to have been very mighty. Did Thor achieve any greater exploit in his dealings with trolls?'
>
> The Bragi replied: 'The story of how Thor went to Geirrod's courts is worth detailed treatment....' [Faulkes transl. 1995: 81]

Snorri sees this as, in the end, a fight with Geirrøðr, even if there are auxiliary fights along the way. He thus actually conceived of the story as quite like the Hrungnir story, which he had just rehearsed. The opening sequence, with the starving of Loki, obviously is in dialogue with Snorri's version of the alienation of Iðunn, which opens *Skáldskaparmál*, and both recall aspects of the Útgarðaloki story, which is in *Gylfaginning*. The first of these is, finally, Óðinn against Þjazi, and the second is Þórr against Útgarðaloki.

Snorra Edda departs from *Þórsdrápa* right here, at the beginning, in the role of Loki. Indeed, actually Snorri has nearly as much to say about the interaction between Geirrøðr and Loki at the beginning of the story as between Þórr and Geirrøðr at the end. Why should Loki be flying about, and why at Geirrøðargarðar? These motifs ultimately motivate the journey, but they serve to offer up a food crisis—the starvation of Loki—the same mechanism that is found in the story of the alienation of Iðunn (this of course makes Þórr traveling weaponless to Geirrøðr a parallel to Iðunn being delivered to Þjazi). Snorri also has Loki accompany Þórr, but his role is smaller than that of Þjálfi in *Þórsdrápa*, since Þjálfi may have helped Þórr get through the river and also participates in giant slayings. The *stef* of *Þórsdrápa* makes this clear: *skalfa Þórs né Þialfa / þróttar stein við ótta* ("Neither Þórr's nor Þjálfi's valor stone (heart) trembled with fear)" (Faulkes ed. 1998: 28; Faulkes transl. 1995: 84). Snorri also explains the *Gríðar vǫlr* ("staff of Gríðr") that helps Þórr and Loki cross the river, and Þórr's possession of a belt of strength and iron glove, as given by Gríðr, in a scene he places early on the journey. Thus, as in *Hymiskviða*, Þórr benefits from a female donor figure.

Snorri quotes lines of *ljóðaháttr*:

Vaxattu nú, Vímur
alls mik þik vaða tíðir
jǫtna garða í;
veiztu, ef þú vex
at þá vex mér ásmegin
jafnhátt upp sem himinn.
(Faulkes ed. 1998, 25)

Rise not thou now, Vimur, since I desire to wade thee into the giants' courts. Know that if thou risest then will rise the As-strength in me up as high as heaven. (Faulkes transl. 1995, 82)

The Uppsala version adds another verse:

Einu neytta ek
alls megins
jǫtna gǫrðum í,
þá er Gjálp ok Gneip,
døtr Geirraðar,
vildu hefja mik til himins.
(Heimir Pálsson ed. 2012, 96)

Once I used all my strength in giants' courts, when Gjálp and Gneip, daughters of Geirrøðr, tried to lift me to the sky. (Faulkes transl 2012, 97)

These verses accord well with *Þórsdrápa* and in general with the vertical orientation of the parts of the myth that deal with the river and the giantesses, and they indicate that the names of giantesses, not to be found in *Þórsdrápa*, were nevertheless firmly anchored in tradition. They certainly hint at the existence of an Eddic poem about the Geirrøðr material, although its focus cannot now be recovered. If there was such a poem, it might also have included the alliterative line spoken by Þórr: *At ósi skal á stemma* ("At its outlet must a river be stemmed" (Faulkes 1995: 82)). I will return to this phrase below.

Even though he presents the story as a visit to and duel with Geirrøðr, Snorri tells of the slaying of the giantesses and even uses the opportunity for the explanation of supposedly proverbial language: *Reynir er bjǫrg Þórs* ("The rowan is Þórr's salvation"). The giantesses have become one scene in a difficult journey, rather like the journeys of Óðinn into the mountain to Gunnlǫð or Hermóðr's journey to Hel, or perhaps even the exchanges with Skrýmir in the Útgarðaloki story. We might regard this way of presenting the mythology as something like a normal narrative mode, but in order to contrast it with the agglutinative mode, we might rather regard it as a selective mode or focused. By this, I mean selecting or focusing on narrative highlights. Thus Snorri's referring to the myth complex as a whole as about Þórr's journey to Geirrøðargarðar allows him to focus three main events, the river-crossing, the encounter with the giantesses, and the duel with Geirrøðr.

And yet, if Snorri is right about that proverbial language, *reynir er bjǫrg Þórs*, it would seem that the crossing of the river might have functioned as a standalone etiological narrative, to answer the question "why is the rowan Þórr's salvation?" The clearest indication of the ability of parts of the entire story to stand alone is the verse exchange with which I began this essay. Haraldr harðráði asked Þjóðólfr only for the high point, for the moment when, just as Sigurðr faced off against Fáfnir, Þórr cast the fiery ingot at Geirrøðr. That was a highly selective mode for approaching the myth complex of the journey to Geirrøðr.

The inclusion of Gjálp but not Geirrøðr (or the river Vimur) in Vetrliði's stanza might suggest the possibility of Þórr's encounters with the giantesses, too, as a standalone episode. Additional support for this hypothesis might be found in Þórr's words *At ósi skal á stemma.* Yes, they are alliterative and could be from a lost Eddic poem, but alliteration was also a feature of proverbial language, such as *kǫld eru kvenna ráð* ("cold are the counsels of women"), to take but one example. So, hypothetically, there could have been an etiological narrative explaining the origin of another proverbial expression ultimately associated with Þórr.

The giantesses must be salient, since Saxo's skeletal telling of the actual myth includes them. Saxo has the Geirrøðr story in Book VIII of *Gesta Danorum*, in what amounts to doubled form. While on what appears to be a displaced version of the myth with Thorkillus leading an expedition of the king and 300 chosen Danish soldiers, including a dangerous river crossing, the expedition comes to the hall of Geruthus. There they see a wounded old man and three hideous women without strength in their backs. Thorkillus explains that the god Þórr had thrown a burning ingot through the guts of Geruthus and that his thunderbolt had broken the bodies of the women. More molten metal, more crumpled giantesses. But here there are three; the third, Eugen Mogk argued cleverly (Mogk 1924), was the one who made the river swell, at whom Þórr hurled a stone ("At ósi skal á stemma"). Again, the salient features are the crossing of the river, the killing of the giantesses, and the molten duel with Geirrøðr. It is surely worth noting, however, that Saxo may imply that the maiming (or killing, if we are in a world of the dead) of the giantesses came *after* the maiming or killing of Geruthus; at least he presents the two encounters in that order: Geruthus, then the giantesses. This ordering certainly suggests the possibility of "standalone" narratives being conjoined in different ways and might even suggest a version in which killing the giantesses was as important or more important than killing the male giant. Or we might say that Saxo's version is to some degree "agglutinative," that is, inclined more to listing than to ordering. Furthermore, the river-crossing is in the "displaced" myth or frame story and is thus cut off from the myth proper, which Thorkillus recounts to his followers.

Indeed, I have argued in these pages that there was a way of thinking about Þórr's accomplishments that was less linear, more agglutinative, more listing than telling, and that this mode may characterize not only the second-person praise poems but also *Þórsdrápa.* In possibly reversing the order of the killings of Geirrøðr and the giantesses, Saxo's version could suggest that the myths involved with Þórr's journey to Geirrøðr lent themselves easily to the agglutinative mode.

Interestingly, these myths were also easily "displaced," that is, moved into the human world, as with the expedition of Thorkillus and the Danish army. The displaced version of the Geirrøðr material is to be found in *Þorsteins þáttr bæjarmagns*, with many details conforming more or less closely to Saxo's version, but in a comic rather than serious vein. *Þorsteins þáttr* is extant in some four dozen manuscripts, including five vellums from the fourteenth and fifteenth centuries (Simpson 1966: 1), and edited versions are those of Rafn et al. (1827), Guðni Jónsson (1954) and Michael Gößwein (2009) (facsimile of AM 589 in Loth 1977), and translation by Hermann Pálsson and Paul Edwards (1968).

As far as I know, it was Eugen Mogk (1924) who first drew serious attention to the possibility that the Geirrøðr in it could be read as the Geirrøðr of the myths, thus putting Þorsteinn into the position of Þórr and making the better part of *Þorsteins þáttr* a displaced myth.[5] Mogk made this observation in connection with his program to reinterpret Snorri's mythography as the product of a literary school at Reykholt and thus could view *Þorsteins þáttr* as another example of literary reworking of the myths, in this case with significant influence from folktale traditions. Mogk read some motifs as relating generally to Þórr's dossier, such as great size and strength, and the magic stone given him by the dwarf; it has magic powers and, significantly, will return to him when he throws it and thus echoes Mjǫllnir, also obtained from a dwarf. Otherwise Mogk finds the main correspondence in the crossing of a dangerous river and ultimate killing of Geirrøðr with a projectile (the stone).

Strangely, Mogk does not see the manifest similarities with the Útgarðaloki myth and only invokes Útgarðaloki once, at the moment when Geirrøðr, finally able to see Þorsteinn, laughs at his small size. But that's a joke that has already been made:

> Þorsteinn gekk þá á veginn fyrir þá ok heilsaði þeim, en þeir ráku upp hlátr mikinn, ok mælti inn mikli maðr: "Sjaldsénir eru oss þvílíkir menn, eða hvert er nafn þitt, eða hvaðan ertu?" Þorsteinn nefndi sik ok kveðst vera kallaðr bæjarmagn, –"en kyn mitt er í Noregi. Er ek hirðmaðr Óláfs konungs." Inn mikli maðr brosti ok mælti: "Mest er logit frá hirðprýði hans, ef hann hefir engan vaskligri. Þykki mér þú heldr mega heita bæjarbarn en bæjarmagn." (Guðni Jónsson and Bjarni Vilhjálmsson, ed. 1943-44, 3: 403)
>
> Thorstein climbed down to meet them and when he greeted them they all burst out laughing. The tall man said, 'It's not every day that we see someone like you. What's your name, and where are you from?
>
> Thorstein gave his name, and added that he was also known as Mansion-Might. 'My family belongs to Norway, and I'm King Olaf's man.'
>
> The tall man smiled and said, 'This regal splendor of his must be a great lie, if he has nobody braver-looking than you. In my opinion you ought to be called Mansion-Midget, not Mansion-Might.' (Hermann Pálsson and Edwards, transl. 1968, 128)

While it is true that in Gylfaginning Útgarðaloki calls Þórr, like Hugi, a *sveinstauli* "boy," earlier Skrýmir had called him and his (male) companions *kǫgursveinar* ("boys in diapers)," and this insult accords far better with *bæjarbarn* than does *sveinstauli*.

Anyone who reads *Þorsteins þáttr bæjarmagns* will be struck by the many other similarities with the Útgarðaloki story. Geirrøðr's abode looks like a royal hall, and there two barely friendly groups engage in contests, including wrestling and coming to grips with a large drinking horn. The participants, here from both sides, bear names that are transparent, like Hugi and Elli, namely Allsterkr and

Fullsterkr on the side Þorsteinn is aiding and Jökull and Frosti on the hostile side. The names do not accord with characters' essences as they do in the Útgarðaloki story, but they certainly evoke the list of *dramatis personae* in that story.

Nora Chadwick (1964) saw that the journey to giantland in *Þorsteins þáttr bœjarmagns* accorded better with the Útgarðaloki story than with the Geirrøðr story, but she argued that they were one and the same story, which is a level of abstraction that is not helpful at the level of text. Jacqueline Simpson's treatment is more focused on the parallels with the Útgarðaloki story, some of which she sees as the result of Celtic influence. But even though he chose to ignore the similarities with the Útgarðaloki story, Mogk's argument could stand on the ending of the story: Geirrøðr dies by projectile. Saxo has fewer direct similarities in his displaced story, but he does have the giants tossing a ball about.

Characteristic of the displaced texts is what we might term either a broadening of mythic focus or a porousness of mythic boundaries, since the displacements call on both the Geirrøðr and Útgarðaloki materials. While it is certainly true that the Geirrøðr material, especially as Snorri transmitted it, is highly intertextual (like many if not most of the myths he recounts), the displaced versions reveal their source material more directly. This directness corresponds with a stylistic mode that is coarsened by exaggeration (Saxo) or the comic (*Þorsteins þáttr*).

To summarize the evidence from another perspective, the Geirrøðr material appears in the following ways. First, there exists a minimum version: Þórr kills Geirrøðr (Þjóðólfr's stanza).[6] Directly opposed to these are maximum versions with selective focus: In one, Loki causes Þórr to journey; Þórr crosses a deadly river with a companion and the help of a giantess's staff; slays giantesses; kills Geirrøðr; kills other giants before and after (*Þórsdrápa*). In the other, Loki causes Þórr to journey; Þórr crosses a deadly river with a companion and the help of a giantess's staff; slays Greip and Gjálp; kills Geirrøðr (Snorri). Then there is what we might call a reduced version: Þórr maims or kills Geirrøðr and three giantesses (Saxo). Finally, there are displaced versions: a Þórr figure travels with companions (across a dangerous river) to an other world (death, giants); witnesses or encounters giants (Saxo); kills Geirrøðr (*Þorsteins þáttr*). I have argued that this variation in presentation allows distinguishing various modes alongside the usual linear narrative: namely "agglutinative," "selective," and "standalone," and that the displaced modes, too, share certain characteristics of plot and style.

I'd like to end with a bit of speculation about what I called the "agglutinative" mode in *Þórsdrápa* and the Þórr-praisers on the one hand and a possible "standalone" mode on the other hand. Together they would accord perfectly with ekphrasis, in which several scenes would be juxtaposed in plastic art; a viewer could switch from one to another, but at any given moment could gaze only on a single scene. Thus the whole story would simultaneously be present but surrounding the current focus. Such a notion would accord well with such versions of the Geirrøðr story as Snorri's or the displaced version. Praising a god in the second person, on the other hand, whatever physical objects might have been involved, is primarily a verbal business, and we can infer that our two late pre-Christian Icelandic poets went in for quantity. Perhaps Eilífr did the same with *Þórsdrápa* so as to be able to invoke even more ethnic kennings, but perhaps, as I just argued, he knew of an agglutinative way of praising Þórr. If so, it is not inconceivable that this was a late pagan fashion, despite the formal analogues that have been adduced to Indo-European poetry.

Notes

[1] The poem is transmitted mostly in the RTW version of *Skáldskaparmál*, which includes a sequence of nineteen consecutive stanzas following just after the prose version of the story. To these, editors add one stanza found elsewhere in *Skáldskaparmál* and clearly relating to the metallic duel between Þórr and Geirrøðr. Editors reach twenty-one stanzas by appending another stanza from *Skáldskaparmál*, which appears to be the *stef*. According to the project website, Marold also includes between the third and fourth stanza in the RTW poem a stanza from the *Third*

Grammatical Treatise tentatively attributed by Finnur Jónsson to Eilífr Kúlnason; this verse would provide a suitable introduction to the river-crossing incident but does not affect a summary of the plot, and I omit it from the following summary (in accordance with Marold's 2007 summary). In accordance with her view that the poem comprises an encomium to Hákon jarl, she ends with a stanza that Finnur Jónnson edited separately in *Skjaldedigtning* as the sole remaining stanza of a poem addressed to him.

[2] As we await Marold's edition, I quote the version of the following stanzas set forth by Faulkes in his edition of *Skáldskaparmál*, based on R (Faulkes 1998), and his translations in his useful *Snorra Edda* translation (Faulkes 1995).

[3] R has *Þrívaldra* here, but TW have the expected form *Þrívalda* (Faulkes ed. 1998: 137).

[4] "Neben den Hymnen nämlich, welche ausschließlich eine einzige Tat des Gottes und diese dann als seine größte verherrlichen, finden sich andere, die in knapper, andeutender Art eine ganze Anzahl von Taten des betreffenden Gottes rühmend aufzählen und aneinanderreihen, 'Aufreihlieder', wie wir sie kurz nennen wollen" (Schröder 1954: 179).

[5] Ursula Dronke (1968) extended the term "euhemerism" to what I here call displacement—that is, an author putting humans in a plot s/he specifically knows to have been about gods—but "euhemerism" seems to me to be best kept as it is usually used, namely the deification of a human (Lindow forthcoming).

[6] The two Eddic stanzas, plus the alliterative line "At ósi skal á stemma," suggest a lost Eddic poem, but although it told at least of the encounter with the giantesses, we cannot speculate further, and I therefore omit it from this summary.

New Perspectives on the Vanir Gods in pre-Christian Scandinavian Mythology and Religion

Jens Peter Schjødt

Introduction

Scholars within the field of pre-Christian Scandinavian religion and mythology have for more than a century been discussing the fact that there are two quite distinct groups of gods in the pantheon,[1] namely Aesir and Vanir. Although the two groups are united against the beings, representing the forces of chaos, first and foremost the giants, they are, at least to some extent, distinguished in the sources. Thus, whereas the Aesir seem to comprise most of the gods, and constitute the 'in-group', so to speak (cf. Schjødt 2008, 392-6 and 2012a, 190), the Vanir group comprises only three members[2] who are part of the same family, namely Njǫrðr and his children Freyr and Freyja. They are not only mentioned as Vanir, but they are clearly thematized as being distinct from the Aesir, since they have been to war with them in the beginning of time, according to *Vǫluspá* and Snorri. Thus the three Vanir just mentioned, were sent as hostages to the Aesir as part of the peace negotiations (*Ynglinga saga*, Ch. 4). In that sense they are strangers among the Aesir, although they apparently live in complete harmony with them without any enmity during the rest of the mythological time, until Ragnarǫk. But at the functional level the opposition between the groups appears, at first glance at least, to continue, the Vanir having as their main functional areas sexuality and riches, or, in one word, 'wellbeing' for society and individuals, at a mythic as well as at a ritual level. The Aesir, on the other hand, in general,[3] seem to be much more attached to warfare, magic, and royal power.

We shall return to the functional centers of the individual gods below, but this distinction, as mentioned, has been recognized by almost all scholars within the field, although it has been interpreted in quite different ways. Traditionally these interpretations can be classified into two main lines: the historicists who saw the two groups of gods and the war between them as vague memories of an ethnic conflict that should have taken place in a period far back in time, but not defined in any precise way. This group comprises such distinguished scholars of an older generation as Karl Helm (1953, 1955) and Ernst Alfred Philippson (1953), and much more recently Lotte Hedeager (2011), and also, in many ways very distinct from those just mentioned, Lotte Motz (1996) to whom we shall return. The other line of interpretation, which we may term 'structural', has as its main proponents Georges Dumézil (1959), Jan de Vries (1956-57), E. O. Gabriel Turville-Petre (1964). Most more recent scholars (e.g. Schjødt 1991, Clunies Ross 1994, DuBois 1999) have accepted this line of research, although differing in important ways from their predecessors. The main characteristic of this group is the acceptance that both the Aesir and the Vanir were an inherent part of the pre-Christian mythology from very early on. The historicists, on the other hand, claimed that the Vanir gods, or some 'vanir-like' gods, were the autochthonous gods of Scandinavia, and that the Aesir represented a group of intruders.[4] The peace negotiations and the exchange of hostages, from this perspective, thus refer to the society as we know it from the later Iron Age that would comprise the autochthonous as well as the intruding groups (and their gods).

There is, however, at least one thing the representatives of the two scholarly groups have agreed upon, namely that the information in the sources, although we have them mainly from Snorri, about the two 'families' of gods, was constitutive for our perception of the pre-Christian Scandinavian pantheon.

In the following we shall firstly deal with a discussion that has taken place within recent years where it is maintained that the Vanir did not constitute a group of gods in pre-Christian times, and secondly we shall attempt to go a bit deeper into one of the main arguments for this rejection.

Did the Vanir ever exist?

Thus the very notion of the Vanir has recently been challenged by Rudolf Simek who, in an article in the *Retrospective Method Network Newsletter* with the title 'The Vanir: An Obituary' from 2010, having originally been published in 2005, suggests that the notion of the Vanir, as a specific group of gods, in the way we know it from Snorri, was not pre-Christian at all. Rather it was a designation that could be attributed to any god in the pantheon, just as is the case with terms such as *goð, tífar,* and *æsir* together with the less frequent *regin, bǫnd,* and *hǫpt.* All these terms could apparently designate any god in the pantheon, and Simek suggests that this was also the case with the term 'Vanir'. His main argument is that the word 'Vanir' is actually quite rare in skaldic as well as eddic poetry where we have only ten instances (Simek 2010, 12), and they are far from always connected to the three gods whom we usually attribute to the group. This is not much to build a case for the Vanir upon, and Simek therefore also states that (*ibid.*):

> The true reason for their popularity is that Snorri gives us, on the basis of these 10 earlier (or possible earlier) sources more detailed accounts of the role of the Vanir, which have in the past mainly been taken at their face value and made into the family of gods commonly known today.

He then goes on to analyze Snorri's accounts and, without going into the details in his argument, he concludes that the idea of a people called Vanir being situated in Vanaland or Vanaheimr was part of the so called learned pre-history of Scandinavia, and thus explicitly part of the world view of the Middle Ages. It was Snorri's invention, and had no background in pre-Christian times. So, even if Simek accepts that the relationship between the three known Vanir and their incestuous marriages "is most likely much older than Snorri's invention of the family of the Vanir" (Simek 2010, 18), a view point to which I shall return, then they were not tied together through the name Vanir. However, if the Vanir family did not exist, then it seems as if there could have been some kind of functional communality that would constitute the group *vis-à-vis* the *æsir*. Simek, therefore, suggests that instead of looking at the Vanir group we could look at the individual Vanir, as he says: "…there is, however, another way of approaching the Vanir/*vanir*, namely to ignore the collective term and look at those gods which are ascribed (by Snorri and otherwise) to this group of divinities" (Simek 2010, 13). However, this also, according to Simek turns out negatively, since Lotte Motz's findings in her 1996 book *The King, The Champion, and the Sorcerer*, "can help [us] to understand the obvious faults in the former division of Norse gods into Æsir and Vanir, as … there is no inherent difference between the gods ascribed to both groups by Snorri" (Simek 2010, 13). I do not agree with this position, and the main part of this paper will deal with this question. Simek concludes his article stating that, "The Vanir were not alive in heathen days, and as a figment of imagination from the 13th to the 20th centuries, it is high time to bury them now…" (2010, 18).

If Simek's argument is correct, it seems, at least at first glance, to have immense importance for our view of the pre-Christian mythology in Scandinavia; and thus it is not surprising that other scholars have commented on it. Thus, in *RMN* 2, 2011, there immediately followed two articles, one by Clive Tolley and the other by Frog and Jonathan Roper.[5] Whereas Tolley is critical towards Simek's conclusions, Frog and Roper support them. Before I come to my main discussion—whether there is a functional tendency which supports the traditional division, or not—we shall therefore briefly look at the arguments put forward by these scholars.

The title of Clive Tolley's article is appropriately "In Defence of the Vanir". Tolley certainly points to some important methodological problems in Simek's argument, although, as we shall return to, he has not 'rescued' the Vanir from Simek's attack. From a methodological point of view, Tolley's sentence "Absence of evidence is not evidence of absence" (Tolley 2011, 20) is probably the most important, together with the recognition of diversity (Tolley 2011, 21). The first point involves the whole problem of *argumenta ex silentio*. We cannot deal with that here in any detail; but everybody who has worked with sources for Old Norse religion and mythology will know that what we have in the extant sources only constitutes a small fraction of what must have existed in the oral tradition of a society in which the daily life as well as the ritual performances must have been dense with 'stories'. Although it is a dangerous path to postulate the existence of details in myths and semantics of mythical beings that have not been transmitted to us, it would be even more dangerous to argue that because something is not transmitted, then it did not exist. That would seem to be a rather naïve way of looking at an oral society in general, and the pre-Christian Scandinavian culture in particular. What is more important, however, is that, as Tolley clearly shows, there are in fact positive arguments for the existence of the Vanir in skaldic and eddic poetry. It is true, as is argued by Simek, that we cannot be certain that the Old Norse sources, or rather the information related in them,[6] are of pagan origin, but this is certainly not a special feature in relation to the Vanir (Tolley 2011, 27), and should rather be seen as a basic condition whenever we attempt to reconstruct elements in pre-Christian Scandinavian religion. The second point about diversity must also be taken into serious consideration, both in general, and in connection to the Vanir: It is certainly possible that at various places, at various times, and perhaps in various situations, various gods could be counted among the Vanir. And this is not an attempt to 'explain away' the inconsistencies in the sources, but quite on the contrary, what we should expect in a society like that of the pre-Christian Scandinavians (Schjødt 2009).

So even if the negative evidence presented by Simek may not be as convincing as perhaps could be expected, it is still possible that he is actually right about the designation 'Vanir'. This said, however, it should also be emphasized that whether or not this is true, both Tolley and many others have argued that the three Vanir form a group which functionally, and perhaps in other respects too, is different from the Aesir.

Frog and Roper are, as mentioned, basically positive towards Simek's results, and they support it mainly through a discussion of the alliterative qualities of the term 'Vanir' which could explain the instances in the poetic sources in which the term is used. They conclude by saying (2011, 36):

> Snorri and the generations of scholars who now follow in his footsteps may have simply interpreted and systematized an ambiguous functionally oriented term of the poetic register. If this is correct, then it is open to doubt whether it is possible to reconstruct the earlier semantic field(s) of the term on which these patterns of alliterative, compositional and associative semantic use developed.

Again we should perhaps emphasize that it certainly is doubtful whether we can reconstruct the semantic field of a certain notion *as it was seen by the pagans*, especially since there can be no doubt that the view was not the same among all individuals. Nevertheless, as we shall see, it does not seem hopeless to reconstruct some sort of semantic center of various deities in pagan times (Schjødt 2013).

So what should we think about the whole situation concerning the Vanir? In my view, Simek's article has definitely problematized, in a fruitful way, the traditional way of dealing with the Vanir, and that we have to approach the problem in a more open way than has been the custom during most of the twentieth century. It is certainly right that by far the largest amount of evidence about the Vanir, as a designation of a particular group of gods, comprising Njǫrðr, Freyr, and Freyja comes from Snorri, and thus, if we belong to the group of scholars who find it particularly interesting to criticize the source value of Snorri, we have certainly been given new ammunition.[7]

On the other hand, as Tolley and many other scholars have clearly shown from various perspectives, it certainly does make sense to see the Aesir and the group that is or was, at least earlier, called the Vanir, as two distinct groups. I shall not repeat my own or the view of other scholars who accept the traditional division, from what Tolley called 'positive' evidence. What I shall do here is simply to discuss that argument of Simek's for which he refers to the analyses by Lotte Motz: that there was no functional difference between the two groups when we analyze the individual Vanir. The remaining part of this article will thus be more about Motz's analysis than about Simek's, although this discussion will also have some consequences for the evaluation of Simek's conclusion. We shall return to that in some concluding remarks.

A functional division?

As mentioned, Motz's idea was basically that there was no functional division at stake between the Aesir and the Vanir. This is well in accordance with her overall theory, namely that the Aesir and the Vanir were gods of two different populations, who reached Scandinavia almost at the same time—in the late Neolithic, but by two different routes, one from Germany up through Jutland, and the other one by sea, either from the south, via the Danish island Bornholm, or from the east, across the Baltic sea to eastern Sweden (Motz 1996, 119-22).[8] These two groups had two different sets of gods; those who reached Sweden venerated the Vanir, whereas those who came through Denmark had a pantheon consisting of the Aesir. The myth of the war between the gods and the peace reconciliation, on the other hand, is placed in the later Iron Ages, when there was a significant move from North to South (1996, 122). As Motz argues, there may be archaeological evidence for these two groups of invaders, and of course it cannot be ruled out beforehand that they actually venerated different gods. However, the argument for this theory is not as convincing as Motz herself and Simek seem to believe. Motz sums up her conclusion concerning the gods, writing:

> The findings of this study do not support the generally accepted view in which the family of the gods is divided into farmers' gods—Vanir—and gods of warriors and kings—Æsir—into gods of fruitfulness and gods of war. The findings point instead to the close relation of the Vanir to the royal office and to the generative and creative powers held exclusively by the Æsir (Motz 1996, 123).

First and foremost it is important to notice that the view that there was a strict social division between those who venerated the Vanir and those who venerated the Aesir into farmers on the one hand and warriors and kings on the other hand is no doubt too simplistic. It is true that some of the scholars who belonged to the school of Dumézil saw it that way but, as Dumézil himself was well aware, the tripartite classification was primarily ideological and not sociological.[9] It was an abstract idea that could be traced back to proto-Indo-European times (whatever that is precisely), which was in certain cultures and instances implemented in the actual political division of actual societies. In the North, we do not know much about the theology of the common people since our sources are mainly related to the upper classes, but we may expect that various local beings were the primary objects of cult. This is not to say that farmers and other 'ordinary' people did not know the gods of the eddic and skaldic poems or Snorra Edda, or that they were not venerated at certain public occasions, but simply that most of these gods seem to be based in the cult of the upper classes,[10] and in some probably rather vague mythological system which in variant forms was known by most people, but hardly played any significant role outside the circles around the kings and the chieftains.[11] We certainly do not know these things for sure, but from a comparative perspective it is probably the most likely scenario. Thus, the 'Dumézilians' who have held the view that certain classes venerated different gods were most likely wrong and it is doubtful whether it is possible nowadays to find many scholars who hold this view. It is obvious that 'fertility of the land' would be immediately more relevant to the farmers than to warriors and artisans and kings, but that is not to say that for such people fertility did not matter, which is the case not least for the kings. Skill and luck in war, on the other hand, were of course more relevant for the warriors than for the farmers, although the ability to defend the country was certainly not irrelevant for the farmers either. Thus all the functions are, as was also the view point of Dumézil, very important for the whole of society, although in different ways and to a differing degree for the individual classes (cf. Schjødt 2012c). Therefore, it is also quite understandable that Freyr or Þórr may have been venerated to a higher degree than Óðinn among farmers, and that they may have played a major role in the spectacular public rituals carried out with the specific purpose of promoting fertility of the soil. Óðinn, on the other hand, was more relevant to kings and warriors and thus in all likelihood was the main figure in rituals dealing with the outcome of battles. But that is certainly not the same as to maintain that Freyr or Þórr was 'the god of the farmers', in the sense that they were exclusively venerated by farmers; or that Óðinn was exclusively venerated by kings: he was definitely more relevant for kings than he was for commoners, but as later folklore seems to confirm, Óðinn as a magician has probably been interesting for a great many people (cf. Mitchell 2009).

Even so, there is no reason to criticize that part of Motz's conclusion: At least the upper classes in all likelihood venerated the Aesir as well as the Vanir. However, when she writes that the gods cannot be divided into 'gods of fruitfulness and gods of war', the case is different. What she is talking about is what has, since Dumézil, been called 'functions'. The problem with Motz is on the one hand that she draws the division between the functions very sharply, probably much more sharply than can be done within any mythology; and on the other hand, in her textual analysis, she often seems to miss the context of the individual piece of information completely, which we shall return to below.

As to the first point, we can state that functions overlap, and the very notion of function is no doubt much more complex than Motz, and probably also Dumézil, believed. Just to give one example: 'fertility' cannot be seen as something that belongs exclusively to a sole 'function'. The three social-ideological functions of Dumézil are all involved here: the prerequisite for fertility—for *ár*—is quite complex, since it involves the protection from the demonic or chaotic beings. In a religion like that of the pre-Christian Scandinavians, crop disease or bad weather would most likely have been seen as an interference of such beings (cf. Witzel 2012, 164); the rhythm of nature was organized by the benevolent gods, whereas disturbances of that rhythm was due to an interference of hostile beings, in the Old Norse world imagined, for instance, as giants. Thus this protection must be in the hands of a god who is strong enough to conquer the giants, and this is obviously Þórr. In that sense Þórr is necessary for a good harvest, although it is because of his strength and his ability to fight. In the same way we can see Óðinn, who often functions as the guardian god of the ruler, as the one who bestows luck to his chosen hero. And since the ruler is responsible for the well-being of the land at all levels,[12] it is another prerequisite for the well-being of the land that his relation to Óðinn is optimal. Finally, the performance of Freyr is also necessary, since he has to drive about in the various landscapes with a priestess, probably performing some kind of sexual act within a ritual framework, as we see it in *Gunnars þáttr helmings* from the *Flateyjarbók*. Rituals of such kind constitute a strong indication that Freyr, with his sexual force, was necessary for fertility. In that perspective it seems obvious that a farmer sometimes had to take all three functions into consideration because they all played a role in that rather complicated process that had to do with fertility, although Óðinn and Freyr were probably only involved in the public sacrifices in which the chieftain or the king was involved. The point here is that the gods involved were not 'fertility gods' in the same way. Þórr is linked to fertility because he is a warrior, Óðinn because he is connected to the ruler, and Freyr because he is connected to sexuality and abundance. Thus they may all be invoked in various rituals with the purpose of promoting fertility, but their contributions to the fertilizing process are quite different. Therefore it is a problem, for example, when Motz, as evidence for the role of Þórr as fertility god, with reference to Adam of Bremen, says: "Farmers sacrifice to Þórr when there is famine in the land so that harvest will improve" (Motz 1996, 107). According to what has just been stated, this does not necessarily indicate that Þórr was primarily a fertility god, but rather that he was the defender of the right order of things against threatening demons. And the same can be said concerning Óðinn and Motz's postulate that he has a particular connection to fertility. Referring to *Ynglinga saga* ch. 43, she mentions that, "At a time of famine King Óláfr trételgja was rendered to Óðinn *til árs...*" (Motz 1996, 107). Yes, because Óðinn is the god of the kings, and because the king is responsible for the prosperity, a sacrifice of kings will be a sacrifice to Óðinn. It has obviously nothing to do with a connection between Óðinn and fertility in particular. Thus the notion of 'function' as a means to characterize the individual gods is much more complicated than is usually thought: there is certainly a difference whether a certain god kills or has sex in order to promote a good harvest.[13]

This agricultural aspect is also a good example of the lack of contextual analysis by Motz. As an argument for Óðinn's relation to farm labor and a relation with the humble classes, making reference to the myth of the theft of the mead in *Skáldskaparmál* she says, "Óðinn mows a meadow and performs the labor of nine thralls for an entire summer" (Motz 1996, 107). The point in this myth however is that whatever Óðinn does in the sequence, it is part of his search for the mead which makes those who drink it wise or gives them poetic abilities. Therefore it is simply not in accordance with the basic idea of the myth to focus on some of the means that are used by Óðinn, because this is not what the myth is about. Quite to the contrary: in nearly all myths in which Óðinn is a main character he either seeks knowledge or he gives it away. In that connection he sometimes kills, he sometimes has sex, and he sometimes uses magical skills. Another example of the lack of context is Óðinn's relation to wealth as treated by Motz (1996, 108-9). After having listed a long series of sources in which the so-called Vanir are connected to wealth and riches, she notes, "The trees of the forest before Óðinn's court bear leaves of gold. The god himself possesses a golden ring which begets eight others every ninth night" (Motz 1996, 108-9). Again we lack the context completely. Óðinn is a mighty king, so of course he is rich; and his ring has surely something to do with the relation between this and the other world, as we see it in the Baldr myth. Rings in general, have some numinous qualities, and the most powerful rings were made of gold. The phenomena, mentioned by Motz, therefore, do not seem to point to any special relation between Óðinn and riches; they just serve to characterize Óðinn as a very powerful king. Thus, in general, there seems to be a lack of ability or willingness to distinguish what is central from what is remote in Motz's analysis. And in this way most of the functions that are enumerated in her book are not adequate when seen in context (Motz 1996, 106-15).

The two problems, just discussed, point to a more general problem that does not only concern Motz, but also many other scholars: as we know, the gods of the ancient Scandinavians were imagined as anthropomorphic. This naturally involves that they had abilities that were characteristic of humans, although in an idealized form. They were all rich—but notice that the Vanir are thematized to a much higher degree as wealthy, than the Aesir; they were all warriors—but the Aesir were thematized to a much larger extent as warriors, as Þórr fights and kills all sorts of demons, while Óðinn takes care of the rage and the strategy of the human armies; and they all had more magical skills than ordinary people—but Óðinn is clearly thematized as the magician par excellence. Thus, it is not a question of whether there was overlap between the functions, since this is exactly what we should expect. What we should look for, I would suggest, in order to learn about the 'functions' of the individual gods, is what distinguishes them from each other, to depict their semantic center so to speak (cf. Schjødt 2013). As more or less human, the gods will inevitably share a lot of characteristics with humans (they have sex, they kill, they perform magic, they even work occasionally), but just like humans not everybody does all these things to the same extent—and certainly not in the same way and for the same reasons.

Concluding Remarks

It is now time to return to the question of the existence or non-existence of the Vanir. If Motz's analysis, as has just been argued, cannot be used as an argument for the view that "there is no inherent difference between the gods ascribed to both groups by Snorri" (Simek 2010, 13) because her treatment of the functions of the individual gods is not reflected sufficiently, then we should accept that the Vanir are not thematized as warriors, whereas the Aesir are not thematized as having sex simply for the sake of it. Whereas Þórr is almost never portrayed as sexually active, this is not the case for Óðinn, but as a rule, when we hear about his seduction of women, he usually has a hidden agenda (getting wisdom, as with Gunnlǫð, or getting a revenger for Baldr, as with Rindr). It therefore does not seem that Óðinn's motives for sexuality can be attributed to lust alone as seems to be the case with both Freyr (for instance in *Skírnismál*) and Freyja (in numerous instances). And Freyr is correctly connected to kings, but he is never thematized as the guardian god of individual kings (Schjødt 2012c). These sorts of distinctions do not become apparent in Motz's analysis. Basically, it seems as if she lacks a clear recognition of how mythological structures create meanings. We need to distinguish between functional and semantic centers on the one hand, and the means the gods use for fulfilling their functions on the other hand. In that way there *is* an inherent difference, although the distinctions are a bit more sophisticated than has usually been thought.

Thus there can hardly be any doubt that, even if Simek may be right about the designation of the Vanir, then the three gods Njǫrðr, Freyr and Freyja do share some characteristics, namely those that have been proposed by so many scholars since the beginning of the twentieth century: wealth, sexuality [incestuous or extremely exogamous], and abundance, characteristics which they do not share with the Aesir. Even if we do ignore the collective term, as is suggested by Simek, then by examining critically Motz's analysis we cannot escape the conclusion that the Vanir are distinguished quite clearly from the Aesir, seen from a functional point of view. Even if the term Vanir was not in existence in pagan times, it does not change substantially the fact that in pre-Christian Scandinavian mythology we deal with two groups of gods who sometimes overlap, whereas at other times they are clearly distinguished, just as is to be expected in an anthropomorphic mythology. It would be wrong to look for an absolute coherence in any mythology. As I have considered in more detail elsewhere, what we can realistically hope to reconstruct is not a coherent mythological or theological system, as this seems to be more of an ideal dream among scholars who are strongly influenced by an older sort of theology, but rather a set of variants which may be part of a deep structure, although with internal contradictions between the various myth-complexes and many 'loose ends' (Schjødt 2009, 2012b, and 2013). In the real world, among real people, such coherence is, as a general rule, absent. Consequently, what we can hope to reconstruct are discursive spaces, understood as frames within which it is possible to say many things about a certain god, but not everything. The Vanir may be warriors or kings and many other things, but what cannot be said is that they are poor or that they are not engaged in the fertility of man and land. In that manner, we may be able to reconstruct a functional and semantic center. On the periphery, the functions of one god may very well overlap with the functions of other gods. Such a semantic center for any specific god should be based on the distinctions between the individual gods, which are more or less clearly expressed in our sources.

The conclusion, in relation to Simek's article would be, then, that even if he should be right concerning the term Vanir, we would still be better off if we had a designation for the gods that we traditionally have seen as belonging to the Vanir group. And perhaps Vanir, then, in spite of all the uncertainties that accrue to it, would still be the most convenient term.

Notes

[1] The term 'pantheon' is used here in a very broad sense. As has recently been pointed out by Terry Gunnell (Gunnell forthcoming), we probably should not think of a pantheon in Scandinavia in the same sense as we know it from the Mediterranean area in Antiquity. Nevertheless, most sources point to some notion of a divine 'society' in which the individual gods have some relations to each other. These relations may not have been very stable and they may have varied from place to place. The term pantheon, when used here, thus only indicates that such relations actually did exist in the worldview of pagan Scandinavia.

[2] A few other gods have been seen as Vanir, however; most conspicuous is Heimdallr who is said to be one of the Vanir in *Þrk* 15.

[3] I use the term 'in general' deliberately, since, as I have argued in other publications (Schjødt 2012b, 2013), there is in mythologies very rarely—if ever—any such thing as absolute coherence between the various statements. Instead of arguing that this or that source is influenced by something foreign we should be aware that we are dealing with a religion that had no dogmatics, i.e. nobody told anybody what and how to believe, so of course there would be, compared to, for instance, Christianity, much more variation, much more overlap, and many more contradictions in the pre-Christian religion (or religions, cf. DuBois 1999).

[4] There have been many suggestions as to who these intruders were and when the war took place, with suggestions reaching from the early Bronze Age (the Indo-Europeans) to the late Roman Iron Age (the Huns) .

[5] I am aware of only these two articles, both of them in *RMN*, but there may be others.

[6] For this distinction between the evaluation of the sources themselves, and the information we can gain from them, see Meulengracht Sørensen 1991.

[7] I am not going to discuss comparison as a methodological tool as I have done so elsewhere (i.e. Schjødt 2012b). The subject is not central for my argument, but I do think that comparisons of the kind carried out by Georges Dumézil or Michael Witzel constitute a strong argument for the existence of a group of gods that are reminiscent of the Vanir as we know them from Snorri, among others.

[8] Motz relies a great deal on place-name material, emphasizing with some right that theophoric place-names in Denmark are much more often connected with the Aesir gods than with those of the Vanir, whereas the opposite is true for the names in most of the Scandinavian peninsula (cf. Brink 2007). There may be other explanations for this distribution. Importantly, the 'meaning' of a certain place name is often not quite clear. For instance, when Motz discusses compounds with *akr*, she says, "Combining the noun *akr*—'ploughland', with the name of a god would surely indicate his powers to bless the soil" (1996, 107), but this is far from obvious. It could just as well be imagined that, because rituals for a certain god were carried out at certain places, for instance fields, the field and its surroundings would acquire names such as Torsakr, Frøsakr, or Onsakr, not because these gods had blessed the soil, but perhaps because the field for some reasons was sacred, and thus would be well suited for carrying out the ritual. It may be hard sometimes to decide how we shall see the relation between cause and effect, and it is certainly not as clear-cut as is suggested by Motz.

[9] It is true that up until the end of the 1940's, Dumézil himself had the view that the classification was rooted in an Indo-European social order. However, during the 1950's he changed his view and became fully aware that the tripartite structure was primarily ideological (Dumézil 1958, 17-8; cf. Jensen and Schjødt 1994, 49-50).

[10] Þórr seems to be an exception, since he appears to have been venerated by all social classes. The explanation could very well be his main function,

namely as the defender of cosmos in a broad sense, i.e. of the 'right' order of things, whether we are dealing with fertility of beast and soil, sickness, bad weather etc. (cf. Schjødt 2012c, 67-73).

[11] The mythological system related by Snorri may have been part of some 'story line' (cf. Witzel 2012), which was known by most Scandinavians and went far back in time, but we cannot be sure. If it was, there is no doubt that it was to a much lesser degree 'systematic' than is the case in Snorri.

[12] Although much doubt has been cast on the information concerning Dómaldi in *Ynglinga saga,* ch. 15, it seems quite clear that the king's luck was important for the fertility of the land.

[13] It is interesting that Motz noticed this problematic, although she draws no conclusions from it. Thus she writes in connection with Freyr's connection to kingship: "Óðinn represents the king in relation to his retainers, frequently landless men who follow in his wake. Freyr, himself, the owner of a hereditary estate, represents the king in relation to the land, as he was seen by men of hereditary property. Freyr and Óðinn may have evolved in different social and probably regional traditions which were blended, imperfectly, at some time in the Middle Ages" (1996, 30). Although the two 'kinds of kingship' which are involved here should more likely be seen as a structural feature than due to various historical situations (cf. Schjødt 2012c), the idea that the two gods represent the king as leader of the war band on the one hand, and the king as responsible for the land, on the other hand, makes good sense.

Edda and Ballad: *Svipdagsmál* and the Uses of Poetic Afterlife

Joseph Harris

Bjarne Fidjestøl's invaluable but incomplete posthumous book on the dating of eddic poetry preserves one paragraph on ballad scholarship since Wolfgang Mohr (1938-39 and 1939-40; Fidjestøl 1999, 318-23) as it intersects with eddic poetry, clearly the initiation of a promising topic but only what Wikipedia would call a "stub" (Fidjestøl 1999, 323; cf. the review, Harris 2000). Filling out that stub, even if not conceived as an attempt at reconstruction of what Fidjestøl might have written, would be a great challenge and possibly an important contribution to eddic dating. A lesser but more attainable alternative would be an "edda and ballad" series that proceeds through individual points of contact between these two oral genres. So far the brave new series numbers only one previous article (Harris 2012; but also see Harris 2013). In the present article I propose to take the balladic afterlife of the eddic *Svipdagsmál* more seriously than is usual in eddic scholarship and out of that to construct an alternative literary history for this eddic poem, one more consonant with the probable roles of oral tradition than is found in standard versions. The ultimate goal for another occasion would be to reassess interpretation of *Svipdagsmál*'s content, not least the mythological content, in view of the proposed new literary history.

Introduction

Svipdagsmál is a modern name covering two poems that appear separately in manuscripts under the titles *Grógaldr* and *Fjölsvinnsmál*.[1] Both poems are in *ljóðaháttr*, and both evince the dramatic character associated with that meter. *Grógaldr*'s single scene shows an unnamed young hero awakening his mother Gróa in her grave; the dead woman of power bestows nine charms and a blessing rooted in stone to protect her boy, as he must follow his fated quest for a certain maiden in an unknown world far away. *Fjölsvinnsmál* opens as an unnamed wanderer approaches a gated community guarded by a giant, the "very wise" Fjölsviðr. After a brief flyting-like passage where the newly arrived gives himself a transparent pseudonym, the bulk of the poem develops a description of this otherworld through a wisdom dialogue comparable to those of the familiar older poems. The hero's goal is to attain his destined maiden, Menglöð, who rules this land. The obstacles facing him—the sticky wicket of a gate and so on—are inventoried by Fjölsviðr, but they suddenly become irrelevant when the giant porter mentions that a person named Svipdagr would have free entry to his mistress. The hero so names himself accordingly and is shortly united with Menglöð. This summary, of course, leaves out all the interesting details and the fact that we are reading good poetry.

The name *Svipdagsmál* was assigned by Sophus Bugge in 1860 to the two poems regarded as fragments of a single composition (Bugge 1860, 140; Grundtvig 1856, 668, 671 had proposed "Svipdagsför"). With hindsight, of course, the two poems do seem fated (like Svipdagr and Menglöð) to converge; yet it was only through a close study of the ballad "Ungen Svejdal" (*DgF* 70) that this was recognized. Initially Grundtvig (1854, 238) identified *Grógaldr* as the source of the first part of the ballad; after that breakthrough, Bugge quickly deduced that *Fjölsvinnsmál* was the source of the ballad's second part (1856). Bugge's conclusion, almost universally accepted now (one exception is Heide 1997), was that the unity of the ballad proved that the two eddic poems were parts of a single composition. This thesis was all the more brilliant when we consider that *nothing* in the transmission or Early Modern history of the constituent poems had suggested to scholars that they belonged together.[2] The hero of *Grógaldr* is unnamed; and the hero of *Fjölsvinnsmál* acquires or reveals his door-opening name only near the end of the second poem. It is true that the name of Menglöð does appear in *Grógaldr* but only in a corrupt and obscure form that went unrecognized before Grundtvig and Bugge.[3] None of the principal manuscripts, all paper, in which the poems or fragments are transmitted, links them; all the manuscripts that have both poems give them their separate titles. In only four of eight manuscripts studied in the published literature do the separately titled poems *happen* to stand next to each other among the shifting orders of other eddic-style poems not in the Codex Regius;[4] in the other four the order is *Fjölsvinnsmál—Hyndluljóð—Grógaldr*. A significant number of manuscripts transmit *Grógaldr* alone. The tradition represented by these manuscripts—only two being somewhat older than the eighteenth century—was that of an elaborated "Sæmundar Edda,"[5] but clearly none of the learned Icelanders of the Early Modern period—the men who carried on this tradition, right through the great Copenhagen edition of 1787-1828—had really understood these puzzling poems. Bugge, whose study of the manuscripts was long regarded as authoritative, believed all to go back to a common vellum original. But Bugge's account has some self-contradictions and obscurities, as I found and then found confirmed by Jónas Kristjánsson (1987). The early twentieth-century study of seven (or eight, see note) manuscripts by Gering and Sijmons is clearer, but it is only in our time that a scholar, Peter Robinson, has been able to establish a stemma and a firmer basis for a critical text. Very recently John McKinnell[6] and Gísli Sigurðsson (1998) have both touched on these manuscript matters but with a different emphasis and purpose from mine.

Anything said about these manuscripts, however, must now be said under correction from Robinson's 1991 unpublished Oxford thesis. Robinson's investigation discovered forty-six manuscripts of one or both of the poems constituting *Svipdagsmál*, far more than any previous scholar, and he was able to collate forty-three of the forty-six—a very significant achievement. Robinson's several published articles, however, use the results of his collations to test and exemplify a program for generating "cladistic" models of manuscript relations (Robinson 1989ab; 1994; 1996) while the dissertation (1991) actually establishes the stemma and prints a critical text. Robinson's accomplishments are, however, not closely related to my rather traditional project here. What I needed was far simpler, an answer to the question: do the large bulk of manuscripts not studied by Sijmons and Gering follow the core seven (or eight) in assignment of titles and arrangement of the poems? Prof.

Robinson kindly came through for me in the spring of 2012 with a copy of his excellent dissertation, and from my reading I am pretty sure the answer is yes: there is no evidence before Bugge of any perception of the unity grounding the two poems.[7]

Edda and ballad

So the most basic things we know about the form and transmission of the so-called *Svipdagsmál* are dependent on or at least strongly colored by its reception in ballad form. In addition to the restoration of the name Menglöð in the first poem, Grundtvig and Bugge also succeeded in using the ballad texts to clarify a series of other details in *Svipdagsmál.* For example, in st. 1 of *Grógaldr* confusing references to women had puzzled the earliest commentators; now that the ballad had supplied a stepmother incident and its curse, they could explain the highly condensed narrative allusions of the eddic verse, and the ballads helped in a number of other corrections of the poor manuscript readings (Bugge 1856; 1860). From the ballad, Grundtvig and Bugge could now postulate a lost journey sequence for the transition from *Grógaldr* to *Fjölsvinnsmál* (Grundtvig 1856, esp. 671-72; Bugge 1860, 132),[8] and in return recognition of the eddic source inspired a revision of Grundtvig's understanding of the relationships among the ballad versions.[9] The full list of improvements and clarifications Grundtvig and Bugge made to *Svipdagsmál* based on the ballad reception is not called for here (Bugge 1856; 1860; 1867; Grundtvig 1856); I suggest however that the balladic afterlife has not yet been fully exploited as a resource for understanding *Svipdagsmál.*[10]

Eddic poetry and the international popular ballad usually constitute two quite separate fields of study even though both basically concern oral narrative poetry that flourished in adjacent—or rather—*overlapping* time and space.[11] For eddic poetry tends today to be dated later than in the classic days of, say, Finnur Jónsson, and traces of outliers of eddic style have appeared in mainland Scandinavia from the high and late Middle Ages. Ballad poetry is *beginning* just as eddic poetry is winding down.

The ultimate stimulus for the ballad in the North is agreed to be the French *carole* and *chanson de histoire*. Beyond this, theories of the Scandinavian derivation still vary, but I take as my chief guide Bengt R. Jonsson, the lamented Swedish genius of historical ballad study (principal reference to 1991a; but also to 1993b and the *Sumlen* series). I summarize briefly his main relevant ideas: The impulses from France did not *diffuse* first to Denmark as filtered through German territory. Instead they *leapt* to Angevin Britain and thence to Norway. The central historical times and places for this act of cultural reception were the Norwegian court in Bergen castle in the second half of the thirteenth century and in the new capital in the Akershus in Oslo, 1299-1319. The latter is the site of an extraordinary convergence of brilliant Northern European aristocrats, including King Hákon Magnússon's German-born queen Eufemia, who sponsored the earliest *Swedish*-language romances, the *Eufemiavisor*—texts which, scholars agree, reveal influences from pre-existing ballads. Bengt Jonsson's model solves a number of problems in the earliest literary history of the ballad by putting Norway at the head of the development of the genre as a whole and not only of the West Scandinavian hero ballads, the origin of which had long been located in Norway by scholarly consensus (see for example, Vésteinn Ólason 1990; 1991).[12]

Our concern here is with only a small portion of Jonsson's model, the Edda-ballad interface. Here is his brief main statement on that:

> [The] connection between eddic poetry and ballads ought to show that some of the eddic lays were known in Norway around 1300 (a fact in harmony with the runic inscriptions found in Bergen) … It is, on the other hand, not very plausible that eddic poetry gave rise to ballads as late as the fifteenth century, which has been suggested even in very recent times. As eddic poetry also was an oral genre, the transformation from eddic lay to ballad represents an encounter between two genres of oral poetry, one older and one younger, two different

> systems of making verse with some formal elements in common. (1991, 157)

I believe this is essentially the correct view. The date "around 1300" is phrased to serve the Akershus portion in this iteration of the theory; elsewhere Jonsson himself locates the Norwegian beginnings of the genre in the 1280s or '90s.

My venture into Scandinavian ballad scholarship in connection with eddic poetry began with an article on *Þrymskviða* and its balladic reception (Harris 2012). I concluded that the Thor ballad originated in Norway, whence it spread to the Faroe Islands, Sweden, and Denmark. The source was an oral Norwegian antecedent of *Þrymskviða*. The surviving Icelandic version in the Codex Regius derives, I suggested, from a Norwegian version brought orally to Iceland too late to be known to Snorri Sturluson. This perhaps explains why *Þrymskviða* scores as one of the oldest eddic poems by objective linguistic tests but as the youngest by subjective cultural criteria.[13] For the actual migration of an older, chanted Thor poem into the sung ballad we need only the prestige of a modern, imported musical style in place of the old-fashioned eddic drone.

The Svipdagr (or Svejdal) ballad—to return to our main subject—was fairly well preserved in continental Scandinavia, but there are no traces of it in Icelandic or Faroese. The Norwegian ballad archives preserve some seventeen variants (Espeland et al. 1997);[14] Swedish preserves two (Jonsson et al. 1983, 204-07 [*SMB* 18]), and Danish around sixteen.[15] This ballad *type* (*TSB* A 45)[16] comprises a considerable amount of variation but does allow a general content sketch. The forms of the hero's name—Svejdal, etc., Sven(nen)dal, Svedendal, Silfverdal—are all plausibly viewed as ultimately descended from Svipdagr; but the heroine is named in only one variant and then without certain relationship to the eddic source.[17] Fjölsviðr has his counterpart in a shepherd or an old man, always unnamed. The fuller ballad versions begin with a scene in which the young hero is playing ball; when the ball lodges in his stepmother's lap and the boy pursues it, she lays the fate upon him never to be at peace before he unites with the unknown maiden who awaits him in a trance-like state. He takes leave of his men, goes to his mother's grave mound, and calls on her for "good advice"; she answers grudgingly but yields up a series of gifts: a horse that never tires on land or sea; a ship that sails on land or sea; a sword that lights his way in a dark wood; and so on, a list with much variation. The hero's journey usually occupies only a few stanzas or is only implicit; but he always meets a guide figure, usually a shepherd, and obtains some help in his quest: the location of the castle, a description of it, the state of the maiden, etc. Obstacles to approach are described, but the hero is told not to worry if he is Svejdal. Sometimes his horse carries him over the wall and right into the courtyard where lions and bears and also a mysterious linden tree, distantly echoing the source, do him obeisance. By messenger or through a window the lady learns of his arrival. Sometimes there is a concerned father, a heathen king, who offers his only daughter, but only if the young man is the real Svejdal. The king's conversion may precede the wedding, where many variants give attention to the rewarding of the shepherd, who is made a knight or placed at the head of the table.

Early nineteenth-century mythologists, ignorant of the ballad connection, liked to expound on *Fjölsvinnsmál* in isolation,[18] and even after 1856 a few insisted on rejecting the connection between the two eddic-style poems.[19] In general, however, post-Bugge scholarship has treated the two as parts of a single poem. Examples are Otto Höfler (1952), Einar Ól. Sveinsson (1971-73; 1975), Jan de Vries (1934; 1964-67), Franz Rolf Schröder (1966), and Lotte Motz (1975; 1993). To be fair, these scholars have been concerned with the *story* and its analogues or with borrowing of topoi and language rather than with the literary-historical question as I want to raise it now.

A new literary history

Let us now reconsider the most basic evidence for the relevant literary history: The oldest recording of "Ungen Svejdal" is in Karen Brahe's Folio Manuscript, 1583, one of the collections of "old songs" made by aristocratic ladies and courtly gentlemen in Denmark beginning *at least* by 1550.[20] The first wave of such collections are "courtly garlands" (c. 1550-80), typified by the famous *Hjertebog* of c. 1553; though it contains some ballads (twenty-one, as registered by *TSB* types) and is known as the oldest ballad manuscript, the real weight of *Hjertebog* lies in other types of song (sixty-two; Colbert 1989, 31). Colbert characterizes the second wave as "antiquarian collections," c. 1580-90; here the proportion of "real" (*TSB*-authorized) ballads to other songs is higher. The second wave may be typified by Karen Brahe's Folio Manuscript, where the ballad-to-other relationship is 197 to 6. As a group the antiquarian collections aimed less at the entertainment of the courtly garlands than at "historical" material; Colbert's excellent chapter emphasizes the role of Anders Sørensen Vedel in the decade or so leading up to his famous printed anthology of 1591. We can conclude, therefore, that "Ungen Svejdal" was probably considered an ancient poem, perhaps even "historical," when its earliest preserved version was written out.

The oldest surviving manuscripts of the poems of *Svipdagsmál* date to about 1680. Even if an ancestor of these paper manuscripts were the *written* source of the ballad, the ballad-maker would have to have operated before about 1500 to account for the spread of the ballad and its reputation as ancient. This dating and the lack of understanding shown by Icelandic *fræðimenn* in the "Sæmundar Edda" tradition strongly discourage any theory that *Svipdagsmál* is an Early Modern imposture. Since there are no traces of *Svipdagsmál* or its parts in *rímur* or Icelandic ballad tradition and almost no traces of them in Iceland at all outside the manuscript tradition itself, the material we know now as *Svipdagsmál* may have been brought to Iceland later than the Codex Regius, entering the "Sæmundar Edda" tradition perhaps about 1300. In any case, the ballad was almost certainly created in Norway, not Iceland.[21]

Most crucially: when the Norwegian ballad-maker took *Svipdagsmál* or its predecessor as his source, that source was still unified. So the disaggregation process that separated *Grógaldr* and *Fjölsvinnsmál* probably took place in Iceland and was a product of the "Sæmundar Edda" tradition, in other words a scribal, not an oral, process.[22] Disaggregation and the separate titles are more likely if the composition was an oral *saga* like the ones performed in

Reykjahólar in 1119 than if the whole was through-composed as poetry.[23] So the ballad-maker's source may well have been an oral **Svipdagssaga*, and that, in Norway.[24] (And I agree with Bengt Jonsson that oral-to-oral is the more likely ballad genesis though there is work to do to carry this through as a principle since significant parts of the West Nordic ballad corpus are traceable to written sagas.) This hand-off from oral prosimetrum to ballad could have taken place as early as the gestation period of the *kæmpeviser* in general, say, the latter half of the thirteenth century, but its terminus ad quem is furnished by the likely oral life of a **Svipdagssaga* in Norway. That likelihood would seem to fade as the fifteenth century approached.

So when it comes to genre, and in terms of its life in oral tradition, I would resist the poetic fusion implicit in Bugge's title and would reorient the separate poems *Grógaldr* and *Fjölsvinnsmál* as parts of a prosimetrum, perhaps performed at a wedding like the two prosimetra that entertained guests at the wedding at Reykjahólar. Certainly no story could be more appropriate to a wedding, a veritable epithalamium in prose and verse. Grundtvig and Bugge have also speculated briefly on a lost *prose* transition from the first poem to the second, and Einar Ól. Sveinsson agrees and adds a few other spots for prose (see n. 24); so my proposal of a prosimetrical form is not new. In general, however, the one-poem view has prevailed despite the unlikelihood of extended narrative in *ljóðaháttr*. The saga-theory would gain some support from the form of late, poetry-bearing fantasy sagas with similar Celtic affinities, such as *Hjálmþés saga ok Ölvis*, a saga extensively mentioned already by the older scholars and in modern times by Einar Ól. Sveinsson (1971-73; 1975). The existence of Norwegian oral *fornaldarsögur* has been argued in connection with ballad evidence at least since Knut Liestøl (1915), and what I am proposing for *Svipdagsmál* and the "Ungen Svejdal" ballads is congruent with established patterns of similar materials.[25] If the entertainment of Reykjahólar in 1119 suggests performance mode and occasion and agrees on the prosimetrical form, the two sagas performed there would have been longer and more varied than should be imagined for **Svipdagssaga*. A better formal comparand might be *Helgakviða Hjörvarðssonar*, a prosimetrum with two comparably long blocks of verse, which even offers some content similarities, including a female-bestowed fate, a destined mate, and a bridal quest.

Dating the ballad as generally as I have—say 1280-1400—does little to date the transmission of the oral **Svipdagssaga* to Iceland, and our literary-historical model needs also to account for the Icelandic burnish of the verse. When we compare the extant *Svipdagsmál* with the ballads, it becomes fairly clear from *agreements* what was taken over into the ballad. But I wonder whether all the *differences* are to be accounted for simply as balladic omissions, simplifications, or adaptations from a source like the extant *Svipdagsmál.* Did the ballad poet, for example, simply substitute gifts for *galdrar*? The gifts of horse and sword, possibly also of ship, can easily be imagined as integral to the *Abenteuersaga* about Svipdagr; compare the sword from the grave in *Hervarar saga.* Would it not be more probable that the oral **Svipdagssaga* had inset poems of a more popular cast than the sophisticated, romantic and mythologically deep poems of the extant *Svipdagsmál*? My hypothesis, then, is that the popular, oral **Svipdagssaga* formed the source for an Icelandic poet, whose revision was the beginning of, or a stage in, the disaggregation of the parts. This Icelandic poet had much other eddic poetry in his head, but I do not believe that he looked up phrases in the Codex Regius. We cannot be sure where every particular item in the extant *Svipdagsmál* originated, whether in the popular verse of the hypothesized saga or in traditions known to and used by the revising Icelandic poet. In the fourteenth or fifteenth century such poetry would have been still essentially oral although circulating in a milieu where the writing down of verse was commonplace.

How—in conclusion—does this proposed literary-historical outline differ from the standard and where does it leave the study of *Svipdagsmál*? Most brief mentions treat *Svipdagsmál* as "a poem" and the ballads as simply "derived" from it;[26] others ignore the ballads altogether.[27] The Norwegian component in the ballad is widely unknown (e.g., Grimstad 1988; Einar Ól. Sveinsson 1971-73, 307; 1975, 51). On the other hand, several scholars, early and later, have imagined a prosimetrical stage in the development of *Svipdagsmál* even if they did not express it that way, and a few have allowed the source question its full complexity.[28] No one has proposed the ballad as the source of the eddic poem, despite the manuscript datings; but a few scholars have glanced, more or less accidentally, at the possibility of a common source.[29] Obviously the more a student of the material admits changes to the form of the *Svipdagsmál* that served as a source for the ballad, the more a comparative reconstructive exercise through triangulation—but also considering *disagreements* with older Icelandic lore—becomes inevitable. Such an exercise might, at some future time, yield some notion of the state of the story and of mythological knowledge in Norway of the early ballad period (Harris 2013).

Notes

1 Major editions, commentaries, and translations consulted: Lüning 1859; Bugge 1867; Detter/Heinzel 1903; Hildebrand 1904; Sijmons/Gering 1903-31; Neckel 1914; Lange 1964; Gísli Sigurðsson 1998; Robinson 1991; Jónas Kristjánsson 1987; Bellows 1923; Hollander 1962.

2 Cf. Einar Ól. Sveinsson 1971-73, 303: "To the best of my knowledge there is nothing to be found in the manuscripts indicating that the copyists were aware of any connection between the two poems, i.e., that they were dealing with two sections of one and the same story. What is more, investigators were long in discovering the fact."

3 Bugge 1856, 667; Grundtvig 1856, 668; Bugge 1860, 130-31; 1867, 338, n. to *Grógaldr* 3,6.

4 Sijmons-Gering 1906 [Einleitung, xiii-xv (§ 9)]. Sijmons-Gering consulted Rask's fragmentary manuscript (*Eddubrot*) only as reflected in his 1818 edition. Bugge's account of the paper manuscripts (1867, lii-lv, lx-lxii) does not, apparently, present the poem inventory of each manuscript that contains *Grógaldr* or *Fjölsvinnsmál* in a usable way, but cf. xlv. Note that Bugge 1867, 343 (head note) says that "i de fleste [mss] følger det [Fjölsvinnsmál] efter Grógaldr, i andere efter Vegtamskviða"; but this appears to be wrong; see the Sijmons-Gering passage (xiv).

5 Bugge 1867: xliv ff [Fortale].

[6] McKinnell (2005, 202 text and n. 24) is wrong in asserting that the constituent poems appear "as a single text in three manuscripts"; they are always separately titled and in only half the eight manuscripts studied do "Groog. und Fjolsvm. unmittelbar auf einander [folgen]"; in the other four "ist die reihefolge Fjolsvm. Hyndl. Groog." (Sijmons-Gering 1906, xiv [Einleitung]).

[7] Robinson 1991 does not parse the material with precisely my question in mind, but he writes about a notebook of Hákon Scheving that Scheving comes closer than any scholar before Bugge to divining the relationship between the two poems.

[8] Grundtvig imagines an original in which the dialogue with Fjölsviðr is divided by the hero's search for the keys to the castle (the tasks); this would explain why he is welcomed "back" (*aptr*) by Menglöð (1856, 671b-72a)—an idea with little to recommend it.

[9] Grundtvig 1856, 672b: he would now put "Ungen Svejdal" right after *DgF* 1 "Thor af Havsgaard" as myth-inspired; he would also rearrange the other ballads with similarities to "Ungen Svejdal" and would demote *DgF* 70 AB to a position behind CDE, C being the most perfect *Opskrift.*

[10] Cf. Einar Ól. Sveinsson 1971-73, 307: "These ballads have, as far as I know, never been subjected to systematic investigation." Grundtvig's 1856 "notes" on the ballad and its relationship to *Svipdagsmál* is the first and still one of the fullest studies, but he concluded: "Den fulde Benyttelse og Forfølgelse af den gjorte Opdagelse vilde kræve en hel Bog" (672a).

[11] Cf. Einar Ól. Sveinsson 1971-73, 306: "It is a fact that when investigators of the Eddic poems approach the vicinity of the ballads, their compasses often seem to cease functioning properly…" The most recent juxtapositioning I have seen of eddic poetry and the ballad is in Kværndrup 2006, 435-57, but the approach is phenomenological, focusing on fate, luck, and honor, rather than literary historical. Colbert (1999, 281) notes the importance for ballad dating of the small group of ballads with eddic sources.

[12] Kværndrup 2006, 148-51, offers a recent summary and evaluation of Jonsson's theory of ballad origins; Colbert (1999) offers a subtle alternative to Jonsson.

[13] Harris 1985, 100-01; Fidjestøl 1999, especially 207-28. Vésteinn Ólason arrived independently at a similar view of the prehistory of *Þrymskviða* (p.c.) and has incorporated it into the in-progress Fornrit edition of the Poetic Edda (§5.9). I thank Vésteinn and Jónas Kristjánsson for a preview.

[14] The Norwegian ballad corpus is made available on the internet (Espeland et al. 1997), but the transcriptions are very late relative to the Danish (beginning in the sixteenth century) and Swedish (both texts from the seventh century) and not easy to assess.

[15] Grundtvig 1854; 1856; 1858-63; Grundtvig et al. 1933-65.

[16] Jonson, Solheim, and Danielson 1978.

[17] In *SMB* 18 A, 24 (Jonsson et al 1983, 205) the heroine is named Spegelklar. Grundtvig (1856, 668b, n.) compares the elements *men* + *glaðr* but concludes that the semantic similarity is accidental. I am more inclined to agree with Robinson that there is some kind of continuity here.

[18] For example, Koeppen 1837, 66; Cassel 1856; Justi 1864. A full bibliography of early scholarship is to be found in Sijmons-Gering 1927, 399, together with their text volume 195.

[19] For example, Bergmann 1874, 31-34, 157-60; Rupp 1871.

[20] I have relied heavily on Colbert 1989, 30-52 (Chap. 2) in this section. Older scholars dated Karen Brahe's Folio Manuscript considerably earlier, c. 1550 in Olrik (1939, 69 [1908, 88]), Steenstrup (1968 [1891], 43), and Grundtvig (1856, 668a ["først optegnet mitdt i 16de Aarhundrede"]). For background on the early collections see Lundgreen-Nielsen and Ruus 1999.

[21] Bugge (1860, 125) thought of Denmark or Sweden as the likely place for the recomposition as a ballad and apparently did not know of any presence of "Ungen Svejdal" in Norway; Einar Ól. Sveinsson (1975, 51) also does not know of the existence of this ballad tradition in Norway. But see my summary, based mostly on Bengt Jonsson, of the current facts and opinions; and see Jonsson 1991.

[22] Bugge (1860, 125) is certain that the ballad's composition was an oral matter ("denne Vise blev fra først af ikke fæstet med Pen i Bog"); but his

theory of the disaggregation of the two parts of *Svipdagsmál* was also oral: "Jeg antager, at *eet Kvad, hvoraf vi have en senere Formation i Visen om Svejdal, er blevet spaltet i to: Grógaldr og Fjölsvinnsmál,* [italics here for *Speerdruck* in the original] og det, som jeg tror, allrede i Folkemunde, og ikke først ved Afskriveres Fejl ..." (1856, 667a).

[23] Bugge (1860, 132) points out the scarcity of narrative verse in *ljóðaháttr* and denies that a longer narrative of the journey could have existed in this meter; Einar Ól. Sveinsson (1971-73, 304) allows for a little more possibility of this, but basically echoes Bugge.

[24] Bugge (1867, 445): the connecting link of the journey will have been in prose. Einar Ól. Sveinsson (1971-73, 304): "... it is ... likely that the gap between the two poems was bridged by prose narrative, whether or not it contained dialogue verses of some kind"; (1975, 53): "Eins og annarstaðar er minnzt á, er nærri vafalaust, að gera má ráð fyrir einhverjum frásögnum í óbundnu máli við hlið og til stuðnings bundna málinu í Grógaldri og Fjölsvinnsmálum, er það augljósast í 'ferðasögu' sveinsins, sem einmitt vantar eins og nú er komið fyrir þessum kvæðum, og er þar þörf þvílíkra frásagna." Einar Ól. Sveinsson imagines a similar prose or prosimetrical passage where the ballads have the farewell to the boy's comrades (1975, 54).

[25] For an excellent survey of scholarship in this area see Mitchell 1991, 139-77, especially 141-46.

[26] De Vries (1964-67, II: 524) can serve as an example: "Kein eddisches Lied hat soviel Berührungen mit der mittelalterlichen Volksdichtung, und es wundert uns deshalb nicht, daß es zu einer Ballade umgedichtet wurde: der schwedisch-dänischen folkevise von Sveidal oder Svendal ... [D]ie *Svipdagsmál* ... bilden den Übergang vom eddischen Heldenlied zur Volksballade." (In this passage de Vries missummarizes *Fjölsvinnsmál* by having "Fjölsviðr" as the hero's false name.)

[27] For example: Motz 1993; Heusler 1906.

[28] Einar Ól. Sveinsson 1971-73: "A cursory glance at Ungen Svejdal's variants does not seem to me to present any difficulties in the way of accepting the Eddic lays as the earlier source, while the relationship could easily be explained by a Norwegian intermediary."

[29] Bugge (1860, 125) already considered that *Grógaldr*, wherever it flourished orally, would not be the same as found in the Icelandic manuscripts, and even the forms of the earliest ballad and of this oral **Grógaldr* were far more like each other than what we see today. Grundtvig (1856, 670b) shrewdly points out that the same fated condition in hero and heroine in the ballad must be the original also of *Fjölsvinnsmál*—an implicit "reconstructive" move. Holtsmark (1972, 586-87) seems to speak of both the standard eddic-to-ballad derivation and also of a common source. Falk (1893, 333) definitely finds it necessary to hypothesize a common source: "For denne rammes vedkommende synes det nödvendigt at tænke sig en for disse to fremstillinger [*Svipdagsmál* and the 'Sveidalsvisen'] fælles sagnbehandling, maaske en mundtlig saga, men i temmelig fikseret form." In some of his reconstructive ideas I can follow Falk (348; 349 "fælles kilde"; 350), but his use of foreign sources before the proximate ones (cf. the derivational model on 334) make his argument as a whole, despite good detailed observations, impossible.

The Role of the Horse in Nordic Mythologies

Margaret Clunies Ross

Introduction

It has long been acknowledged that horses played an important role in early Nordic religious cult and ritual, just as they appear to have done among the Germanic peoples more generally (Gjessing 1943; Ellmers 1972). They are also represented frequently as images on objects such as standing stones and rock carvings from the pre-Christian period in Scandinavia, usually together with anthropomorphic subjects in various guises and undertaking diverse activities (Fuglesang 2007, 211, 215-16). Horses are also often mentioned in Old Norse literature, much of which was composed in its present form after the introduction of Christianity, and so may not always accurately reflect pre-Christian attitudes and behavior. Nevertheless, the considerable numbers of references to horses, especially in early poetry, and the often-repeated topics in the literature in which horses are involved, provide a basis of confidence for generalizations about the roles horses are likely to have played in early Scandinavian life and cult. Such evidence, together with visual and archaeological witnesses, is thus available to a modern mythographer desiring to assess the role of the horse as a cultural symbol in the system of human communication represented by Nordic mythologies. This chapter addresses that subject and analyzes the key intersecting cultural paradigms through which the figure of the horse gains meaning in early Nordic culture.

Many studies, both old and new, have argued for the central role of the horse in Indo-European myth, religion and real life (e.g. Puhvel 1955; Sauvé 1970; Anthony 2007) and this status has also long been accorded to the horse in Germanic myth and cult (Tacitus, *Germania* 10, Winterbottom 1975, 42-3; de Vries 1956, I, 364-7). Both older and more recent archaeological research has added extensive evidence from graves and other locations from the Bronze Age up to and including the Viking Age (Steuer 2003) in confirmation of the importance of the horse to early Scandinavian society, particularly to people of high social status. There is abundant evidence for the intimate relationship between men, women and horses in high status graves from the Vendel and Viking periods in Denmark, Sweden and Norway (Sundqvist 2001). Horses are often buried beside warriors, as, for example, on a Vendel chieftain's funeral pyre at Rickeby, Vallentuna, Uppland, Sweden, where a horse lies beside the warrior, together with four dogs at his feet (Sten and Vretemark 1988). The skeletons of large numbers of horses, and various kinds of horse trappings, including harness mounts, parts of decorated bridles, stirrups, wagons and other evidence of the importance of these animals to their human owners, have been excavated from the major Viking-Age ship graves of the Oslo fjord region of Norway, including those at Borre, Oseberg, Gokstad and Tune. At Oseberg, for example, there were up to twenty decapitated horses (Price 2008, 265). Horses are also evident in other types of graves; Price (2008, 268-9 and Figure 19.4) illustrates a reconstruction of a Birka chamber grave that shows a couple buried together seated on a chair, with two harnessed horses in a separate area below what appears to be the human living area of the chamber. A lance has been thrown across the seated figures to strike deep into the wood of the platform upon which the horses rest.

It has been usual for archaeologists to interpret the large numbers of animal bones in such graves as evidence of ritual sacrifices made during mortuary ceremonies performed for high-status individuals as they made the transition between life and death. This interpretation has conformed both to some of the evidence from the graves, where the animals are often decapitated, and to the writings of early ethnographers, such as Adam of Bremen (IV, 26-7; Schmeidler 1917, 259-60) and Ibn Fadlan (Duczko 2004, 139-41), who claim to have been told, in Adam's case, or seen, in the case of Ibn Fadlan, the sacrifice of animals along with humans at Viking-Age rituals, in the latter case at a mortuary ceremony among the Rus people on the River Volga. In many societies, including that of Scandinavia, the symbolic significance of sacrifice involves a rite of passage between worlds (Clunies Ross 1994, 191-7; Schjødt 2008, 59-52, 177, 184-202, 335-52), so the sacrifice of animals, such as horses and dogs, closely associated with their human owners, would probably have been understood by early Scandinavian peoples as ensuring the transition of individuals who had recently died from the world of the living to that of the dead. Animals and birds frequently found in early Scandinavian graves, such as the horse, the dog, and the cock or hen (cf. Gräslund 2004; Schjødt 2007; 2008, 344-5, n. 28), then arguably function as liminal beings that act as mediums between worlds.

Inferences such as these, drawn from the evidence of the existing remains of mortuary installations, fit well with what historians of religion and anthropologists have inferred from archaeological and other kinds of evidence for the role of the horse in pre-Christian Scandinavia. To date, the chief focus of this research has been on the horse's role as a dynamic mediator between worlds (Schjødt 2003, 431; 2008, 419; Loumand 2006) on the ground that it is a being 'endowed with mobility which enables it to mediate between all spheres' (Schjødt 2008, 419). Schjødt was here discussing the significance of the horse Grani in the legend of the hero Sigurðr, but his remark has general applicability. Somewhat earlier, the anthropologist Kirsten Hastrup analyzed representations of space in medieval and post-medieval Icelandic culture in terms of center and periphery (Hastrup 1985, 147-51; 1990, 254), and concluded that horses 'belonged to a separate space; they were tamed yet left more or less wild and out-of-doors for the entire year. They had both will and character…, and were endowed with both physical strength and a power of orientation in the wilderness which man had to traverse on horseback' (1990, 254). This statement hints at the horse's role as a mediator with logically opposed characteristics, something that will be further explored later in this chapter.

The horse's ability to travel between actual, physical environments, carrying either a human rider or pulling a cart or wagon, must have been central to its representation in myth as a liminal figure capable of mediating between worlds. However, there are other dimensions to the figure of the horse in myth and literature which suggest that the essential mediatory position of horses in early Nordic thought was both more complex and more ambiguous than has previously been accepted, and that the horse's role as a mediator allowed these complexities to remain unresolved or suspended, while at the same time the evident anomalies in the horse's position, which will be discussed in the rest of this chapter, meant that it was a being 'good to think with' about human society in general, because the binary yet oppositional categories of thought with which it was associated were fundamental to the character of the pre-Christian Nordic mythological system. This is why an understanding of the horse's role as a mediator helps us to understand the dynamics of Old Norse religion as a whole. As often, these mediating functions can best be expressed by means of a series of pairs of cultural categories in binary opposition, the most important of which will occupy the remainder of this chapter.

Binary categories involving the horse in pre-Christian Scandinavia

The analysis of myth as like a natural language in which categories in binary opposition are invested with symbolic meanings that may, upon analysis, reveal what the myths are 'about' in terms of a holistic understanding of mythological systems has been a methodology associated with the rise of structural anthropology in the mid-twentieth century. It is connected particularly with the ideas of the French anthropologist Claude Lévi-Strauss (Lévi-Strauss 1977-8; Leach rev. Lang 1996). The analysis that follows is structuralist in its broad approach, but is informed by an ethnographic particularism based on a thorough knowledge of Old Norse texts from the medieval period. The key binary pairs with which the horse is strongly associated have been identified as fundamental in many mythological systems (Leach 1976, 9-16, 55-64) and have also been traced in early Nordic mythologies (Clunies Ross 1994, 79-84; Schjødt 2008, 410-21). They include the binary pairs animal:human, nature:culture, wild:tame, male:female, dominance:submission, edible:inedible, and sacred:profane.

Animal:Human and Nature:Culture

As Kirsten Hastrup observed of Icelandic horses, they have or are thought to have 'both will and character'. In the Old Norse poetic corpus it is striking how often horses are not only associated with elite anthropomorphic beings, be they gods, heroes or other high-status individuals, but are themselves often endowed with names and genealogies just as humans are. According to the *Gylfaginning* section of Snorri Sturluson's *Edda*, the goddess Gná, for example, is quick to assert the pedigree of her horse, Hófvarfnir 'Hoof-thrower', when challenged by some Vanir as she rode through the air, saying that he was begotten by the stallion Hamskerpir on the mare Garðrofa (Faulkes 2005, 30).[1] The *þulur Þorgrímsþula* and *Kálfsvísa*, recorded in some manuscripts of the *Skáldskaparmál* section of Snorri's *Edda* (Faulkes 1998, I, 88-90), comprise lists of mythical and legendary horses and (in *Kálfsvísa*) their riders. The first stanza of *Kálfsvísa* (Anon *Kálfv* 1[III]) provides an example:

Dagr reið Drǫsli en Dvalinn Móðni,
Hǫð Hjálmþér en Haki Fáki.
Reið bani Belja Blóðughófa
en Skævaði skati Haddingja.

Dagr rode Drǫsull and Dvalinn Móðnir, Hjálmþér Hǫðr and Haki Fákr. The slayer of Beli <giant> [= Freyr] rode Blóðughófi and the champion of the Haddingjar <legendary family> [= Helgi] Skævaðr.

We must assume from such evidence that, although horses were primarily classified as animals, they were also considered to have human-like traits and to have been thought of as individuals. Their identity as individuals was intimately bound up with that of their human owners, who, importantly, were usually also their riders. Horses had personal names, which were remembered, and associated not only with the names of their human riders, but also with mythic and legendary narratives in which the horse and rider combination played a vital part. Thus horses had history, just as much as gods, heroes and humans, and in fact shared and participated in mythic history with anthropomorphic beings. They could thus be considered beings with culture. We no longer know some of the mythemes recorded by *Kálfsvísa*'s linked god- and horse-names, but the audiences of such rigmaroles certainly must have.

Horses and men could be thought of as growing up together and sharing lives. The close bond between a horse coeval with its owner and the human who owned it is expressed in a passage of the *fornaldarsaga Hervarar saga ok Heiðreks*. The prose text provides an explanation of a stanza the author quotes from the poem generally entitled *Hlǫðskviða* (often translated into English as *The Battle of the Goths and the Huns*), which tells of the birth of the hero Hlǫðr:

> Hlöðr var þar borinn í Húnalandi
> saxi ok með sverði, síðri brynju;
> hjálmi hringreifðum, hvössum mæki,
> mari vel tömum á mörk inni helgu.
> (*Hlǫðskviða* st. 76 (Anon (*Heiðr*) 7[VIII] (*Heiðr* 88)

Hlǫðr was born there in the land of the Huns, with short-sword and with sword, with long mailcoat; with ring-adorned helmet, with sharp sword, with a horse well tamed in the holy forest.

The prose text explains that the stanza refers to weapons that were being made and horses that were born at the same time that the hero was born "ok var þat allt fœrt saman til virðingar tignum mönnum" [and all this was gathered together in honor of men of noble birth] (Tolkien 1960, 46-7). Such attitudes make the frequent presence of the skeletons of horses alongside their owners in graves very understandable: beings that have lived together lie together in death.

Where we do know myths and legends in which horses participate, it is observable that they play central roles in the narrative just like anthropomorphic supernatural beings. In this respect they are unlike most other animals, which do not normally behave as independent actors in mythic narratives but rather function as members of an anthropomorphic being's entourage or equipment, like the goats that pull Þórr's chariot or the cats that perform the same function for Freyja, and the menagerie that inhabits the World Tree Yggdrasill, itself a metaphorical horse. An exception to this generalization is provided by a group of predators arrayed against the Norse gods in the context of Ragnarøkr: dogs, wolves and the World Serpent, Miðgarðsormr. Examples of horses that play independent roles in Norse myth include the narrative of the stallion Svaðilfari's role in the genesis of Óðinn's eight-legged horse Sleipnir (Faulkes 2005, 34-6), to be analyzed further below, and the role of Grani, according to some sources the son of Sleipnir, in the adventures of Sigurðr, in which he displays independent will, as, for example, in his refusal to carry Gunnarr through the flame wall to Brynhildr, as well as human-like emotion and behavior in his mourning the death of Sigurðr (cf. *Guðrúnarkviða* II, 5/5-8).

Another possible reflection of the early Nordic conceptualization of horses as independent beings with will is the fact that there are very few kennings whose referent is horse in skaldic poetry (cf. Meissner 1921, 111). When I first discovered this, I was quite surprised,[2] because I know there are many kenning patterns in which a word for 'horse' functions as the base-word of a kenning for some other referent; for example, a majority of ship-kennings have a *heiti* for horse as base-word (Meissner 1921, 208-12) and so do kennings for the gallows (Meissner 1921, 435). Although any conclusion about the reason for this surprising exclusion must remain speculative, I am inclined to attribute the absence of skaldic kennings for the horse to its special status as a dynamic, independent mediator. It may be that such a status rendered the horse ineligible to participate in the kenning system because of its variable symbolic significance.

The same absence of horse-kennings that we find in mythic narrative can also be detected in other kinds of narrative in skaldic poetry. In Sigvatr Þórðarson's *Austrfararvísur* 'Verses of a Journey to the East', for instance, the skald describes the privations of his journey into the wilds of Västergötland, undertaken c. 1019, using several forms of transport: by boat, on foot and on horseback. Whereas he uses a number of kennings for ship in the stanzas about his boat journeys, when it comes to the stanzas, 11-12, that refer to travel on horseback, he uses no kenning for a horse, but several horse-*heiti*, including *jór*, *blakkr*, *fákr*, *hross* and *hestr*.

Another interesting link, that places horses as much in the cultural as the natural world, is their mythic role in regulating the heavenly bodies, a crucial phenomenon that allowed the gods and humans to establish the cultural markers of time (cf. *Vǫluspá* 6). In this connection horses are associated with pulling the sun and moon across the sky in wagons or chariots, as stanzas 11-14 of the eddic poem *Vafþrúðnismál* tell us, information echoed by Snorri in *Gylfaginning* (Faulkes 2005, 13), and as the late Bronze-Age Trundholm sun-chariot famously reminds us. Thus horses are represented in Old Norse myth as human-like animals with culture, and, significantly, as we will shortly see, their cultural activities in myth are predicated upon the two real-life cultural inventions that allowed humans to exploit horses, namely their capacity to be tamed so that humans could ride on their backs, and their ability to be harnessed to pull wagons and carriages (cf. Anthony 2007, 59-82, 193-224).

Wild:Tame

The oppositional binary pairing 'wild' and 'tame' articulates special qualities that are to some extent subsumable under the binaries animal:human and nature:culture, and to some extent particular to the horse in Old Norse mythology. As we have seen above, the recognition of the horse as a creature of culture depends on its being tame rather than wild, yet, as with most originally wild things, there is an element of risk associated with interacting with the tamed animal, in that its wild nature or the riskiness of riding it as a form of locomotion may show through. Fear at the prospect of danger if the animal runs amok or its rider falls off is an emotion that can sometimes be associated with the figure of the horse in Old Norse literature. This is well expressed in stanza 16 of Þjóðólfr of Hvinir's *Ynglingatal*, generally dated to the late ninth century, in which the legendary Swedish King Aðils is said to meet his death after falling from a horse (*drasill*). The poem takes responsibility for the death away from the horse and ascribes it to a sorceress, while in Snorri's *Ynglinga saga*, the king is said to fall while riding the horse round the *dísarsalr* at a sacrificial feast to the *dísir* (*Heimskringla* I, 57-9).

The human effort expended in taming a horse and keeping it tractable is often indicated in Old Norse texts through the verbs of action by means of which this particular human-animal relationship is conveyed. In these expressions the human or divine being is always the grammatical subject, the horse always the grammatical object (often indirect), thus showing linguistically who's boss. Relevant verbs include *tama* 'tame', *ríða* 'ride', sometimes 'drive' (in a wagon), *aka* 'go, drive, travel', *reka* 'drive' (often of pack-animals or a herd, possibly also of goading horses to a fight; cf. Marold 2008). By contrast, the verb *draga* 'drag, draw, pull' is used of the action of pulling a wagon or other type of carriage; here the position of grammatical subject, by contrast with the verbs already mentioned, is usually occupied by the horse or other beast of burden.

A selection of illustrative examples from early Old Norse poetry and (in one case) a runic inscription from Gotland reveal the grammatical and syntactic signs of the horse's mediatory role.

Kjalarr of tamði
heldr vel mara

'Kjalarr <= Óðinn> tamed horses very well' (Þórðr Sjáreksson Fragment 3/ 3, 7 (ÞSjár Frag 3/3, 7[III]), eleventh century)

Kostigr Heimdallr ríðr … hesti … at kesti

'Excellent Heimdallr rides … a horse … to the pyre' (Ulfr Uggason, *Húsdrapa* 10/1, 3, 4 (ÚlfrU *Húsdr* 10/1, 3, 4[III]), c. 1000)

Svá er friðr qvenna, þeira er flátt hyggia,
sem aki ió óbryddom á ísi hálom,
teitom, tvévetrom, oc sé tamr illa

'The love of those women who think to deceive is like [someone] driving a frolicsome, three year-old horse not wearing ice-spikes on the slippery ice, and one that has been badly broken in'. (*Hávamál* 90/1-6)

óc Óðins sonr í iotunheima

'Óðinn's son [= Þórr] drove into giantland' (*Þrymskviða* 21/7-8). Here the beasts that are pulling Þórr's carriage (*hafrar* 'he-goats') are mentioned earlier in the stanza.

iu þin(n)Uddr rak

'Uddr drove (or 'incited') this horse' (runic inscription on runestone of Roe, Gotland, c. 800; possibly, *vide* Marold 2008, a reference to horse-fighting).

'Scinfaxi heitir, er inn scíra dregr
dag um dróttmǫgo'

'He is called Skinfaxi, who pulls the shining day over human beings' (*Vafþrúðnismál* 12/1-3).

One interesting exception to the grammatical and conceptual patterns established here is provided by two lines in *Grímnismál* stanza 49/1-5. Here the god Óðinn is speaking about the different names he assumed in the course of various adventures or when performing particular roles:

Grímni mic héto at Geirraðar,
enn Iálc at Ǫsmundar,
enn þá Kialar, er ec kiálca dró;

'They called me Grímnir 'Masked one' at Geirrøðr's, but Jálkr 'Gelding' (?) at Ásmundr's, and then Kjalarr 'Feeder (?)' when I drew a sledge'.

Here Óðinn as speaking subject refers to himself as drawing a sledge. Nothing is known of the myth alluded to here, but it was clearly familiar to Þórðr Sjáreksson and his audience (see the first quotation above) and it seems to have involved Óðinn as some kind of horse trainer and possibly as taking on himself some of the tasks, like pulling a sledge, more usually assigned to horses or other animals such as reindeer. The name Kjalarr occurs also in a *þula* of Óðinn's names (Þul *Óðins* 1/5^{III} and Note [5]).

This mysterious mytheme provokes another thought: together with Freyr, Óðinn is the Norse god most frequently associated with horses. Without delving into the possibility that people in Scandinavia believed that Óðinn sometimes took the form of a horse, one can say that the roles of god and horse could sometimes be merged (something we also detect in the sacred:profane binary) and that some myths and some names for the god, like Jálkr and Hrosshársgrani (a name Óðinn assumes in *Gautreks saga*), suggest that people thought of this god as having horse-like qualities. If so, the binary opposition of the terms animal:human and nature:culture could sometimes evidently be mediated and achieve a kind of fusion, as we perhaps see in visual images of Óðinn riding Sleipnir – the two become one.

Male:Female and Dominance:Submission

These two binary pairs, while almost universal in human thought, are particularly strongly represented in Old Norse myth and literature more generally. They have been very well studied and documented by a number of scholars (*inter alia* Ström 1974; Meulengracht Sørensen 1983; Clunies Ross 1994; Schjødt 2008). However, the ways in which they are inflected when it comes to the subject of horses has not been much discussed, as far as I am aware. Firstly, it is notable that almost all the named horses that figure in Old Norse myth and legend are stallions and their riders are male gods and heroes. If mares are involved in Norse myths, as they sometimes are, they are hardly ever named, nor are they represented as having autonomous will and intelligence. (The significance of riding a mare will be discussed below.) Mares thus belong on the natural side of the binary divide, as one would expect from the general nature of Old Norse myths, in which females are equated with nature and males with culture (Clunies Ross 1994, 79-84, 103-7, 127-8).[3] However, the binary pair wild:tame cuts across the nature:culture and male:female binaries in a very interesting way when it comes to the subject of horses, because the male horses that are accorded cultural status in Old Norse myth are all tamed, necessarily so if they are to participate in the mythic or heroic activities of their male owners and riders. Even in the horse fights referred to a good deal in Icelandic sources (Solheim 1956), the horses fight under the control of their human owners. Thus the position of stallions in the dominance:submission binary is equivocal; they are dominant male beings with culture, yet they are also submissive, because they have been tamed and learnt to accept the bit and reins, a saddle and a rider. In this pairing, the anthropomorphic rider usually dominates the ridden stallion.[4]

It is likely that this particular binary opposition may explain the close connection of the horse with *níð* or shaming insult, in addition to the stallion's obviously phallic character, which is well evidenced from many sources including *Vǫlsa þáttr.* Because the male horse could be associated with both sides of the binary dominance:submission, the figure of the stallion could easily be made to suggest either dominance or submission, and sometimes both at the same time. The slipperiness of the binary here allowed people to focus on one or the other value but to hint at its opposite. Such a facility served both poets and ordinary Scandinavians well, given that the composition of *níð* was a punishable offence in early Norse law, so ambiguous statements were at a premium. There are a number of skaldic poems that play on the horse's mediation of the male:female and dominance:submission binaries, and I will give only one example here.[5] This is a *lausavísa* by the eleventh-century Icelandic skald Sneglu-Halli directed at a rival poet, Þjóðólfr Arnórsson. The text and interpretation are based on Kari Ellen Gade's edition in Clunies Ross *et al.* 2007- (SnH Lv 11[II]):

Sýr es ávallt;
hefr saurugt allt
hestr Þjóðolfs erðr;
hanns dróttins serðr.

'There is always a sow; Þjóðólfr's horse has a completely filthy prick; he is a master-fucker.'

While the first line of this *helmingr* is rather difficult to interpret precisely, it opens the door to the general farmyard sexuality Halli associates with Þjóðólfr and implies at least bestiality with a sow as a last resort if nothing better offers. The rest of the *helmingr* probably suggests that Þjóðólfr lets his stallion fuck him, that is, the role of anthropomorphic dominance and animal submission is reversed. However, it is possible that the last two words should be understood as the compound *dróttinserðr* 'having been used sexually by the master', in which case Þjóðólfr is accused of having anal intercourse with his own stallion. Gade favors the first interpretation, as do I.

In this context, the symbolism of the *níðstǫng* 'shame-pole', reported in Old Norse texts of various kinds, fits perfectly. Much has been written about the significance of this object, which comprised a decapitated horse's head set atop a wooden pole. From the extant descriptions, a *níðstǫng* could be erected by one man to shame another or to cause him harm. In *Egils saga* (Sigurður Nordal 1933, 171) the pole is intended to send the guardian spirits of Norway adrift from their normal places of residence and drive King Eiríkr blóðøx and his queen Gunnhildr out of the country. The meaning of the *níðstǫng* derives from focussing the horse-related binaries male:female and dominance:submission and underlining the horse's ambivalently mediating role in them. The *níðstǫng* comprises male and female elements: the pole is phallic and male, and so a symbol of phallic aggression, but the horse's head is arguably female or feminized (Meulengracht Sørensen 1983, 29). It represents the person or persons again whom the *níð* is directed. In some sources, such as *Vatnsdœla saga* (Einar Ól. Sveinsson 1939, 88) the horse's head is clearly that of a mare, and this is probably true of other sources too, *Egils saga* using the term *hrosshǫfuð*, in which the first element *hross* usually refers to a stud horse or mare. As with Sneglu-Halli's *lausavísa*, the symbolism is similar: the aggressor is (or is like) a stallion fucking his male adversary, who is (or is like) a mare and thus feminized. Feminization is denoted not only by the actual mare's head, but by the cultural qualities that were supposed to accompany feminization in submissive males, namely cowardice and sexual perversion (*ergi*). The *níðstǫng* itself is thus a kind of material representation or objectivization of the symbolic rape of a submissive mare-like man by a dominant stallion-like human rival.

High Status:Low Status

It follows from the binaries that locate male horses, together with gods and heroes, on the cultural side of the divide with the natural, that they should also be associated with high rather than low status. As we have already seen, there is plentiful archaeological and pictorial evidence to back up this connection, including the well-documented presence of horses in high-status graves throughout Scandinavia. Sometimes skaldic encomia for early Scandinavian rulers can support the close connection between high-ranking humans and horses, like stanza 11 of the Icelandic skald Glúmr Geirason's *Gráfeldardrápa* (Glúmr *Gráf* 11[I]), composed in the late tenth century in honor of the Norwegian king Haraldr gráfeldr. The stanza records the king's death in battle.

Varð á víðu borði
viggjum hollr at liggja
gætir Glamma sóta
gerðs Eylimafjarðar.

'The guardian of the fence of the steed of Glammi <sea-king> [ship > shield > warrior], benevolent to horses, had to lie on the wide shore of Eylimi's fjord [Limfjorden].'

It is significant that the main trait the poet mentions here about his dead lord is that he was *viggjum hollr* 'benevolent [or possibly 'loyal'] to horses'. While it is not possible to know of the way or ways in which Haraldr favored horses, his close connection with them is evidently regarded as both characteristic of him and a praiseworthy trait.[6]

Inedible:Edible and Sacred:Profane

These two binary oppositional pairs are connected in the case of the horse, which indicates that the animal was consciously tabooed in early Northern society (cf. Leach 1972, 44-6). One might think that, logically, if horses belong mainly with culture, they should be inedible, as being human-like and therefore likely to be classified as 'non-food', but in fact there is good evidence that they were edible in early Scandinavia and other parts of the Germanic world, though restrictions appear to have sometimes been imposed on when they could be used as food. The most striking circumstances in which horse meat could be eaten involves the sacred sphere, and it may well be that the horse's role as a dynamic mediator between nature and culture explains what seems to have been the very powerful symbolic significance of horse meat as a ritual food. This significance is amply attested in a variety of written sources, including accounts in several historical works that tell of how the Christian King Hákon Aðalsteinsfóstri is reluctantly forced by his pagan subjects at sacrificial feasts in Hlaðir and in Mærr to eat horse-meat, first in the form of a stew, whose vapours he inhales and then by nibbling on a piece of horse liver (Snorri Sturluson *Heimskringla*, *Hákonar saga góða* chapters 13-18, Bjarni Aðalbjarnarson 1941, 166-72; cf. Jón Hnefill Aðalsteinsson 1992). Another important witness is *Íslendingabók*'s identification of the eating of horse meat (*hrossakjǫtsát*) as one of the pagan practices, along with the exposure of babies, that newly converted Christian Icelanders were allowed to continue for a short time but then had to discontinue (Jakob Benediktsson 1968, I, 17; cf. Dillmann 1997). There is also comparative evidence from other parts of the Germanic world that the eating of horse meat was particularly associated by Christians with core pagan religious rituals. A report to Pope Hadrian by a group of papal legates who had visited England during the reign of King Offa of Mercia, dated 786, makes special mention of how the Anglo-Saxons perform strange mutilations on their horses and that *Eques etiam plerique in vobis comedunt, quod nullus christianorum in orientalibus facit. Quod etiam evitate.* 'Also many among you eat horses, which no Christian does in the East. Give this up also.' (Dümmler 1895, no. 3, 27, lines 12-13; Whitelock 1979, 838).

The extent to which the practice of eating horse meat should be connected to other attested sacral roles of the horse is not entirely clear, but what is clear is that some horses, at least, were considered to belong to the sacred rather than the profane sphere, and were closely associated with certain of the pagan gods and their *hof* or places of worship. Poetic and pictorial evidence suggests a close connection with Óðinn, while later prose sources, such as *Óláfs saga*

Tryggvasonar in *Flateyjarbók*, *Vatnsdœla saga* and *Hrafnkels saga*, emphasise that horses were involved in the cult of Freyr. In this context it is instructive to dwell briefly on a detail in an episode in *Flateyjarbók* because it shows how several of the binaries mediated by the figure of the horse in Old Norse myth are likely to have influenced a particular practice, at least in its literary reflex if not in reality.

In an episode of *Flateyjarbók* entitled *Óláfr konungr braut goð Þrænda* 'King Óláfr broke up the gods of the people of Trøndelag' (Gudbrand Vigfusson and Unger 1860-8, I, 400-1), the narrative tells how King Óláfr Tryggvason is determined to destroy the image of Freyr to which local pagans still sacrifice and to desecrate the *hof* that contained images of Freyr and other gods. Most of the narrative is taken up with how Óláfr destroyed the Freyr idol, but one detail is interesting: the king and his men arrive at the *hof* before the pagan party can get there and they see, in the vicinity, a group of *stóðhross* 'stud horses' which are said to be Freyr's possession (*er þeir sǫgðu at Freyr átti*). The king then mounts the stallion of this stud (*konungr steig á bak hestinum*), orders the stud of females to be captured, and rides the stallion to the *hof*, where he dismounts, enters the building and cuts down the gods' icons from their stalls.

This action can be understood partly in the light of the binaries we have been discussing here. The stallion of the stud is to be identified with the god, Freyr, to whom he is ritually bound, just like Freyfaxi in *Hrafnkels saga*. By mounting and riding this stallion, King Óláfr deliberately breaks an implicit prohibition upon the riding of the horse by anyone other than the god and so profanes the horse and the god together. At the same time he asserts his domination, as rider, ruler and bringer of Christianity, over horse, pagan god and the pre-Christian religion itself.

The association between pagan gods, their sanctuaries and studs of horses, with their attendant stallions, and the means by which this ritual complex could be profaned during the period of conversion to Christianity receives an interesting confirmation from the Anglo-Saxon historian Bede's account of the conversion of King Edwin of Northumbria and his court in 627 (*Historia*

Ecclesiastica ii, 13, Colgrave and Mynors 1969, 183-7). The story is well known, but the details of interest to this discussion are less often commented on: namely, the actions of Edwin's chief priest (*primus pontificum*) Coifi in desecrating his former idols (*idola*) and sanctuary (*fanum*). His actions bear a considerable similarity to Óláfr Tryggvason's, with this difference: Coifi was a priest, not a king, and as such, as Bede tells it, not allowed to bear arms or ride except on a mare (*non enim licuerat pontificem sacrorum uel arma ferre uel praeter in equa equitare*). In symbolic terms, then, priests were feminized by being deprived of two high-status male attributes, the bearing of arms and the ability to ride a male horse. Coifi immediately breaks the taboo on both these things by mounting the king's own stallion (*emissarium regis*), wearing a sword and carrying a spear, which he uses to hurl into the sanctuary, thereby profaning it.[7] He then orders it to be destroyed and burnt. Coifi is thus a surrogate for King Edwin and takes upon himself the responsibility for the destruction of the gods of the old religion, whereas in the *Flateyjarbók* narrative, King Óláfr bears that responsibility in his own person. In both cases, however, a stallion is the mediator between the spheres of the old and new religions.

Conclusion

There are many ways in which horses were (and are) entities good to think with in Old Norse myth and culture more generally. By examining their often equivocal status across a relatively small number of fundamental binary oppositional pairs, it can be seen that their roles as dynamic mediators between and across these terms reveal some of the basic building blocks of the Old Norse conceptual world. This analysis has been by no means exhaustive, and, for reasons of space, I have ignored some well-known binaries in Norse mythology such as life:death in which horses play an important role as dynamic mediators.[8] However, I hope to have demonstrated that the horse's role as a mediator is not confined to his ability to move between different spatial worlds in Old Norse myth and society, but is central to many fundamental conceptual nodes that can be discerned at work in these cultural forms. In conclusion, I offer a close reading of the myth of the genesis of Óðinn's horse Sleipnir as one in which the majority of the binaries investigated here, including animal:human; nature:culture; wild:tame and dominant:submissive, all contribute to the myth's meaning.

Excursus: The Genesis of Sleipnir

The story begins (Faulkes 2005, 34-5) when a certain builder (*smiðr*) appears before the gods and offers to build them a fortress (*borg*) in three seasons that would be strong enough to keep out their giant enemies. This builder appears to be an agent of culture, but he is actually a giant (thus of the natural world in Norse myth) and his identity becomes clear from the nature of the payment he demands if he finishes on time: the goddess Freyja (after whom giants are always lusting) as his wife, along with the sun and moon, which the gods established to regulate time and the seasons of the year. This request breaks fundamental but unstated rules of divine society, in that the gods' women are never willingly given in marriage to giants (Clunies Ross 1994, 48-50), nor would the heavenly bodies be given to them, and so it alerts the gods that things may not be as they seem. Thus they stipulate that the builder must forfeit his payment if he fails to finish on time and, in order to ensure his failure, they say that he cannot have the help of any man, but must work alone.

The builder persuades the gods to let him have the help of his stallion, Svaðilfari, thus employing an animal, not a man, but using him for the cultural purpose of hauling up gigantic blocks of stone to the building site, presumably harnessed to a wagon. Svaðilfari's role is that of a tame draught animal engaged in a work of construction. When it appears that the builder will finish the work within the stipulated time, the gods act to prevent this happening: they put pressure on Loki to transform himself into a mare, that is, a natural being by virtue of both animal nature and gender, and to distract the stallion by offering him sexual intercourse during the evenings when the animal was usually employed hauling stones. This strategy works: Svaðilfari allows his untamed, natural impulses to get the better of the work ethic that has been imposed on him, and he runs around all night in the woods, a place of nature, with the 'mare' Loki. The fortress is not finished in time, the giant reveals his true nature by flying into a rage, which provokes Þórr, the god who keeps the giants in order by smashing them with his hammer, to mete out this very punishment to the builder, who is killed. As often in Norse myths, this last action is morally equivocal: the gods had to break the oaths that they had sworn in order to call up Þórr, but, on the other hand, the builder had deceived the gods both about his own giant identity and on the subject of his stallion's supernatural strength.

Svaðilfari's and Loki's sexual adventure had an awkward natural consequence: 'somewhat later he [Loki] gave birth to a foal' (*nokkvoru síðar bar hann fyl*). The male god who was forced to transform himself into a female horse suffered the natural consequences of sexual intercourse with the male counterpart to 'her' animal nature. But, interestingly, the transgressive character of Loki's act (looked at from a dominant, male point of view this was an act inviting *níð*) was translated into the superiority of the product, the foal Sleipnir, who became Óðinn's horse, the best among gods and men. Yet Sleipnir was marked as a being of abnormal genesis in that he had eight legs. Usually, beings with excessive numbers of limbs are of giant descent, like Starkaðr (cf. *Víkarsbálkr* st. 32, StarkSt *Vík* 32[VIII] (*Gautr* 40)), and Sleipnir indeed had giant ancestry (Loki himself had a giant father, while Svaðilfari had giant strength and was the horse of a giant). In this case, however, instead of having his four extra legs ripped off, as it is reported that Þórr did to other beings with too many limbs (Lindow 1988), Sleipnir's eight legs were retained and seem to have given him superior speed and strength.

Notes

1 The names Hófvarpnir (doubtless a variant of *Gylfaginning*'s Hófvarfnir) and Hamskarpr (a variant of Hamskerpir) occur in a *þula* or list of horse-names attached to some manuscripts of Snorri's *Edda* (Þul *Hesta* 4/5-6[III]). All citations from eddic poetry are from the edition of Neckel, rev. Kuhn 1983, while citations from skaldic poetry are from the new skaldic edition,

Clunies Ross *et al.* 2007- and its database at abdn.ac.uk/skaldic/db.php. The edition's sigla for the stanzas cited are presented in parentheses after the poem's or stanza's title and the volume number in which the citation will appear or has appeared is given as a superscript roman numeral. I thank the following editors for allowing me to cite their published or forthcoming editions of certain stanzas or poems: Kari Ellen Gade for *Kálfsvísa* 1, Þórðr Sjáreksson Fragment 3, Sneglu-Halli Lausavísa 11, and Bjarni Kálfsson, Lv 1; Hannah Burrows for *Hlǫðskviða* st. 76; Edith Marold for part of Úlfr Uggason *Húsdrápa* 10; Alison Finlay for Glúmr Geirason *Gráfeldardrápa* st. 11.

2 Evidently, so was Meissner, who remarked (1921, 111) 'Auffallend ist das Fehlen von Pferdekenningar; nur drei sind unten verzeichnet'.

3 Nevertheless, horses are found reasonably often in female graves in pre-Christian Scandinavian funerary sites and there is strong evidence of the connection between female graves and wagons, which are likely to have been pulled by horses, as we see depicted on the Oseberg tapestries (Roesdahl 1978).

4 I leave aside the complicating factor of castration, which produces a gelding, but I assume that a gelded male horse is equal to a female in classificatory terms.

5 Other examples include Mgoð Lv 1[II], a *lausavísa* attributed to Magnús inn góði Óláfsson and Anon (*ÓTHkr*)[I], an anonymous *lausavísa* composed about the Danish king Haraldr Gormsson and his steward Birgir, in which the former is represented as a stallion and the latter a mare.

6 An amusing stanza from a poet accompanying King Sverrir Sigurðarson on one of his campaigns, complaining about higher-status men having to walk when servants and cooks are riding horses, is Bjarni Kálfsson, Lv 1 (BjKálfs Lv 1[II]). The humor here depends upon the audience's acceptance of the association between riding horses and high social status.

7 Some scholars have speculated that Coifi's action in throwing the spear reflects traces of the cult of Woden in Anglo-Saxon England (cf. Mayr-Harting 1991, 26; see also Wallace-Hadrill 1988, 72, note to Colgrave and Mynors1969, 184, ll. 35-36).

[8] Obvious examples are Óðinn's ride to Hel on Sleipnir intent on recovering the dead Baldr (*Baldrs Draumar* 2) or, according to Snorri in *Gylfaginning* (Faulkes 2005, 46-7), his son Hermóðr riding for the same purpose.

Mythologizing the Sea: The Nordic Sea-Deity Rán

Judy Quinn

The subject of this essay is the representation of the sea in Old Norse mythology, not as it is conceived from the point of view of the Æsir, but from the point of view of people. My main source for this will be poetry, supplemented by some material from sagas to use as something of a foil for *Snorra Edda*, whose three main parts, with their varying agenda, present quite different mythologies of the sea. According to the eddic poem *Vǫluspá* and Snorri's elaboration of its content in *Gylfaginning* (11), the primordial sea was created from the blood of the giant Ymir when his body was dismembered to form land. The sea is also the habitat of the *miðgarðsormr*—whose being to some extent defines the span of the earth by encircling it—and whose fatal animosity towards Þórr is played out in combat on both sea and land. In this conception, the sea exceeds land in power and expanse, rising to cover it entirely at *ragna rǫk*, and receding afterwards to expose it again, having recreated it as beautiful and productive terrain for the new generation of gods to live in (*Vsp* 59-62).[1] The verdant landscape the outflow exposes retains the bounty characteristic of the sea: fish and the birds that prey on them (*Vsp* 59), and edible crops that require no sowing (*Vsp* 62). The gods who do not survive *ragna rǫk* are killed not by the engulfing sea but in direct combat with the animated forces who also control, or in some sense are, the sea. It is from the sea that the forces inimical to the gods at *ragna rǫk* launch their attack: according to *Vǫluspá* 50-51, the breaking of the ship Naglfar from its mooring as the *miðgarðsormr* churns the waves is one of the first signs of impending chaos and another ship, coming from the east, is captained by the turn-coat Loki.

Yet in other respects the sea does not seem a necessarily hostile environment to the Æsir: according to *Grímnismál* (st. 7), one of their halls is called Søkkvabekkr, or Sunken Benches, where the goddess Sága and Óðinn enjoy a drink every day, sipping from golden cups while cool waves splash above them.[2] And in the reciprocal feasting arrangement between the Æsir and the sea-deity Ægir—whose name is also a common noun for "sea"—there seems to have been an impulse towards rapprochement between gods and the divine beings of the sea, though it is not fully articulated in extant sources. After Ægir's visit to them, the Æsir retinue are, according to Snorri's account in *Skáldskaparmál* (*Skm* 1),[3] willing to go *en masse* to a feast in Ægir's hall out on the island where he lives, a venture that would seem unimaginable if the venue were in the traditional terrestrial domain of giants in the east—where, we are told by Snorri, Þórr was occupied meanwhile culling the hordes of land-giants. Ægir's hospitality is also expressed by his provision of a brewing cauldron, its huge capacity to hold valuable drink consonant with the containment of sea-water by the force of the ocean, at least in the pattering of concepts discernable in skaldic kennings. Ægir is therefore best understood as a personification of the sea—and for that reason I refer to him in this essay as a sea-deity—even if he is counted among the *jǫtnar* in some *þulur* (Lindow 2001, 47-48).

For men, the sea has a different meaning. It bites into the landmass they inhabit, as the opening of *Ynglinga saga* reminds us: "Kringla heimsins, sú er mannfólkit byggvir, er mjǫk vágskorin" [The ring of the world, which people inhabit, is deeply scored by bays] (*Heimskringla* 9). From the point of view of men, the sea is depicted as a treacherous surface to be traversed for fame and gain, its treachery personified to some extent by Ægir—especially in common-noun guise—but in a more animated fashion and more often by the female figures of the sea-deity Rán[4]—whose name as a common-noun means "robbery" (though it is a neuter noun in that case)—and the daughters of Rán and Ægir, whose names are mainly synonyms for waves. Although, as we shall see, poets developed the character of Rán in different ways, to the extent that her mythological function can be summarized, it seems to have been as a robber of life from men but not gods. Specifically, she personifies death by drowning and is aligned mythologically with the valkyrie, who personifies death in battle, as well as Hel, who personifies death in unspecified circumstances. Like Hel, she appears to be an independent agent, in partial distinction to the valkyrie who is sometimes portrayed as doing Óðinn's bidding in determining men's fate in battle. But like the valkyrie, Rán is depicted in some sources as a seducer of men, choosing sailors to take down to her underwater home.

The main sources for Rán are poetic—though there are some references to her outside of verse as well—and a little needs to be said about these sources before going further. Skaldic poetry in particular is full of references to the sea and sea voyages and therefore represents a valuable quarry of information about how Scandinavians both envisaged the sea and how they mythologized it. Among mythological kennings whose referent is the sea, the blood of Ymir is in fact referenced in only a handful of expressions—in a fragmentary verse by Ormr Barreyjarskáld (*Skm* v. 123); or allusively in *Þórsdrápa* 6 (*Skm* v. 85) as "Þorns svíra snerriblóð" [swirling blood of [a giant's] neck] or "undir háls jǫtuns" [wounds of the giant's neck] in Egill Skallagrímsson's *Sonatorrek* 3 (*Skj* B1 34). References to the *miðgarðsormr* in poetic depictions of the sea are rare. When poets conceptualized the sea, the tension between duelling gods and giants seems to have been less relevant than the danger of death they themselves faced in encounters with it. Of course in Christian devotional poetry, the ship and sailing across the sea took on different religious meanings—a sea journey is often the metaphor used for the course of earthly life—and that in part accounts for the very high number of references to the sea in the skaldic corpus.[5] There still is, nonetheless, abundant evidence of deeper traditions of imagining the sea which are not dependent on Christian symbolism; certainly the archaeological record of ship burials suggests a strong connection between death and the domain of the sea. As a source for mythological information, poetic texts naturally need to be treated with some caution since the requirement for alliteration could, in practice, lead poets to a choice of words that was determined more by metrical demands than semantic ones, and this consideration is even more pronounced in the case of poetry in *dróttkvætt,* where certain syllables also needed to assonate within lines; in addition, the interchangeability of base-words is intrinsic to the process of kenning formation. Nonetheless, in many of the examples involving Rán, it might be argued that it is the metrical pattern of the line which has been built around the mythological allusion rather than the other way round.

The Sea

Experientially, the sea is fundamentally a different kind of domain to land since being liquid rather than solid it is both surface and depth: the surface of the sea, like land, is traversable. Both surfaces are subject to changes in weather conditions that make journeying more difficult, but in the case of the sea, the very shape of the surface can change: it can toss about whatever is on it and in its movement towards a land mass can lash the coast and make the transition back to land of whatever is floating on it fraught with danger. To whatever is able to live beneath its surface, the movement inherent in this environment does not pose a problem, but to those hoping to cross its surface, the forces that make the sea swell and break into waves and troughs, it presents mortal danger. Staying on the surface of the sea is also more physically demanding than dwelling on the surface of the land: while the area beneath the earth's surface is strongly associated with the world of the dead, it is generally not too difficult, according to Old Norse sources, to keep away from zones where transit is effected, such as grave mounds. When it comes to the sea, however, the permeable zone extends across its entire surface, and human life is extinguished more or less immediately below the surface. Not surprisingly then, it is the surface of the sea that is the focus for most expressions relating to it, with an emphasis on the bravery and skill of those who manage to traverse it without being pulled beneath it to a watery grave.

Poetic Expressions for the Sea

Heiti, or simplex poetic terms for the sea, capture something of the sea's otherness as an environment, its movement and the dangers it presents. According to the *þulur* preserved in manuscripts of *Snorra Edda*, it is called, among other things, "salt, ægir, lǫgr, geimi, súgr, svelgr, hríð, gymir, órór, snapi, gnat, djúp, hylr, iða, hvítingr, sólmr" [salt, ocean, liquid, extensive one, sucker, swallower, storm, yawner, unquiet, snatcher, crashing, deep, pool, eddy, white one, weller] (*Skáldskaparmál* vv. 475-78).[6] This semantic range registers both the expansiveness of the sea and its powerful undercurrents that can draw what is on its surface downwards into its depths. These features are less apparent in kennings, which to a large extent tame the sea in the interests of valorizing the sailor who effects transit across it.

The formation of allusive kennings generally relies on a paradoxical relationship between base-word and referent, yet in the construction of most kennings referring to the sea, that paradox is intensified as a land-based perspective is assimilated into the construction by the use of base-words depicting features of terrestrial geography. The sea can be called:[7]

reggstrind	[ship-land]	Anon *Óldr*
dorgtún	[yard of the trailing fishing-line]	Bjbp *Jóms* 3[I]
svanvangr	[swan-plain]	Gsind *Hákdr* 5[I]
jǫkla akr	[meadow of ice-floes]	Eyv Lv 13[I]
otrheimr	[otter-world]	Þloft *Tøgdr* 1[I]
láð þangs	[kelp-land]	Steinn *Nizv* 2[II]
fjall humra	[lobsters' mountains]	SnH Lv 6[II]

While the determinants all belong to a marine environment, in almost all sea kennings the base-words are familiar elements of the landscape. Perhaps surprisingly, there are only a few exceptions, in which the base-word is a liquid, such as "húnlǫgr" [liquid of the mast-head] (Hókr *Eirfl* 8[I]) or the infrequent mythological kenning, "Ymis blóð" and its more abstract counterpart, "dreyri vengis" [blood of the land] (Ótt *Hfl* 3[I]). In an unusual example where the base-word is another liquid, the sea is described by Sturla Þórðarson (*Hrafn* 12[II]) as "útverja bjórr" [beer of the fishing outposts], an image, like those below, which exaggerates the domestic nature of the maritime landscape:

hvalsrann	[the hall the whale]	Anon *Pl* 3[VII]
úthauðr knarrar	[the outlying land of the knǫrr]	Bersi *Ólfl* 1[I]
setr flausta	[abode of ships]	Anon (*SnE*) 17[III]

The determinants of sea kennings are often legendary sea-faring kings, whose domains seem to retain the notion of land-like territory even while pointing to a marine referent. The sea is:

garðr Gestils	[the court of Gestill]	GSvert *Hrafndr* 1[IV]
sjǫt Hǫgna	[the dwelling of Hǫgni]	GunnLeif *Merl II* 31[VIII]
Ræfils fold	[the earth of Ræfill]	ESk *Øxfl* 10[III]
Leifa lǫnd	[lands of Leifi]	Bragi *Rdr* 4[III]
hlíðir Meita	[the slopes of Meiti]	Arn *Hryn* 18[II]
glójǫrð skíðs Gylfa	[the glowing earth of Gylfi's ski]	Anon *Óldr* 23[I]

Imagining the vast ocean as a sea-king's domain serves to tame it and to render its surface tractable: the poet Hofgarða-Refr Gestsson described the smooth plane of the sea as "Glamma skeið" [the race-course of the sea-king] (Refr *Ferðv* 5[III]). Even when the determinant is a marine or coastal creature, seascapes are still very much projections of landscapes:

reyðar rann	[hall of the finner-whale]	Anon *Brúðv* 4[VII]
búð ǫggs	[booth of the redfish]	EVald *Þórr* 2[III]
lýskáli	[pollack-shed]	Anon *TGT* 26[III]

álvangr	[eel-plain]	Rv Lv 9[II]
láð vǫgnu	[land of the dolphin]	Anon *Óldr* 28[I]
vǫllr lunda	[plain of puffins]	Sturl *Hryn* 6[II]
land hróka	[land of cormorants]	ÞjóðA *Magn* 6[II]

And that orientation obtains for the depictions of features of the marine environment as well. Seaweed is "lyng lýsu vangs" [the heather of the cod's field] (Sigv Lv 1[I]), while waves are "fannir Heita" [snowdrifts of Heiti [a sea-king]] (Styrkárr Frag 1[III]).

This land-based conception of the sea is particularly strong in kennings which depict the sea as a surface to be traversed—an orientation that was no doubt reassuring to sea-farers—where it is again the terrestrial that dominates the imagery. From this perspective, the sea is:

kjǫlslóðir	[keel-tracks]	ÞKolb *Eirdr* 13[I]
trǫð fleyja	[path of vessels]	Eþver Lv 1[V]
varrláð	[plain of the oar-stroke]	ÞKolb *Eirdr* 13[I]
fornar slóðir hafskíða	[the old tracks of ocean skis]	Mark Lv 1[III]

Confidence in the illusion sometimes wavers, however, as is shown by Einarr Skúlason's periphrasis for the ocean, the "bifgrund" [trembling ground] (Frag 14[III]). Indeed the propensity of waves to swell to dangerous proportions is acknowledged in kennings for waves as "marfjǫll" [sea-mountains] (Mark *Eirdr* 31[II]) and for a large swell as a "sægnipa" [sea-peak] (Refr *Ferðv* 3[III]). Swells and troughs could appear to the sailor as "gnípur húna" [crags of the mast-heads] (Mark Lv 1[III]), surrounding the ship as a "hár hranngarðr" [high wave-enclosure] (Steinn *Óldr* 10[II]). According to *Landnámabók*(132-34), an unnamed Hebridean poet is said to have composed a poem called *Hafgerðingadrápa*, the phenomenon of "hafgerðingar" [tremendously high waves] also described in *Konungs skuggsjá* (1983, 27-28), when a sailor finds himself hedged in by huge seas.[8] In these conditions, the "garðr"

[yard] of the ship surrounds but hardly contains the threatening elements beyond.

In sea kennings which are not focused on the traversability of the sea's surface, the point of view is sometimes raised above the land-base, surveying the surrounding sea as an encircling force—sometimes glittering like a necklace but more frequently described as a constraining force, isolating land masses and inhibiting travel between them. The sea is:

glæheimr	[the glistening world]	ÞKolb *Eirdr* 4[I]
men Lista	[necklace of Lista]	Sigv *Austv* 9[I]
hringr foldar	[ring of the earth]	Anon *Óldr* 4[I]
holmgjǫrð	[islet-belt]	Eþver Lv 1[I]
svalfjǫturr Selju	[the cool fetter of Selja]	ESk Lv 14[III]

Another of Einarr's kennings for the sea, "haustkǫld holmrǫnd" [autumn-cold island-rim] (Frag 12[III]), serves as a reminder that winter constrained sea travel and made insular communities even more isolated.[9] The great uncertainty and hostility attributed to the sea that is evident in the *heiti* quoted earlier is also expressed by some kennings, such as:

meingarðr margra jarða	[harmful enclosure of many lands]	HSt *Rst* 30[I]
inn ljóti landgarðr	[the hideous land-enclosure]	Anon *Mberf* 7[II]
læbaugr	[the deceit ring]	Hár Lv 2[I]
sverrigjǫrð landa	[swirling girdle of lands]	ESk Frag 13[III]
it grimma hrannláð	[the grim wave-land]	SnSt *Ht* 35[III]
élsnúinn þjalmi Manar	[the storm-twisted noose of the island]	ESk Frag 16[III]

The sea is also characterized as disarmingly boisterous and noisy, as resounding, roaring, rushing and swollen:

hrynslóð vǫgnu	[rushing path of the orca]	Anon *Óldr* 7[I]
hrynbrautar áls	[the resounding road of eels]	ESk *Øxfl* 8[III]
glymfjǫturr skers	[resounding fetter of the skerry]	Mark Lv 1[III]
rymvǫllr reyðar	[roaring field of the whale]	HSn Lv 2[II]
hár hryngarðr Hléseyjar	[the high roaring enclosure of Hlér [an island]]	ÞjóðA Hár 6[II]
grund gjálfrs	[the land of the surge]	Sturl *Hrafn* 16[II]

Only occasionally does the perspective change to imagine the dangerous domain beneath the traversable surface, with sea-ice described as "álhiminn" [sky of the channel] (Eyv Lv 14[I]), "næfr hallar hœings" and "nykra borgar næfr" [roof-shingle of the salmon's hall and roof-shingle of the water-monsters' stronghold] (Anon *Nkt* 4 and 68[II]).

This place beneath the surface of the sea is the home of fish, seaweed, sea-monsters and sea-deities, who sometimes emerge onto its surface to cause havoc for sea-farers. The twelfth-century poets Earl Rǫgnvaldr Kali Kolsson and Hallr Þórarinsson referred in *Háttalykill* 54[III] to the "raustljótar snótir svanvengis" [ugly-voiced women of the swan-meadow] and, in the same century, Gísli Illugason spoke of the "glymbrúðr hafs" [roaring bride of the ocean] (*Magnkv* 15[II]). A century earlier, the poet Snæbjǫrn described "níu brúðir skerja hrœra út fyrir jarðar skauti" [nine skerry-brides churning [the sea] out beyond the edge of the land] (Lv 1[III]) and another, Sveinn, pictured the "élreifar dœtr Ægis" [the storm-happy daughters of Ægir] (*Norðrdr* 1[III]) weaving about and enticing the sailor.[10] In his *Ferðavísur*, another eleventh-century poet, Hofgarða-Refr Gestsson, described the perils of a sea journey, with a struggling vessel tearing its breast as it escapes the devouring mouth of White-Rán:

En sjágnípu Sleipnir
slítr úrdrifinn hvítrar
Ránar rauðum steini
runnit brjóst ór munni. (*Skm* v. 127)

[But Sleipnir of the sea-crest [> ship], spray-driven, tears its red-stained breast away from Rán's white mouth.]

Refr also referred to the "spray-cold *vǫlva* of Gymir" (a sea-giant or another name for Ægir), who often brought ships down into the depths of the ocean:

Fœri bjǫrn, þar er bára
brestr, undinna festa
opt í Ægis kjǫpta
úrsvǫl Gymis vǫlva. (*Skm* v. 126)

[Gymir's spray-cold *vǫlva* often brings the twisted-rope-bear [> ship] into Ægir's jaws where the wave breaks.]

The "*vǫlva* of Gymir" is usually understood to refer to Rán, who through the choice of base-word acquires the attribute of foreseeing men's fates in addition to being present at the moment of their death, the components of the kenning merging the characteristics of female personifications of fate. The interchangeability of supernatural female figures as base-words in kennings of this kind in fact gives rise to a kind of conceptual blending of *vǫlva* with valkyrie and with giantess and this occurs in other instances as well. All of these female supernatural beings were understood to have power of some kind over the lives of men and more specifically, over the timing of their death (Quinn 2006).

Rán also figures as the base-word in a number of kennings for woman, some of them exploiting the resonances of this enticing but dangerous sea-deity. Rán's association with the ruthless killing of men is probably why Bragi Boddason, in the ninth century, chose her as the base-word in his kenning for the valkyrie, Hildr, in *Ragnasdrápa* 1: "ofþerris æða ósk-Rán" [the desiring- (or desired-) Rán of the excessive drying of veins] (*Skm* 250). When Hallfreðr vandræðaskáld Óttarsson imagined the love-making between the woman he desired and her husband, he described her as gloomy "dýnu Rán" [Rán of the eiderdown] (Lv 15 ^{V}), a depiction which encodes both the intimacy he assumes and the peril he courts.[11]

Sometimes reference to Rán is less charged with mythological meaning, as in this lausavísa (16) by Rǫgnvaldr:

> Orð skal Ermingerðar
> ítr drengr muna lengi;
> brúðr vill rǫkk, at ríðim
> Ránheim til Jórdánar . . . (*SkP* II, 594)

[The outstanding warrior will remember Ermingerðr's words for a long time; the stately lady wants us to ride Rán's world to Jordan...]

No doubt the poet wanted to impress the Viscountess of Narbonne—perhaps for the boy who learned to sail in the rugged north-west Atlantic playing up the danger of his sea voyage across the Mediterranean is part of this—but this kenning is one example in which assonance might have been the primary motivation for the choice of word.[12] There is little doubt from the syntax of the following example from Snorri Sturluson's *Háttatal*, however, that Rán is essential to the conception of the line, as the subject of the first and second clauses:

> . . . ne Rán við hafhreinum
> háraust—skapar flaustum –
> (hrǫnn fyrir húfi þunnum
> heil klofnar) fríð—deilu. (*Háttatal* st. 19)

[Noisy Rán does not create peace for the sea-deer [> ships]; she causes conflict for cruisers, the entire wave breaks before the slender bow.]

In another anonymous verse quoted by Snorri in *Skáldskaparmál*, the poet invests in the imagery of the sea across all four lines, making the choice of Rán semantically purposeful as well as an instrument of assonance:

> Hrauð í himin upp glóðum
> hafs; gekk sær af afli;

bǫrð hygg ek at ský skerðu;
skaut Ránar vegr mána. (*Skm* v. 356)

[The embers of the ocean were tossed towards heaven; the sea moved with strength. I think that prows cut the clouds; Rán's path struck the moon.]

This dramatic depiction of turbulence at sea also engages with the extraordinary light-reflecting qualities of water, as waves breaking high above the ship are described as glittering as though gold were thrown up into the air (Faulkes 1998, 296).

Rán and Death

I want to turn now to examples that engage a specific aspect of Rán as a mythological figure, the identification of her not just with the physicality of the sea—its iridescence and its power—but with death at sea. In *Sonatorrek*, Egill expresses his profound grief after his son Bǫðvarr has been drowned at sea (sts. 6-7):

Grimt vǫrum hlið,
þat's hrǫnn of braut
fǫður míns
á frændgarði;
veitk ófult
ok opit standa
sonar skarð,
es mér sær of vann.

Mjǫk hefr Rǫ́n
of rysktan mik;
emk ofsnauðr
at ástvinum;
sleit marr bǫnd
minnar ættar,
snaran þǫ́tt
af sjǫlfum mér. (*Skj* BI, 34-35)

[The breach which the wave caused in my father's kin-stronghold was dire; I know that gap stands open and unfilled, the loss to me of my son, caused by the sea. Rán has treated me very roughly; I am stripped of beloved friends; the sea has slashed the bonds of my family, the twisted strand from myself.]

Rán as an animation of the sea is clear here, the personification extending to willful and targeted action against an individual. Towards the end of the poem, Egill returns to this idea of a person's interaction with animated nature, as he describes his attitude to the inevitability of his own death (st. 25):

> Nú erum torvelt,
> Tveggja bága
> njǫrva nipt
> á nesi stendr,
> skalk þó glaðr
> góðum vilja
> ok ó-hryggr
> helja bíða. (*Skj* BI, 37)

[Now it's difficut for me. The sister of the enemy of Tveggi [Óðinn > Fenrir >Hel] stands on the headland. I shall, nevertheless, await Hel, glad, in good spirits and without dread.]

In this almost cinematic image, Hel stands on a headland awaiting the doomed man. Such a mythological posture invites an association between herself and Rán, between death at sea and death generally. These stanzas are remarkable for the degree to which Egill characterizes death as an encounter with a supernatural female. While he focuses on his own mental preparation for the encounter, other poets imagine what thoughts might be passing through the mind of the animated being herself. In *Ynglingatal* 7, Þjóðólfr ór Hvíni describes how Hel—again alluded to as the sister of the wolf—had to choose King Dyggvi for death:

> Kveðkat dul,
> nema Dyggva hrør
> Glitnis Gnǫ́
> at gamni hefr,
> þvít jódís
> Ulfs ok Narfa
> konungmann
> kjósa skyldi.
> Ok allvald

Yngva þjóðar
Loka mær
of leikinn hefr. (*SkP* I, 19)

[I declare it no secret, that the Gná of Glitnir has the corpse of Dyggvi for her pleasure; for the sister of the Wolf and of Narfi [> Hel] had to choose the king. And Loki's girl [> Hel] has outplayed the sovereign of the people of Yngvi [the Svíar]].

The formulation, *kjósa skyldi,* might otherwise be expected in connection with a valkyrie rather than Hel, another example of the merging of these figures in the poetic imagination. The sense of the stanza is nonetheless clear: death—personified as a female—has got her way in claiming the king for herself. What is disconcerting, especially in relation to Hel, is the idea that she takes men into death for her personal pleasure, and in this respect the personification again has parallels with that of the valkyrie. By its very nature, death in combat—the most celebrated form of death in Old Norse poetry—involves the figure of an antagonist. Rather than attributing the act of killing to this hateful victor, however, Old Norse poets describing heroic deaths sometimes availed themselves of the convention of ascribing agency to death itself, thus amplifying the glory of the valiant (but ultimately vanquished) warrior and occluding the figure of the victorious enemy. Personifying death itself, and identifying her motivation as erotic desire, worked to transform martial defeat into seduction by a powerful supernatural force, an altogether more satisfying motif in the discourse of heroic eulogy.

In a later stanza of the poem, *Ynglingatal* 18, describing the death of King Yngvarr, the idea of the natural world's pleasure at the death of a king is reiterated:

. . . Ok austmarr
jǫfri sœnskum
Gymis ljóð
at gamni kveðr. (*SkP* I, 40)

[And the Baltic Sea sings the song of Gymir [a sea-giant] in delight at the Swedish ruler.][13]

The kenning *Gná Glitnis* in *Ynglingatal* 7 is usually taken to refer to Hel in parallel with the other two kennings in the stanza.[14] If that is so, its resonances extend Hel's mythological profile considerably. Glitnir is a glittering hall (mentioned as Forseti's home in *Grímnismál* 15), whose goddess, according to Þjóðólfr, enjoys the company of corpses. The idea that death personified awaits the pleasure of men's company in a shimmering chamber chimes with other representations of Rán, rather than those of Hel, and perhaps there is a productive merging of figures here as well.

Other poets express a more laconic attitude to the poetic trope of visiting Rán. In an episode in *Sneglu-Halla þáttr*, the Icelandic poet Sneglu-Halli is described as coming up with a cunning ruse to frighten away other potential travellers from an already full vessel he wishes to catch from England to Norway. He tells those who already have a berth that he's just had a dream in which a drowned man came up to him and said:

> Hrang es, þars hávan þǫngul
> heldk of, síz fjǫr seldak;
> sýnt er, at ek sitk at Ránar;
> sumir ró í búð með humrum.
> Ljóst es lýsu at gista;
> lǫnd ák út fyr strǫndu,
> því sitk bleikr í brúki,
> blakir mér þari of hnakka;
> blakir mér þari of hnakka. (*Sneglu-Halla þáttr* 292)

[It's chaos there, where—since I gave up my life—I grab hold of tall seaweed. It's obvious I'm living at Rán's; some share their living space with lobsters. It's light enough to visit whiting. I have land off-shore—that's why, pale, I sit on a pile of seaweed. Kelp keeps flapping around my neck . . . kelp keeps flapping around my neck.]

The repetition of the last line, as in *galdralag,* emphasizes the spookiness of the vision. In this comic vignette he plays down the frightening aspect of being drowned—though scaring the other passengers is his ultimate aim—and concentrates instead on the domestic nature of life in the sea-deity's hall, a medieval version of

Davy Jones's locker. Again, the transparency of the medium of sea-water is noted as a feature of Rán's brightly-lit environment. These ideas are also taken up by the poet Friðþjófr, preserved in the *fornaldarsaga* about him. In these stanzas he reflects on the prospect of being drowned by comparing his erotic chances with Rán with his land-based seductions:

Satk á bólstri
í Baldrhaga,
kvaðk hvat kunnak
fyr konungs dóttur;
nú skal Ránar
raunbeð troða,
en annarr mun Ingibjargar.

. . . sjá skal gull á gestum,
ef gistingar þurfum,
þat dugir rausnar-rekkum,
í Ránar sal miðjum.
(*Friðþjófs saga* 15-16; *Skj* BII, 294-95).

Nú hefr fjórum
of farit várum
lǫgr lagsmǫnnum
þeims lifa skyldu,
en Rán gætir
rǫskum drengjum
siðlaus kona
sess ok rekkju.
(*Friðþjófs saga* 46; *Skj* BII, 294-95
[only in AM 510 4to]).

[I sat on a bolster in Baldrshagi, I recited what I could for the king's daughter; now I shall tread the dangerous bed of Rán and someone else will tread Ingibjörg's bed. . . . In the middle of Rán's hall, gold shall be visible on the guests, if we have to be accommodated there—that befits magnificent warriors. Now the sea has taken four of our men who should have lived; but Rán, unconventional woman, provides a seat and a bed for brave warriors.]

The description, *siðlaus kona,* might also be rendered "woman without social graces", an understatement, of course, on the part of the drowned guest. In another verse, Friðþjófr describes drowning men as sinking down into the bottomless sea (*Friðþjófs saga* 16; *Skj* BII, 294).

Rán in Saga Prose

The literary motif which figures drowning as an embrace by a female personification of the sea is found as well in family sagas. In *Fóstbræðra saga*, for instance, surviving a risky sea voyage is described in terms of the brothers Þorgeirr and Þormoðr escaping the embrace of the daughters of Rán: ". . . reyndu Ránar dœtr drengina ok buðu þeim sín faðmlǫg . . ." [. . . . the daughters of Rán tried to embrace them. . .] (*Fóstbræðra saga* 135). And in the extended sequence of evening visits by dripping revenants described in *Eyrbyggja saga*, the following explanation is given for their return:

> Menn fǫgnuðu vel Þóroddi, því at þetta þótti góðr fyrirburðr, því at þá hǫfðu menn þat fyrir satt, at þá væri mǫnnum vel fagnat at Ránar, ef sædauðir menn vitjuðu erfis sins. (*Eyrbyggja saga*, 148)
>
> [People welcomed Þóroddr warmly, thinking it was a good omen, because at that time they believed that if men who had drowned at sea attended their own funeral feast, they had been well received by Rán.]

Notwithstanding that sanguine explanation, the drowned are evidently reluctant to abandon fireside warmth for life under the sea, no matter how accommodating Rán is being regarding their attendance at the departure ritual for them from the land of the living. Sagas also contain two instances of an idiomatic expression, *mælir rán ok regin*: "to speak Rán and divine powers" against someone, which seems to mean to defame someone.[15] There has been much debate about what the word *rán* may refer to in this context: in a doublet with *regin*, it seems more likely to be the sea-deity Rán (Jóhannesson 1950, 92) than the common noun *rán*, but it is hard to know from surviving evidence what the special resonance of the name Rán might have been here, beyond its alliterative appeal.

Rán in Eddic Poetry

More immediately illuminating are the references to Rán in eddic heroic poetry, where she is depicted as working in league with her daughters and a giantess called Hrímgerðr to capture men from their ships. In *Helgakviða Hjǫrvarðssonar,* Helgi's companion Atli, who has earlier called Hrímgerðr "nágráðug" [corpse-greedy], confronts the giantess (st. 18):

Þú vart, hála, fyr hildings skipum
ok látt í fjarðar mynni fyrir;
ræsis rekka er þú vildir Rán gefa,
ef þér kœmið í þverst þvari.

[You were, giantess, in front of the prince's ships and you lay in wait in the mouth of the fjord; you wanted to give the prince's men to Rán, if a spear had not pierced your flesh.]

Another description of an encounter with Rán and her daughters is provided by *Helgakviða Hundingsbana I,* stanzas 28 to 30:

Svá var at heyra, er saman kómu
Kólgu systir ok kilir langir,
sem bjǫrg við brim brotna myndi.

Draga bað Helgi há segl ofarr,
varðat hrǫnnum hǫfn þingloga,
þá er ógorlig Ægis dóttir
stagstjórnmǫrum steypa vildi.

Enn þeim sjálfum Sigrún ofan,
fólkdjǫrf, um barg ok fari þeira;
snøriz ramliga Rán ór hendi
gjálfrdýr konungs at Gnipalundi.

[So it could be heard, that the sisters of Kólga [waves] and the long keels clashed, as if the cliffs might break apart from the force of the surf. Helgi ordered the tall sail hoisted higher up; the crew were not reluctant to engage in the meeting with breakers when the unlovely daughter of Ægir wanted to capsize the horse of the stay-bridle [> ship]. Still, from above, battle-daring Sigrún [a valkyrie] protected them and their ship; the king's beast of the roaring sea [> ship] was wrenched with great force out of Rán's hands at Gnipalund.]

Further definition to the role of the sea-deity is provided here, since she is in direct competition with the valkyrie who protects each of the Helgis. In *Helgakviða Hjǫrvarðssonar*, the valkyrie Svava provides air cover for the hero and his troops in their sea-battle. When the giantess discovers this, she describes the protecting valkyrie as hateful to her (st. 28), for having frustrated her own plan to have Helgi for herself; just one night, she pleads, as compensation for Helgi's killing of her cliff-dwelling father (st. 24). The idiom of Hrímgerðr's *senna* with Atli also casts her desire as unashamedly sexual (sts 20-21), albeit played out rhetorically between mare and stallion and involving rather violent rib-straightening. Interestingly, even though Atli fears she will bob up beneath their ship, he repeatedly uses land-based images to articulate men's attempted control of the threat she poses: she should be buried deep in the earth with trees growing up from her breast, Atli says (st. 16). Eventually Helgi is able to control her with hel-runes, which, it is specified, are effective on both land and sea (st. 29), and her apparent ability to move between land and marine environments which so unsettles them is resolved when she is turned to stone. De-animated and returned to her element by men, she is no longer able to move at all.[16] In *Helgakviða Hundingsbana I* too, a valkyrie is pitted against Rán in a tussle to control the fate of the hero. In this company, Rán seems to represent the ineluctable tug of mortality, a force that can only be countered by the temporary protection of a valkyrie whose medium is air rather than land or sea.

Rán in Snorra Edda

When Snorri turns to expressions for the sea in *Skáldskaparmál*, he foregrounds the mythological explanation for its origin—as the blood of the giant Ymir—that he had related in *Gylfaginning*, both in his prose list and in the first stanza he quotes by the poet Ormr:

> Hvernig skal sæ kenna? Svá at kalla hann Ymis blóð, heimsœkir guðanna, verr Ránar, faðir Ægis dœtra fleira er svá heita: Himinglæva, Dúfa, Blóðughadda,

Hefring, Uðr, Hrǫnn, Bylgja, Bára, Kólga; land Ránar ok Ægis dœtra ok skipa ok sæskips heita, kjalar, stála, súða, sýju, fiska, ísa, sækonunga leið ok brautir, eigi síðr hringr eyjanna, hús sanda ok þangs ok skerja, dorgar land og sæfogla, byrjar. Svá sem kvað Ormr [Barreyjarskáld]:
Útan gnýr á eyri / Ymis blóð fara góðra. (*Skm* 36-37)

[How shall the sea be referred to? By calling it Ymir's blood, visitor to the gods, husband of Rán, father of Ægir's daughters, whose names are Himinglæva, Dúfa, Blóðughadda, Hefring, Uðr, Hrönn, Bylgja, Bára, Kólga; land of Rán and of Ægir's daughters and of ships and of terms for sea-ship, of keel, stem, planks, strake, of fish; sea-kings' way and roads no less ring of the islands, house of the sands and seaweed and skerries, land of the fishing tackle and of sea-birds, of sailing wind. As Ormr Barreyjarskáld said: "Out on the sand-bank of good vessels, Ymir's blood roars."]

Snorri also promotes his own account of Ægir as *heimsækir guðanna* even though no kenning of this type is found in the corpus. Despite the preponderance of female personifications of the sea in kennings, Snorri orients the evidence to Ægir, consonant with his organizational principle in *Skáldskaparmál*, as Margaret Clunies Ross has shown (1983), to make anthropomorphized natural phenomena members of male-led mythological families.

The eleven stanzas following Ormr's contain kennings for the sea with the combinations of base-words depicting landscape features and determinants that are either sea-creatures or sea-kings, such as I surveyed earlier, with four of the eleven containing animated kennings involving sea-deities (vv. 125, 126, 127, 133). The names of the nine daughters of Rán and Ægir listed by Snorri are either common nouns denoting waves or words connoting their bright upward surge: "Himinglæva" [Sky-bright] and "Hefring" [Riser]. Only "Blóðughadda" [Bloody-haired] signals the man-devouring side of her nature as it is seen in other sources, though the imagery is abstract. In stanzas where these names are deployed, the personified wave is ascribed agency, and often rather willful agency. These kenning formulations that depict Rán's familial relations, however, attest to the taste in skaldic poetry for riddling identifications, and no imaginative energy seems to have gone into depicting this particular giant household. For all intents and purposes, Rán, Ægir and their many daughters are a family in taxonomic terms only.

When an explanation for the kenning, "the fire of Ægir", is provided in some versions of *Skáldskaparmál* (it is not in the Uppsala manuscript), a household of sorts is, however, momentarily glimpsed:

> Fyrir því er gull kallat eldr Ægis? Þessi saga er til þess, er fyrr er getit, at Ægir sótti heimboð til Ásgarðs, en er hann var búinn til heimferðar þá bauð hann til sín Óðni ok ǫllum Ásum á þriggja mánaða fresti. Til þeirar ferðar varð fyrst Óðinn ok Njǫrðr, Freyr, Týr, Bragi, Viðarr, Loki; svá ok Ásynjur, Frigg, Freyja, Gefjun, Skaði, Iðunn, Sif. . . . En er goðin hǫfðu sezk í sæti þá lét Ægir bera inn á hallargólf lýsigull þat er birti ok lýsti hǫllina sem eldr ok þat var þar haft fyrir ljós at hans veizlu svá sem í Valhǫllu váru sverðin fyrir eld. . . . Rán er nefnd kona Ægis, en níu dœtr þeira, svá sem fyrr er ritat. . . . Þá urðu Æsir þess varir at Rán átti net þat er hon veiddi í menn alla þá er á sæ kómu. Nú er þessi saga til þess hvaðan af þat er, gull er kallat eldr eða ljós eða birti Ægis, Ránar eða Ægis dœtra. (*Skm* 40-41)
>
> [Why is gold called Ægir's fire? The origin of it is this story: Ægir, as was told before, went as a guest to Ásgarðr, and when he was about to return home, he invited Óðinn and all the Æsir to visit him in three months' time. On this journey were Óðinn and Njǫrðr, Freyr, Týr, Bragi, Viðarr, Loki; and the Ásynjur, Frigg, Freyja, Gefjun, Skaði, Iðunn, Sif . . . And when the gods had sat down, Ægir had brought onto the floor of the hall brilliant gold, which

> brightened up and lit the hall like fire, and this served as lighting at his feast, just as swords had at Valhalla instead of fire. Rán is the name of Ægir's wife and their nine daughters, as was written before . . . then the Æsir became aware that Rán had a net in which she might catch all the men who went to sea. So this is the story of the origin of gold being called fire, or light, or brightness of Ægir or of Rán or of Ægir's daughters.]

When, later in the treatise, Snorri quotes an anonymous verse describing Rán's path hitting the moon (v. 356), he reiterates the family bond he seeks to foreground, both before and after the quotation, reinforcing his conceptual scheme:

> Rán, er sagt er at var kona Ægis, svá sem hér er . . . Dœtr þeira Ægis ok Ránar eru níu ok eru nǫfn þeira fyrr rituð: Himinglæva, Dúfa, Blóðughadda, Hefring, Uðr, Hrǫnn, Bylgja, Drǫfn, Kólga. (*Skm* 95)

> [Rán, who is said to be Ægir's wife, as here: . . . the daughters of Ægir and Rán are nine and their names have already been written: Himinglæva, Dúfa, Blóðughadda, Hefring, Uðr, Hrǫnn, Bylgja, Drǫfn, Kólga.]

In this list, *Drǫfn* is substituted for *Bára,* although both names occur in a later maximized list in a *þula* of words for "wave" (*Skm* v. 478).

Rán's net is also mentioned in the prose of the Poetic Edda (in the prose prologue to *Reginsmál*) and in *Vǫlsunga saga* (ch. 14), when it is borrowed by Loki to catch the dwarf Andvari, who, at the time, has taken the form of a fish. Interestingly, there is no kenning that draws on this imagery. Like Freyja's feather-coat, which she herself never seems to need, perhaps Rán's net is just a borrowable attribute, an extension of her powers that can be lent out, useful to the Æsir when they go fishing for mythological gain, but unnecessary to her since she can just flex her extensive surface if she wants to capsize a boat. In that sense, Rán is both the sea and in the sea; and in the latter context, she takes a woman's form.

The Sea in Riddles

Perhaps it is not surprising that the mythologizing of the sea lies behind one of the most elusive riddle complexes in Old Norse poetry, the verses quoted in *Hervarar saga ok Heiðreks* eliciting the solution "waves", which have recently been edited by Hannah Burrows. There is also a riddle in the eddic corpus which invites the female personification of a wave as the answer (in the question which exposes Óðinn's disguise in his interrogation of the *vǫlva* in *Baldrs draumar*):

> . . . hverjar eru þær meyjar, er at muni gráta
> ok á himin verpa hálsa scautum?
>
> [. . . who are those girls who weep from desire
> and who cast up to heaven the sheets of their necks?]

As Burrows observes, the referential meaning of the collocation of *háls* ("ridge", "neck", "sail") with *scaut* ("headdress", "square cloth", "sail") is not easily construed. Given that riddles often allude to white-capped waves as having headdresses, however, it seems plausible to read the line as alluding both to wave-maidens tossing their metaphorical white headdresses "or the more literal ships that venture out on them" (Burrows 2013, 211). Once again, the personification works concurrently as a characterizing figure and metaphorically as the body of water itself. The girls' weeping in relation to desire (*munr*) is also puzzling—most commentators interpret their behavior as a response to grief over lost love—though here again the description, in the riddling idiom of the stanza, may be metaphorical rather than physical, with "weeping" referencing the girls' watery nature rather than their sorrow. If so, they would be released from a narrative of grief and express instead the desire familiar from portrayals of Rán and some valkyries as well as Hel in the example discussed earlier, with the seduction of sailors serving as a euphemism for drowning. If a warrior's death in battle induced an imaginative transformation of defeat into the honor of being selected by an other-worldly woman, how much more in need of transformation might a sailor's sad fate have been, being shipwrecked and drowned at sea? The depictions of frolicking waves that lured sailors to join them, or of Rán drawing men down to her beneath the surface of the ocean, allowed poets to transform tragic loss of life into the consolation of powerful elemental forces pulling men irresistibly towards them.

In this connection, the wave riddles preserved in manuscripts of *Hervarar saga ok Heiðreks* offer an interesting trove of associations, made richer by the proliferation of verses in some manuscripts. As the examples below show, female personifications of the sea were imagined as nubile, alluring, self-willed, determined and destructive:[17]

> Hverjar eru þær brúðir, er ganga í brimskerjum
> ok eiga eptir firði för?
> Harðan beð hafa þær inar hvítföldnu,
> ok leika í logni fátt . . .
>
> Hverjar eru þær ekkjur, er ganga allar saman . . .
> Sjaldan blíðar eru þær við seggja lið
> ok eigu í vindi vaka . . .
>
> Hverjar eru þær snótar, er ganga syrgjandi
> at forvitni föður?
> Hadda bleika hafa þær inar hvítföldnu,
> ok eigut þær varðir vera . . .
>
> Mörgum mönnum hafa þær at meini orðit
> við þat muna þær sinn aldr ala . . .

[Who are those brides who go along in the surf-skerries and have their journey along the fjord? They have a hard bed, the white-hooded ones, and they play little in the calm . . . Who are those women who go around together? . . . Seldom are they gentle with the band of men, and they are awakened in the wind . . . Who are those women who go sorrowing to the curiosity of their father? They have pale hair, the white-hooded ones, and those women do not have husbands . . . To many men they have caused harm, and in this way they must spend their lives . . .]

Roused into action by the wind, waves swell in wild weather, when the sailing of ships on the sea is particularly dangerous. The animation inherent to the riddle form lends itself to elaborated metaphor with the embrace the wave-maidens offer rough and the bed they entice men into as hard as the sea-bed they wash over. While the wave-maidens are specifically connected to their (unnamed) father rather than to their mother, they clearly operate independently of any paternal direction, travelling in groups to the apparent bemusement of their father. In this perhaps we might see a reflex of the flighty valkyries of the eddic heroic poems who neglect the task assigned to them by Óðinn and follow their own desire instead. Relentlessly breaking and flowing back into the ocean, the life of waves may be everlasting but it is only "life" in a figurative sense, their status of being without husbands as notional as the family Snorri posited for his classification of personifications of the sea. It is their desire for men that is the salient characteristic. This marauding band of seducers, in the face of whom an ordinary mortal has very little chance of escape, inverts the familiar Viking stereotype in terms of gender, and presents the wave-maiden as arbiter of a mariner's fortune.

Being the sea as well as appearing in sexualised female form, these personifications enlivened the literary imagining of the sea in medieval Scandinavia and gave expression to the force that resided beneath the ocean's surface and frequently broke through it. That men's experience of that force centred on disaster and death is unsurprising given their dependence on sea-travel; that said, many of the kennings quoted earlier in this essay occur in descriptions of sailors' triumph, as their ships rode the waves and they defied death-at-sea.

Notes

[1] All quotations of eddic poems are from the fifth edition by Neckel and Kuhn, with normalized orthography; the titles of poems are abbreviated following their practice. Translations of eddic and skaldic poetry are my own.

[2] For a discussion of Søkkvabekkr in Old Norse mythology, see Ursula Dronke's contribution to Dronke and Dronke (1997, 27-45).

[3] Quotations and references to *Skáldskaparmál* are to Anthony Faulkes's edition, abbreviated to *Skm*; references to quotations of verse follow Faulkes's numbering.

[4] There is some evidence that Rán was considered to be a goddess: she is listed among the Ásynjur in a *þula* preserved in AM 748 Ib 4to and AM 757 4to (*Skm* vv. 433-4). In a verse preserved in *Laufás Edda*, attributed to Þórðr Sjáreksson, Rán appears to be the referent of the kenning "ásynja fljóðs" [goddess of high-water] (*Skj* BI, 304), though the head-word in this case may simply be denoting any female. Like Ægir, Rán is primarily a personification of the sea and both figures defy straightforward categorization as either a god/goddess or a giant/giantess.

[5] For a survey of imaginative traditions involving sea-imagery in classical and medieval Christian literature, see Peter Dronke's contribution to Dronke and Dronke (1997, 2-26).

[6] Translations of excerpts from *Skáldskaparmál* are adapted from Faulkes (1987).

[7] In the examples gathered here, the identification of works containing kennings follows the abbreviations of the names of poets and poems used in *SkP*, with the superscript number indicating the volume of the edition (published or planned).

[8] I am grateful to Judith Jesch for providing me with a copy of her as yet unpublished paper from 2009 on Old Norse poetry associated with Scotland, in which *Hafgerðingadrápa* is discussed.

[9] Einarr was clearly an enthusiast for sea kennings, with over fifty examples preserved across his extant oeuvre.

[10] On the interpretation of this stanza, see Faulkes (1998, 257) and Kock (NN§2989H).

[11] In both of these examples, the word *Rán* participates in the formation of *hendingar* but not in the alliterative structure of the lines. The same pattern occurs in two further kennings with *Rán* as the base-word: "auð-

Rán" [wealth-Rán], a kenning for woman in *Brúðkaupsvísur* 18[VII] and "folk-Rán" [battle-Rán], within a kenning for "warrior' in Þorleifr jarlsskáld Rauðfeldarson's *Hákonardrápa* 1[I].

[12] Another instance of the name *Rán* being deployed for metrical as much as mythological reasons is Gunnlaugr Leifsson's *Merlínússpá*, I, 89[VIII], where the sea is described as "Ráns vegr" [Rán's way].

[13] Compare Edith Marold's translation of the line: ". . . to the delight of the Swedish ruler"; the interpretation of the preposition is not discussed in the Notes (*SkP* I, 41).

[14] For a survey of interpretations of the kenning, see Marold (*SkP* I, 19-20), who notes that "most interpreters justifiably view this phrase as a reference to an erotic relationship between the dead and the goddess of death" (20).

[15] See *Qlkofra þáttr* 92 and *Fljótsdæla saga* 246.

[16] There is a further possible reference to Rán in the context of a magical spell in the eddic poem *Grógaldr* (st. 6), though the form of the name in this case appears to be masculine (Rani); (see Bugge 1867, 339).

[17] The edited texts of lines from waves riddles are quoted from Burrows 2013, 216 (*Heiðreks gátur* 24, 23, 21 and 22).

Comparative Historical Focus

From History to Myth: The Ingvar Stones and *Yngvars saga víðfǫrla*

Lars Lönnroth

Yngvars saga víðfǫrla—the saga of the far-travelling Yngvar—describes an expedition by Swedish vikings into exotic Eastern lands where they encounter dragons, giants, cyclopes, seductive but deadly witches and other mythical creatures. The text, which is preserved in two late medieval manuscripts, is generally classified as a *fornaldarsaga* and several scholars have regarded it as postclassical fiction.[1] Unlike other *fornaldarsögur*, however, this one claims to be an account of an actual viking expedition that is known to have left Sweden in the eleventh century and is generally believed to have perished around 1040 somewhere along the Eastern trade route. About thirty commemorative runestones from that time, the so-called Ingvar stones, located in the area around Lake Mälaren in Sweden, testify to the existence of the expedition itself and its leader, Yngvar víðfǫrli, or Ingvar, as he is usually called in the inscriptions.[2]

In 1981 Dietrich Hofmann showed that the saga text, in spite of its fantastic content, is based on a chronicle in Latin from the late twelfth century by Oddr Snorrason, who was a monk in Þingeyrar monastery and who also wrote a Latin biography of King Olav Tryggvason. Oddr, in his turn, based his account on oral traditions that can, at least to some extent, be traced back to Sweden and the time of Ingvar víðfǫrli (Hofmann 1981). Several scholars have therefore tried to look behind the fictional appearance of the saga in order to figure out what actually happened to Ingvar's expedition.[3] It seems highly unlikely, however, that these efforts will lead to convincing results, since there are almost no facts to go on. Ingvar and his men are not mentioned in any reliable Eastern source, although attempts have been made to find traces of their expedition in works as different as the Russian *Primary Chronicle* from the twelfth century, an inscribed Russian stone cross from the eleventh century and the so-called *Georgian Chronicle* from about the same time. A lot of energy has been wasted on these attempts, I think. Last year, for example, the Government of Georgia in Caucasus and the Historical Museum of Stockholm cosponsored a large and expensive conference called "Early Contacts between Scandinavia and Georgia, Caucasus", at which several papers were devoted to speculations that Ingvar's expedition ended up in Georgia in 1041. Such speculation may well further the friendship between Sweden and Georgia by providing a good excuse for wonderful dinners with eloquent speeches and a lot of excellent Georgian wine, but it is doubtful whether scholarship is very much advanced.

What I will try to do in this paper is not to propose a new theory about what happened to Ingvar and his men but instead to identify some of the narrative patterns and mythical traditions that have formed *Yngvars saga víðfǫrla* into what it is today: a strange mixture of history and myth, Latin clerical learning and Old Norse folklore. I shall also try to explain why this saga was written.

But let us first look at the runic inscriptions on the Swedish Ingvar stones in order to see what people probably knew about Ingvar's expedition around 1040 when most of these inscriptions were made. Most of them just say that such and such a person, usually a member of a prominent family in the local community, left with Ingvar and died abroad. Several of the inscriptions say that the person commemorated on the stone travelled to the east on a ship and died (or was killed) far away in "Serkland"(*a sirklanti*), although one inscription says that death occurred in "Greece" (*a kriklanti*). Quite a few of the inscriptions also contain a cross and some of them end with a Christian formula, "may God help his soul" (*kuþ hialbi ant hans* or *kuþ hialbi salu hans*). Nothing much can be concluded from these runic monuments except that a fairly large number of people must have travelled with Ingvar on ships towards the east, and that many of them never came back but were believed to have met their fate in foreign lands, possibly "in Serkland", wherever that may be.

Two inscriptions, the Tystberga stone and the Gripsholm stone, both in Södermanland, contain short commemorative poems in Eddic metre suggesting that heroic legends existed already at this time about the fate of the expedition. The Tystberga poem says the following about a father, Holmsten, and his son, Rodger, who had both left Sweden with Ingvar:

Hann hafði vestarla
um varit længi,
dou austarla
með Ingvari.

"He"—presumably the father, Holmsten—"had been in the West for a long time, they"—presumably both father and son—"died in the East Way with Ingvar".

The meaning is evidently that the father had travelled as a viking on both the Western and Eastern Way, but he as well as his son had finally died together with Ingvar, probably in some kind of battle.

The more impressive, imaginative and often quoted Gripsholm poem, placed on a large stone raised in memory of Ingvar's brother Harald by their mother Tola, reads as follows:

þæir foru drængila
fiarri at gulli
ok austarla
ærni gafu,
dou sunnarla
a Særklandi.

Which in free English translation has been rendered as follows:

They fared bravely
afar after gold
and in the East Way
fed the eagle,
died in the South Way
in Saracen lands.

"They" in the poem must either refer to the brothers Ingvar and Harald or to all members of Ingvar's expedition. Both monuments, but especially the Gripsholm stone, suggest that Ingvar's expedition consisted of adventurous vikings who travelled for their own gain and participated in bloody battles, an activity that could metaphorically be described as "feeding the eagle", since eagles and ravens were supposed to feed on the bodies of dead warriors. Furthermore, both poems agree that "Serkland" is the name of the country where the members of the expedition were supposed to have met their fate.

But what is meant by "Serkland"? This is by no means clear, although most scholars have understood the name as either the land of the Saracens, i.e. Muslim Arabs, or the land where people wear long gowns or *särkar*, as many Arabs did but also other people who lived around the Mediterranean or in the Middle East during the Middle Ages. In Icelandic *fornaldarsögur* the name Serkland is used in a vague and general way about far away exotic countries, inhabited by strange heathen races and dangerous beasts but not necessarily by Arabs or Muslims.[4] My conclusion is that the name "Serkland" on the Swedish Ingvar stones could mean a lot of things, and that the people who erected these runestones probably did not have a very clear idea about the country where Ingvar was supposed to have perished among the heathens. What they did know, or thought they knew, was that Ingvar and his companions, like Raoul Wallenberg, were great heroes who went on a mission or quest somewhere in the east and never came back. It is in honor of such men that monuments are erected and legends are told.

Let us now turn to *Yngvars saga*, a text preserved in two Icelandic vellum manuscripts, Gl. Kgl. Sml. 2845 4° and AM 343a 4°, both dating from the fifteenth century but evidently based on an older original, written at some time between 1200 and 1400.[5] The text consists of fourteen chapters. The first four, which we may call Part I, read like an Icelandic *konunga saga* and provide a background for Yngvar's expedition. He is presented as the son of a high-ranking Swedish chieftain related to the royal family and with ambitions to rule the country. When Yngvar is denied the title of king he decides to set out on an expedition towards the east "to find himself a kingdom in some foreign land."

The next four chapters, Part II, describe the actual expedition. Yngvar and his men travel on thirty ships to Garðaríki where they stay for three years under the protection of the Russian King, Jaroslav, but they then decide to explore a big but unnamed river in search of its sources. They encounter various supernatural adversaries such as dragons and giants but then stay for a while in the city of Citopolis or Scythopolis, where the beautiful queen Silkisif falls in love with Yngvar, offers him her country and the title of king and lets herself be converted by him to the Christian faith. Yngvar accepts her offer but wants to continue the travel project and return later for the wedding, so the expedition moves on along the river to the city of Heliopolis, where he and his men help a certain King Júlfr, also called Hrómundr, in a war against his brother King Bjólfr, also called Sǫlmundr.

The travellers also come to the Red Sea and a huge gap or gulf, reminiscent of Ginnungagap, near the end of the world and close to a place called Siggeum, where there is a large hall inhabited by malevolent devils. Finally they end up at a place where most of them, including Ingvar himself, fall sick and die, after having gone to bed, against Ingvar's advice, with some seductive but dangerous women. Yngvar's dead body is carried back to Scythopolis, where the beautiful Silkisif mourns him and arranges for his funeral. She asks his surviving companions to return to Sweden and come back with missionaries so that her people may be converted to the Christian faith and a church be built for Yngvar's body to rest in.

The following five chapters, Part III, describe a new expedition carried out along the same route by Yngvar's son Sveinn. It recounts various new encounters with demonic and supernatural creatures: cyclopes, dragons, giants, birdmen with beaks instead of noses. When the travellers arrive in Scythopolis, Sveinn marries Silkisif and is promoted to king. He has brought with him a Swedish bishop by the name of Róðgeirr who helps him and Silkisif with the missionary work of converting their subjects. This third part ends with the establishment of a church dedicated to Yngvar in

Scythopolis. Bishop Róðgeirr at first does not want to dedicate the church to a man who has not worked miracles and therefore cannot be regarded as a saint, but Silkisif convinces the bishop that Yngvar was indeed a holy man who always loved God even if he had not worked any miracles. And so Yngvar is buried in the church with great ceremony and masses are sung for his soul.

The fourteenth and final chapter describes the informants and the sources used for the saga as a whole. The text then continues as follows:"En þessa sǫgu hǫfum vér heyrt ok ritat efter forsǫgn þeirar bækr, at Oddr munkr inn fróði hafði gera látit at forsǫgn fróðra manna, þeira er hann segir sjálfr í bréfi sínu, því er hann sendi Jóni Loftssyni ok Gizuri Hallssyni" [We have heard and written down this story in accordance with the books that the wise monk Oddr had prepared [*literally:* let be made] from the tales of [*or:* at the request of] wise men, as he himself explains in the letter which he sent to Jón Loftsson and Gizurr Hallsson]. The two last-mentioned men are the two most important chieftains and, at the same time, church leaders in Iceland towards the end of the twelfth century. Furthermore, it is said that "Oddr claims to have heard this saga from the priest called Isleifur and also from another called Glúmr Þorgeirsson [or Þorgilsson] and from a third called Þórir. Isleifur said he heard *Yngvars saga* from a merchant who claimed to have heard it at the court of the Swedish king. Glúmr had heard the story from his father, Þórir from Klakka Sámsson, and Klakka had heard it from his older kinsmen".

It would seem from this last chapter as well as from various linguistic details that the saga is based on a now lost text in Latin by Oddr Snorrason, who had probably been commissioned to write it by the prominent chieftains Gizurr Hallsson and Jón Loftsson, since he sent them a letter about his sources. Oddr in his turn based his narrative on three separate oral sources. Somebody has later translated Oddr's Latin text into Icelandic, but the translator may possibly also have had access to oral sources of his own, since he claims to have *heard* the story, not just seen it in a book. At least part of the oral tradition may have come to Iceland through a merchant who had some contact with the Swedish court, but there are also indications earlier in the saga that it may have come from an Icelander named Garða-Ketill, said to have been one of the most prominent members of Yngvar's expedition. It is thus evident that *Yngvars saga* is based on several different sources, Norse as well as Latin, oral as well as written, and this conclusion is borne out by the fact that alternative versions are sometimes presented within the text, for example that Júlfr and Bjólfr are also referred to as Hrómundr and Sǫlmundr.

The literary and folkloristic patterns in the saga also seem to be of several different kinds and have different origins. First, the saga appears to be influenced by various Old Norse myths and folktales about travels in the North or East to Giantland, Bjarmaland or Kvænland by Þórr, Þorsteinn bæjarmagn, Ǫrvar-Oddr and various other heroes—a narrative pattern that goes back to the mythological poems of the Edda but was further developed in the *fornaldarsögur* and also in the learned literature of the Scandinavian Middle Ages (Lindow 2012). The closest parallel to *Yngvars saga* among these texts is probably the story of Thorkillus the Far-Travelled in Book 8 of Saxo's *Gesta Danorum*. In both cases, an expedition is led by a hero through strange wild countries with dark caves and alluring dwellings where they may find treasures but also many dangers. Giants, dragons, dangerous women and birdlike monsters confront the travelers and test their wits, virtues and skills in various ways. The members of the expedition, before these confrontations take place, are often warned by the wise hero not to do this or that, stay away from greed, gluttony, heathen rituals or sexual temptations. When some of the men do not heed the hero's warnings, they become sick or die as a result of their stupidity. It is evident that most of these stories, in their present form, have an edifying purpose: they serve as medieval *exempla*. Like Saxo's Thorkillus, Yngvar is presented as a paragon of Christian virtue, even though he is finally defeated by the evil machinations of women.

It is also obvious that some of the folkloristic motifs in *Yngvars saga* are not from Old Norse but from Classical mythology and may be traced back to Medieval Latin authorities such as Isidor of Seville.[6] This is true for example of the cyclopes and the birdmen and one of the dragons that attack Yngvar's men, since that dragon is called Jaculus, just as a similar monster in Lucan's *Pharsalia.* The dangerous women are reminiscent of amazons and they live where amazons were said to live, that is in Scythia, according to Classical sources. The cities Heliopolis and Scythopolis have Greek names, meaning "the city of Scyths" and "the city of the Sun", and are inhabited by people who speak Greek, as both Queen Silkisif and King Júlfr turn out to do.[7]

The entire story of Silkisif's conversion and the building of Yngvar's church in Scythopolis has a hagiographic touch typical of religious medieval literature. As Dietrich Hofmann has argued, basing his arguments partly on an earlier article of mine (Lönnroth 1963), Oddr Snorrason's reason or at least his excuse for writing his Latin text was probably that Yngvar was thought of as a Christian missionary of royal descent and in that respect similar to the apostolic hero of Oddr's Latin biography of Olav Tryggvason.[8] In his prologue to this biography, Oddr had pointed out that Olav Tryggvason, unlike Olav the Saint, was not known to have worked miracles but should nevertheless be regarded as a man of God and venerated as a great missionary king who had done much for the Christian faith.[9] This is of course the very same argument that Silkisif uses against Bishop Róðgeirr when she convinces him that Yngvar is a holy man and that the church in Scythopolis should be named after him. Yngvar is also explicitly compared to Olav Tryggvason in chapter three of *Yngvars saga.*

Why was it important for Oddr to show that great secular leaders like Yngvar víðfǫrli and Olav Tryggvason could be considered holy men, even though they were not known to have worked miracles? This had to do with the political situation in Iceland, Norway and the rest of Europe at the time when Oddr's Latin *Yngvar's saga* was written. There was at this time an enormous conflict going on all over Europe about the power over the church between *regnum* and *sacerdotium*; between, on the one hand, secular kings and leaders who wanted to remain in control of the churches and, on the other hand, the papacy and bishops loyal to the pope, who wanted to make the church completely independent of secular power. Icelandic bishops such as Guðmundr Arason defended the pope and the independence of the church, but the monks of

Þingeyrar monastery were, as we know from other sources, on the side of *regnum*, that is of secular control over the church. Also on the side of *regnum* were King Sverrir of Norway and the famous Icelandic chieftains Gizurr Hallsson and Jón Loftsson, the two church leaders to whom Oddr sent his *Yngvars saga*.[10] For these defenders of secular power it was important to show that secular leaders such as Yngvar or Olav could be great missionaries, protectors of the Church and holy men, even though they were not saints and did not work miracles.

Accordingly *Yngvars saga* in Oddr's Latin version had a didactic and political purpose, just as his Latin biography of Olav Tryggvason did. But how shall we explain this peculiar blend of Norse myth, Classical myth and politically motivated hagiography? Is it a blend that existed in the oral tradition even before Oddr Snorrason, was it made by Oddr himself or perhaps by his translator, or somebody later on in the manuscript tradition?

It seems obvious, first of all, that oral traditions about Ingvar's expedition existed early in both Sweden and Iceland, or at any rate long before Oddr wrote his Latin work. This much is clear from the runic inscriptions, especially the poem on the Gripsholm stone, and also from the detailed references in the last chapter of *Yngvars saga* to Oddr's oral sources. Originally, these traditions probably consisted of adventure stories about brave vikings who went out in pursuit of gold and died in battle in some faraway Eastern country after having "fed the eagle", as it is said in the Gripsholm inscription. At some stage, however, these traditions must have become part of a clerical heritage, promoted by learned servants of the Church and used for edifying purposes. This can be concluded from the fact that all three of Oddr Snorrason's principal informants—Ísleifr, Glúmr and Þórir—appear to have been priests[11] and thus probably familiar with at least some of the Classical and hagiographic motifs in the saga.

Within the saga itself, the Icelander Garða-Ketill, one of Yngvar's companions, is presented as a witness to the most important events, and the events are often reported from his point of view. It is said explicitly that it was he who brought the story about Yngvar's expedition from Sweden to Iceland. There are, however, reasons to be skeptical of this information about Ketill's role. First, no such person is attested in other Icelandic sources. Second, his name may be derived from the cauldron (*ketill*) which he steals from a giant in one of the more dramatic episodes of the saga. It seems more likely that the story was brought to Iceland by a merchant who had heard it in Sweden, as one of Oddr's informants told him, but this information probably cannot be trusted either.

In the last chapter of *Yngvars saga* it is said that some storytellers (*nokkurir sagnamenn*) think that Yngvar was the son of king Eymundr Óláfsson, but this is a tradition that the saga does not accept. It is admitted, however, that king Eymundr had a son by name of Ǫnundr who, in several ways, was quite similar to Yngvar. In this connection, the saga refers to a Latin source called *Gesta Saxonum* which can be identified as Adam of Bremen's Church history, written around 1070. Adam is here quoted as saying that "fertur, quod Emundus, rex Suenonum, misit filium suum Onundum per mare Balticum, qui postremo ad Amazonas interfectus est" [Emund, King of the Swedes, sent his son Onund across the Baltic Sea to the Amazons and was killed by them]..This information is further explained in a later scholion (119), in which Adam claims that Onund was sent by ship to Scythia in order to win more land for the Swedes, but that he and his entire army died after having drunk from wells poisoned by the Amazons of Women Land.[12] It would seem from Adam's wording that he probably identified the home of the Amazons, Scythia or Woman Land (*terra feminarum*), with Kvænland, a territory in north-eastern Finland, the name of which could easily be misunderstood as "the land of *kvánir* (i.e. women)"[13]. This legend about the fate of Onund or Ǫnundr, a man who appears also in *Yngvars saga* although not as a member of Yngvar's expedition, looks like another version and possibly the very origin of the edifying legend of how Yngvar and his men fell victim to the women and died. It appears obvious, at any rate, that Adam's legend about Ǫnundr Eymundarson has somehow influenced the legend about Ingvar at an early stage in the tradition.

There is, however, an even more striking but until now unnoticed parallel between *Yngvars saga* and Adam's Church history.

When Yngvar's men reach the big hall inhabited by devils near the end of the world, they learn that King Haraldr of Sweden once came here and perished with all his men in the big gap of the Red Sea (*fórst hann í Rauða hafs svelg með sínu föruneyti*). In Adam's Church history a similar story is told about another King Haraldr, namely Haraldr Harðráði of Norway, who is said to have explored the Northern Sea at the end of the world and almost perished in the "awful abyss of the gap."[14] This story also appears to have found its way into the Ingvar legend but in a distorted form which may suggest that we are dealing with oral variants of the same legend: thus the Norwegian king Haraldr has been transformed into a Swedish king Haraldr and the abyss at the end of the world has been moved from the Northern Sea to the Red Sea.

To this may be added that cyclopes and other classical monsters that appear in Adam's description of the northern lands beyond Scandinavia. I think there can be no doubt that the world picture presented by Adam and the world picture presented in *Yngvars saga* are, on the whole, one and the same, in spite of many differences in minor details. It is a world that is not very similar to the real world, but it is typical of clerical minds in the Middle Ages and it appears to be shaped both by oral and by literary traditions. This is what we could expect in view of the fact that both Adam and Oddr refer to other clerics as oral sources for the stories they presented in Latin.

It is now time to draw some tentative conclusions. The origin of *Yngvars saga* must be sought in early Swedish speculations about the fate of Ingvar's expedition. The Christians who erected the Ingvar stones and prayed for the souls of their lost relatives evidently believed that malevolent heathen forces in some faraway country had somehow destroyed the expedition. The legend that grew up as a result of such speculation eventually incorporated many well-known folkloristic motifs from Old Norse myths and oral *fornaldarsögur* about travels to Geirröð, Útgarðaloki and other monsters of Giantland, but the Ingvar legend was also influenced by stories that probably circulated at the Swedish court about other princes that had travelled abroad and perished, or almost perished, in foreign lands—stories that were also known to Adam of Bremen. These stories could be used by Christian clerics such as Adam, Saxo and Oddr for edifying and political purposes, and as a result the legends also included many traits from classical myth and hagiography. From this material Oddr Snorrason created a Latin text that could be used to promote the cause of secular Icelandic chieftains such as Gizurr Hallsson and Jón Loftsson who opposed the papacy and the bishops and wanted to stay in control of the church in Iceland. Oddr's translator—or some other Icelandic scribe—may have added more motifs and formulas from *fornaldarsögur* to make the narrative even more exciting to a late medieval audience, but most of the saga could very well be—and I think probably is—a product of the eleventh and twelfth centuries.

Regardless of the age of the text in its present form, however, it is in my opinion not possible to draw any conclusions at all about the actual travel route or ultimate fate of Ingvar's expedition. None of the persons who originally made runic inscriptions about Ingvar or composed stories about him or adapted them for religious or political purposes appear to have had any reliable knowledge about such matters. They may have been just as ignorant about the fate of Ingvar as most Swedes were about the fate of Raoul Wallenberg before the fall of the Soviet Union. Even now we know very little about what actually happened to Raoul Wallenberg in Russia after his disappearance behind the iron curtain in the 1940's, and I think we know even less of what happened to Ingvar viðfǫrli in the 1040's.

Afterword, August 2013

A few days before the deadline for sending this article to the editor, I received a newly published article containing a novel and very interesting theological interpretation of *Yngvars saga* (Antonsson 2012). Like Dietrich Hofmann and myself, Antonsson does not read *Yngvars saga* as a historical source but as a fantastic text with an edifying purpose, but he argues that this purpose was religious rather than political. In his opinion, Oddr's *Yngvars saga*, as well as other works by the Þingeyrar monks around 1200, was "marked by a creative use of biblical typology and Christian symbolism" (Antonsson 2012: 129) and fundamentally concerned with the problem of Man's redemption from sin: "The adventure and exploits of Yngvarr and his men can thus be viewed metaphorically as a journey of mortals through the travails of the profane world in search of salvation" (Antonsson 2012: 111).

It is not possible for me at this time to discuss Antonsson's learned arguments in detail, but I suspect that he has exaggerated Oddr Snorrason's use of typology and other forms of theological thinking. I also think that he has underestimated Oddr's ambition to entertain his audience with an exciting adventure tale while at the same time promoting the political agenda of Gizurr Hallsson and Jón Loftsson. Their goal was certainly not to make a canonized saint out of Yngvar—a goal that would have been unattainable and hence ridiculous—but to promote the idea that pious secular rulers should have an important say in ecclesiastical matters. That is why the monks of Þingeyrar, as well as their secular sponsors, eventually became strongly opposed to Bishop Guðmundr Arason's attempts to abolish secular influence on the church of Iceland (Cf. Lönnroth 1963:92)—an important fact that Antonsson appears to have missed.

On one important point, however, I think that Antonsson has advanced our understanding of *Yngvars saga.* This is when he argues that the arrival of Yngvar and his men to the Red Sea and struggle with demonic forces there—an arrival that makes no sense at all from a geographical point of view—should be understood against the background of the biblical story of how the children of Israel, led by Moses, crossed the Red Sea on their way from Egypt to the promised land (*Exodus* ch.14). Yngvar may have only a superficial similarity to Moses, but King Haraldr of Sweden, who perished in the gap of the Red Sea together with his army, should probably be understood as a new version of Pharaoh's men who perished in the depths of that same water as they were persecuting the children of Israel (Antonsson 2012: 82-87). What Antonsson's interpretation misses, however, is that this episode, as told in the saga, is only in part biblical, because it also contains elements from the Old Norse myth about Ginnungagap and legends about travels to Giantland.

Notes

[1] See Emil Olsson's introduction to his edition, *Yngvars saga víðfǫrla* (Copenhagen, 1912).

[2] The inscriptions are included and commented in Olsson's edition and in Mats G. Larsson 1990.

[3] See in particular Melnikova 1976; Larsson 1987, 1990; Shepard 1984-85; Glasyrina 2002.

[4] See for example *Fornaldar sögur Norðurlanda* 1954: I, 373-380; III, 364, 379; IV, 182,190.

[5] See in particular Hofmann 1981 and Olsson 1912.

[6] Paul Edwards and Hermann Pálsson 1989:7.

[7] See Glasyrina 2002.

[8] Hofmann 1981: 217-21; cf. Lönnroth 1963: 90-94.

[9] Lönnroth 2000: 257-64.

[10] Lönnroth 1963: 91-93; Hofmann 1981: 215-20.

[11] Glúmr is referred to also in his capacity as a reliable witness to miracles in a pious text by Oddr's monastic colleague Gunnlaugr Leifsson, *Biskupa sögur* 1858, I: 42.

[12] Cum rex Sueonum Emund filium suum Anundum misisset in Scythiam ad dilatandum regnum suum, ille navigio in terram pervenit feminarum. Quae mox venenum fontibus immiscentes, ipsum regem et exercitum eius tali modo peremerunt; Adamus, Gesta Hammaburgensis ecclesiae pontificum (Scholion 119).

[13] Cf. Armas Luuko 1964.

[14] Haraldus [---]latitudinem septentrionalis occeani perscrutatus navibus, tandem caligantibus ante ora deficientis mundi finibus inmane abyssi baratrum retroactis vestigiis pene vix salvus evasit. Adamus, Gesta, Descriptio insularum aqualonis, cap. 38.

Odin of Many Devices: Jonas Ramus (d. 1718) on the Identity of Odin and Odysseus

Jonas Wellendorf

If one seeks a common Western European origin myth, the most obvious candidate would be the story of the fall of Troy and its consequences. The oldest European classics, the Homeric poems, are closely tied up with this story, and in Classical Antiquity, the Romans saw themselves as descendants of fugitives from the burning city—an idea most powerfully expressed in Vergil's *Aeneid.* Learned medieval writers strove in the wake of the *Aeneid* to forge links between their own origins and the Trojan story world. Thus the Matter of Troy came to form a solid foundation for subsequent mythopoesis. A successful connection with the Troy legend could supply medieval and early modern nations that did not possess a long and venerable tradition of historiography with a framework within which they could fashion an identity for themselves, creating a past which extended far back and which could be compared, sometimes favorably, with that of the Romans, providing answers to fundamental questions such as 'Where do we come from?' and 'Why are we here?'

Surveying the large-scale medieval accounts of the origins of peoples, it soon becomes apparent that the vast majority commence with a migration that establishes a whole people or some important individuals in a new location, sometimes far from their point of origin. In his mid sixth-century work about the origins and deed of the Goths, *Getica*, e.g., Jordanes describes how the ancestors of the Goths, led by a certain Berig, left the island of Scandia in the far north of Europe and migrated southwards (eds. Giunta and Grillone 1991, 12). In the late seventh century, the anonymous account of the origin of the Lombards, *Origo gentis langobardorum*, tells of how the Winili, who later became the Lombards, migrated southwards from Scandanan and eventually settled in Lombardy (ed. Bracciotti 1998, 105–109). In the early eight century, Bede tells in his history of the church of the English people of how Saxons, Angles, and Jutes left the Continent and settled in England (I, 15, eds. Colgrave and Mynors 1969, 48–52).[1] This migration model is not restricted to speakers of Germanic languages; thus, the Irish *Lebor Gabála Érenn*, 'Book of the Taking of Ireland', describes the prolonged wanderings of the Gaels that eventually result in their permanent settlement in Ireland, and the (eighth-century?) Armenian historian Moses Khorenats'i tells of the migration of the Hayk, the eponymous ancestor of the Armenians (*Hay*) to Ararad (trans. Thomson 1978, 85–88). In these two last mentioned works, the migration is closely linked up to Biblical history.

Against this background it is not surprising that the Scandinavians also knew of and used the migration myth as a basic model for describing the early history of their region. The migration to and settlement of Iceland in the late ninth and early tenth century looms large in Icelandic historical works, beginning with Ari fróði's *Íslendingabók* and its description of Ingólfr's settlement in Iceland (ed. Jakob Benediktsson 1986, 5). The saga of the Gotlanders follows a similar pattern in its description of the settlement of Gotland from mainland Sweden by Þieluar (ed. Peel 1999, 2). Among the most famous Nordic treatments of this theme, one finds the migration myth in which Odin (Óðinn) and a group of followers move from a location close to the center of the world (in Troy or north of the Black sea) to Northern Europe, where they eventually settle in Sweden and acquire a reputation for divinity. This euhemerist superstructure to the mythology is very likely to be a learned construction invented by readers familiar with origin myths of other peoples and fuelled by a desire to trace a line of descent far back in time. It is therefore unlikely that the versions of the migration myth contained in medieval mythographical and historiographical writings accurately reflect a migration myth that originated with the pagan Scandinavians. The migration myth is most elaborately presented in the Snorronic writings, i.e. in the prose *Edda* and in *Ynglinga saga*, the first saga in the *Heimskringla* compilation of kings' sagas, although these two writings tell very different stories about the migration. The myth has also left clear traces in other Nordic writings of earlier and later date.[2]

The exact chronological point of origin for this construction is difficult to determine with accuracy, but the processes of (medieval) etymologization and *interpretatio romana* or *graeca* are likely to have initiated or at least inspired its development. Through this interpretative process, the main gods of the Germanic speaking peoples were equated with important Roman gods, which is seen most clearly in the names of the days of the week where, e.g. *Dies Mercurii* (The day of Mercury > French mercredi) became OE *Wodnesdæg* (The day of Woden > English Wednesday) and ON *Óðinsdagr* (The day of Odin > Norwegian onsdag).[3] The adoption of theophoric names of the days of the week by speakers of Germanic, and hence the equation of Germanic gods with those of the Romans, has traditionally been dated to the fourth century, but Shaw (2007) has proposed arguments in favor of a much later date, namely the seventh or eighth century. It is also in the late eighth century that we find, for the first time, Odin (or at least his counterpart Wotan) explicitly situated in the cultural sphere of Greece. This information is given as an aside by Paul the Deacon in his history of the Lombards in connection with what he terms an 'amusing [or perhaps silly] story' (*ridiculam fabulam*, I, 8) about how the Lombards received their ethnic name from a certain Godan (i.e. Wotan), "who is called Mercury by the Romans and who is worshipped as a god by all the peoples of Germania, though he is deemed to have existed not around these times but long before, and not in Germania but in Greece" (I, 9).[4]

The names of the days of the week and Paul the Deacon both testify to the common identification of Odin/Wotan with the Roman god Mercury, who is in turn equated with the Greek god Hermes by the end of the eighth century (or perhaps somewhat earlier). But the encoding of Odin's name in the name of one of the days of the week by no means fixed his identity as the Germanic god corresponding to Mercury, and an abundant number of other identifications of Odin can be found elsewhere in Scandinavian literature. In one study, Battista (2003) has shown how Old Norse hagiographic texts identified Odin with no fewer than five different

Roman gods, namely Mercury, Mars, Jupiter, Hercules, and Saturn. The question of identity is only complicated by Odin's famed proclivity for assuming various names and keeping his identity secret when travelling (cf. *Grímnismál* sts 46–50, eds. Neckel and Kuhn 1983, 66–67). In the *þulur*, some one hundred and fifty names for Odin are listed (see Kuhn 1978, 289–294).[5] Commenting on the multitude of Odin's names, King Gylfi/Gangleri exclaims in *Gylfaginning*: "What a terrible lot of names you have given him [i.e. Odin]! By my faith, one would need a great deal of learning to be able to give details and explanations of what events have given rise to each of these names" (transl. Faulkes 1995, 22).[6] In response, Hár presents two explanations for the abundance of names for Odin. He first appeals to the multitude of human languages, claiming that it is a basic need of humans to be able to address their god in their own language. Hence the names, Hár claims, illustrate how Odin is invoked in many different languages. The implication of this is that Odin should be considered a nearly universal god venerated by all humanity, something which might also be implied through the process of *interpretatio* if one understands it as a process of identification rather than equation. But since many of these names are clearly formed with Old Norse roots and give meaning in that language, it is difficult to imagine that this explanation is proposed in earnest. The second explanation is that it is Odin's adventures in various parts of the world that have given rise to the different names. This explanation is also the one Gylfi/Gangleri alludes to in his comment cited above. Curiously, the explanation that makes most sense within the mythological system as it is known to us, namely that Odin himself adopted many different names in order to travel *incognito*, is not presented as a possibility, though *Gylfaginning* explains the many names of Freyja in this way a few pages later.[7]

In the early eighteenth century, the complexity of Odin's identity was increased considerably in a strikingly original but relatively neglected Nordic refraction of the Troy migration myth. In this late offshoot of the efforts to see the Trojan war as the catalyst of nations, the Norwegian mythologist, amateur historian, and parish priest Jonas Ramus (1649–1718) strove to situate the Norse Æsir, Odin in particular, within a Trojan framework when he argued that Odin, the king of the Norse gods, was identical with the widely travelled Odysseus.

In medieval Western Europe, the most important text dealing with the matter of Troy was probably Dares Phrygius's *De excidio Troiae* 'On the destruction of Troy'. The text itself claims to be an eyewitness account of the fall of Troy by a certain Dares the Phrygian, who fought on the side of the Trojans and kept a written day to day record of the events as they happened (ed. Meister 1873, 52). As a supposedly firsthand account of these dramatic events, it was considered to be more reliable than other textual testimonies. As a story about Troy it also had an advantage over other texts such as *Ilias latina* and even Vergil's own *Aeneid* in that it told the whole story about the siege of Troy (as well as the events that led up to it) rather than just a small part of it. Dares was believed to have been a Trojan, and his sympathies naturally lay with the Trojans. The medieval creators of myths of origin often followed Dares and were therefore also often biased in favor of the Trojans. Trojan fugitives fled the burning city, travelled the western world, and gave impulse to the origin of great dynasties.

In the prose *Edda*, we are offered a special twist of this Trojan fugitive pattern in which the migration takes place long after the Trojan War has ended. Here the migration myth has the character of a noble exodus rather than a flight from a burning city. Some of the details of this Norse account are hard to grasp, but the general idea is well known. I will therefore not to go into detail on this point.[8] The Trojan fugitive pattern is just one of several possible Trojan foundations for the elaboration of national myths of origin. Another and, I believe, older framework is provided by the story of the often-delayed homecoming of Odysseus. After the long siege of Troy had ended with the victory of the Greeks, they set out for home. Many had a difficult journey,[9] but that of Odysseus was particularly long and troublesome. It took a full ten years before he eventually reached his home at Ithaca—but much of this time was spent in the company of beautiful women who loved him and provided for him in every possible way. The episodic character of many of the stories of Odysseus's wide travels provided rich opportunities for those who sought to develop a myth of origin for a particular site or people. In the course of his travels, Odysseus 'the destroyer of cities' (πτολίπορθος, *Odyssey* 8, l. 3 and elsewhere) would have become the founder of many cities and the progenitor of many noble houses. Rulers of the Etruscans, for instance, were already said by Hesiod to have descended from Odysseus (*Theogony* ll. 1011–1016, ed. Solmsen 1983, 48; Malkin 1998, 156–177),[10] and alternate versions of the story of the origins of Rome also feature Odysseus in important roles (reported by Dionysius of Halicarnassus in *Antiquitates Romanae* 1.72, ed. Jacoby 1885, 115–117).[11] He was also claimed to have played a central part in foundations further afield. The ancient geographer Strabo, e.g., had claimed that Odysseus founded Lisbon (3.2.13, ed. Meineke 1909, 202). Not long afterward, Tacitus reports that Odysseus was the founding father of a city by the name of Asciburgium situated on the Rhine, and that monuments and tombs inscribed with Greek letters have been found in that area. Tacitus does not vouch for the veracity of this information—"I intend neither to confirm nor refute these claims: let each man believe or disbelieve them according to his own disposition," he writes.[12] Others, including Jonas Ramus, were more favorably disposed toward an Odyssean origin of Asciburgium. He explained the name etymologically as Asi-purgion: The city of the Asians, i.e. Trojans. Why Odysseus, a Greek from Ithaca, would name a city after his enemies, the Trojans, will become clear later.

To sum up so far: Medieval accounts of origin typically include a migration from one location to another. This migration would often, but by no means always, be situated in a biblical (as in the case of the Irish and Armenians) or Trojan framework. In the case of a Trojan foundation, two main possibilities for subsequent mythopoesis offered themselves: A Trojan fugitive pattern and a Wandering Odysseus pattern. The latter appears to be older, while the Trojan fugitive pattern enjoyed the greatest popularity in the medieval period because of the general bias in favor of the Trojans. However, as times changed and knowledge of Greek improved in the Western world, interest in the second model increased once again.

Jonas Ramus presented an elaborate argument for the identity of Odysseus and Odin. His argument is an excellent example of how the Norse gods and the stories told about them lived on long after the end of the Middle Ages and formed new divergent or alternative versions of the well-known mythological story world. As scholars sought to penetrate these myths in order to arrive at some sort of understanding of their origin and meaning, they contributed to the perpetuation of the mythic dynamics, and the mythology lived on, at least on desktops and in drawers. In 1693, at the age of forty-four, Ramus published his first work of historiography, entitled *Nori Regnum: Hoc est Norvegia antiqva et ethnica, sive historiae Norvegicae prima initia, a primo Norvegiae Rege, Noro, usqve ad Haraldum Harfagerum,* 'The rule of Nor: That is the Old Pagan Norway, or the first beginnings of Norwegian history, from the first Norwegian king, Nor, until Harald Hair-Fair'. In this work, he briefly adumbrated the novel theory that Odin and Odysseus were one and the same (1693, 5). In 1702 he published a full 200-page monograph entitled *Ulysses et Otinus Unus & idem Sive Disqvisitio Historica & Geographica, qvâ, ex collatis inter se Odyssea Homeri, & Edda Island. Homerizante, Othini fraudes deteguntur, ac detractâ larva in lucem protrahitur Ulysses* [Odysseus and Odin [are] one and the same or, a historical and geographical treatise in which through a juxtaposition of Homer's *Odyssey* and the comparable Edda of the Icelanders the deceits of Odin are revealed and, the mask having been pulled away, Odysseus is dragged forth into the light] in which he argued his case with great conviction. In the course of his wide travels, Odysseus adopted the name of Odin and visited the shores of Norway. Here he became the progenitor of the earls of Hlaðir. The very elaborate arguments proposed by Ramus testify to his wide reading of classical literature as well as the works of more recent historians, geographers, and antiquarians. He also used some Norse texts, particularly the prose *Edda* ascribed to Snorri Sturluson that had been published by Resen with parallel Latin and Danish translations in 1665, to corroborate his claims. Many Old Norse texts still awaited publication in Ramus's day, and this naturally meant that the range of Old Norse texts available to him was rather limited. He also had the disadvantage of not having easy access to medieval manuscripts, since his parish Norderhov, in Buskerud, inland Norway, was situated far from the main centers of learning at that point in time. However, his hinterland position did not prevent his works from being read. In 1711, *The Reign of Nor* was published in a Danish translation as *Det gamle hedenske Norge* [The Old Pagan

Norway],[13] while his treatise on Odin and Odysseus was published three times in 1702, 1713, and 1716; in the later editions he refined and expanded his arguments.[14] Ramus wrote both these historical works in Latin, the international language of scholarship in his day, but he also left behind a considerable number of writings in Danish on history, biology, and dialectology. He achieved his greatest success with a piece of devotional literature called *Naadens Aandelige Markets-tid* [The Spiritual Market Time of Grace] (1680).[15]

Ramus was, in other words, an industrious writer, but he is all but forgotten today.[16] Some of his contemporaries, the manuscript collector Árni Magnússon and the royal historiographer of Norway, Tormod Torfæus, were critical of his historiographical efforts, and Árni Magnússon feared that Ramus "or someone like him" would be appointed royal historiographer of Norway should Torfæus pass away, "and write some nonsense which confuses the half-taught and disgraces the occupation of the learned."[17] In 1771, fifty-four years after the final edition of Ramus's treatise, Peter Frederik Suhm summarily dismissed Ramus's efforts in his own monograph on Odin, stating that he had presented "many shrewd and ingenious but not particularly conclusive proofs" of the oneness of the two.[18] When Ramus's mythological work is mentioned by scholars of our era, it is presented as a curiosity rather than as a serious attempt to arrive at some sort of understanding of Old Norse mythology. Examples of this are Holm-Olsen (1981, 36–37) and Lassen (2011, 35). This conspicuous lack of press might be connected with the fact that not all libraries possess copies of *Ulysses et Otinus* and that it has never been translated.[19]

It will probably be difficult to find a modern reader who is convinced by Ramus's argument, but his work merits more attention than it has hitherto been granted. When mentioned, Ramus's treatise is generally compared with Rudbeck's *Atlantica*,[20] which appeared in Sweden between 1679 and 1702. Rudbeck's massive *Atlantica* was the talk of the day in this period, and it is unlikely that Ramus would not have known of this work. However, he claims in the first edition of his work that he has not had the occasion to examine Rudbeck's work.[21] Furthermore, there is a significant difference in the attitude of the two authors to their material. While Rudbeck, Ramus's Swedish contemporary, claimed to have identified the cradle of humanity and the root of civilization in Sweden, Ramus's work is much less patriotic: he does not assign the Norwegians or Norwegian soil a particularly noble or praiseworthy role in the history of man. The guileful Odysseus comes to the Norwegian shores and, under the name of Odin, fools the Norwegians into venerating him as a god. Ramus's claim is that he has seen through the deceit and trickery and that he can reveal the true identity of the impostor. This is clear from Ramus's preface, where he presents his thesis in a rhetorical style that is slightly more elevated than the one used elsewhere in his book:

> That Greek one, Odysseus, who is completely made up of trickery and deceits, and who was never one and the same wherever he went but often made up another name or another fatherland for himself and who, like Proteus and Vertumnus, always assumed varying appearances, has long enough deluded not only Polyphemus but the whole Northern world under the name of Outinus. Now at last, however, the mask of the impostor, the one under which he has hid unrecognized for almost 29 centuries, is to be drawn off. It is said about Otinus [Odin], among other things, that he once assumed the shape of a serpent. But now we will see Odysseus slither forth from that old serpent skin under which the treacherous and deceitful Otinus [Odin] has resided long enough.[22]

This passage hints at Ramus's central argument, which he presents it in full in the second section of the second chapter of his treatise. Here he discusses Odysseus's encounter with the Cyclops Polyphemus (1716, 41–46). In this episode, told in book 9 (ll. 105–566) of the *Odyssey*, Odysseus famously hid his true identity and claimed that his name was No-one, Οὖτις (Outis) in Greek: "No-one is my name; mother and father and all the other followers call me No-one."[23] The name No-one appears twice in this passage, once in the nominative and once in the accusative. The accusative form given in the Greek text is Οὖτιν, but Ramus points out that the expected accusative form is οὔτινα rather than οὖτιν. Beginning with this unexpected form, Ramus argues that Οὖτις cannot be the pronoun meaning 'no one' and that it therefore is incorrect to translate Οὖτις as 'No-one'. Instead, Οὖτις (with the accusative form Οὖτιν) is a proper name and should be left untranslated. Ramus is not the first one to have fastened upon οὖτις in its various forms, and he cites Ptolomy Hephestion, to whom the ninth century patriarch Photius in his *Bibliotheca* attributed the opinion that Odysseus had been called Οὖτις by his parents and friends because he had large ears—Greek οὖς means 'ear' (1716, 41). On these grounds, Ramus suggests that Outis is a pet name of Odysseus used by his friends and family, and he suggests that, when travelling, Odysseus often sought to hide his true identity by using his pet name 'Outis'. The people of the North, having little knowledge of Greek, used the oblique form and simply called him Outin or Odin:

> From what has been said, it is thus clear that Odysseus, when on his journey, wanted to be called Outis [acc. *Outin*] so that he could travel without being recognized: as he uttered this name in Greek in the oblique case, our ancestors, who were ignorant of the Greek language, also called him Outin in nominative. All our books of history are full of that name, proclaiming that some Outin, Otin or Odin, whom they have translated as Otinus [acc. *Otinum*] in Latin, once came to us in the north from Asia. Yet although it has hitherto been unknown to us, who he were, we now, at last, begin to discern the man from the name, and we can assess the lion from its claw.[24]

At its core, Ramus's argument thus rests on a linguistic misunderstanding, yet, where the *Odyssey* attributes the misunderstanding to the Cyclops, Ramus attributes it the ancient Scandinavians.[25]

Ramus is generally careful not to base his arguments on the resemblance of names only, and on one occasion even cautions explicitly against this procedure (p. 89). On another occasion he jokingly proposes that Circe and her Island Aeaea (Gr. Αἰαία, written Ajaia by Ramus) is a permutation of the Norwegian

Locations on Odysseus's route	Identification by Ramus
Troy	Troy
City of the Cicones	Ismarus in Thrace (pp. 49–50).
Land of the Lotus Eaters	By the southern shore of the Gibraltar strait (pp. 52–54).
Land of Cyclopes	Cape Finisterre, Galicia (pp. 54–61).
Island of Aeolus	Somewhere in the United Kingdom, perhaps by the Severn or the Humber Estuaries (pp. 62–67).
Land of the Laestrygonians	Ramus is uncertain and proposes a number of locations from Uxellodunum, near the river Dordogne in SW France, to Lemvig in NW Jutland (pp. 75–83).
Island of Circe	An unidentified Danish island (pp. 91–92).
City of the Cimmerians	In the far North of Europe (pp. 97–105).
Island of the Sirens	Ramus does not identify this island, although he discusses various Norwegian legends about fairy isles (Hulderland) and other remote islands, including Røst, Værøy, Lovund, and Jomfruland (pp. 109–116).
Scylla and Charybdis	Moskstraumen, the famous tidal maelstrom just south of Lofoten. Ramus argues that the maelstrom is divided in two and that the Northern part between Lofotodden and Ambaaren[26] is to be identified with Scylla while the Southern part, between Mosken and Verøy, is to be identified with Charybdis (pp. 116–130).
Thrinacia—island of the Sun	Although Ramus expresses doubts about the identification of this location, he proposes Træna, outside Mo i Rana (pp. 137–140).
Ogygia—island of Calypso	Hinnøya, the island on which Harstad is situated today (pp. 143–150)
Scheria—island of the Phaecians	Ramus finds that Ireland is not an unreasonable identification of this location (pp. 161–163).
Ithaca	Ithaca

Kierrinka aa eya, i.e. Kjerringa å øya [the old woman/hag on the island] (p. 92–93). However, his proposal that Circe is to be equated with Hyrrokkin (written Hirokin by Ramus) is earnest, and he adduces elements from the account of Baldr's funeral in *Gylfaginning* as well as other arguments that, in his view, strengthen this idea (p. 92–96). His skeptical attitude regarding similarities of names or words also leads him to adduce many additional arguments for the identification of Odin and Odysseus, in addition to that of the name

Outin/Outis. First, he argues that his theory is supported by chronology and geography. The chronological part of the argument is passed over relatively briefly, but he claims that Odin arrived in the North soon after the end of the Trojan War (p. 47); the geographical argument is much more elaborately presented and takes up a large portion of his work. Ramus seeks to identify the locations Odysseus is said to have visited *en route* from Troy.[27] These locations he finds strewn between Thrace in Greece and Lofoten in Northern Norway.

Ramus takes the stories told in *The Odyssey* and in the prose *Edda* more literally than most of today's readers, and he believes both that Odysseus/Odin had a protracted journey home after the fall of Troy and that he arrived at the shores of Northern Europe. Nevertheless, he is not an uncritical reader of his texts and is by no means a literalist. He readily acknowledges that his texts might contain errors or untruths, and particular pieces of information are sometimes explained as possible misunderstandings of Homer (1716, 44) or as falsification in the prose *Edda* (1716, 169). His main explanatory model, however, is founded on the story of Odysseus as it is told in the *Odyssey*, partly by Odysseus himself, and he sees it as a story that is fundamentally historical in nature.

Odysseus did undertake a prolonged journey, but much of what is related in the text stems from Odysseus's tall tales about wanderings at sea. His famed proclivity for tricks and machinations thus provides Ramus with a key. One of Odysseus's epithets is πολύμητις (e.g. *Odyssey* 9,1, ed. Allen 1917, 148) 'of many devices, counsels, machinations'. This quality makes him an unreliable narrator *par excellence*, and Ramus therefore seeks to penetrate Odysseus's lies and uncover what really happened. However, even if this characteristic of Odysseus's is the key that opens the interpretative pathways to Ramus, others, perhaps even those who accepted the basic premises of his argument, will find that the very same key locks the pathways that Ramus saw opened. The unreliability of the narrator soon makes it difficult to disentangle the (supposedly) historical elements of the narrative from those made up by Odysseus. Ramus, for instance, does not doubt that Odysseus spent one year feasting and sleeping with 'the loveliest of all immortals' Circe, but he argues that when Odysseus later had to explain to his wife Penelope why he tarried so long on Circe's island, he made up the parts about the enchantment and how his men were turned into pigs (1716, 87).

If one were to accept the identification of Odin with Odysseus, many questions would soon arise—and Ramus, of course, has answers for some of them. One central problem is that the prose *Edda* indisputably links the Norse gods with the Trojans (ed. Faulkes 2005, 6, 13, 55; 1998, I, 5–6). According to medieval etymology, the very name of the Norse gods, the *Æsir*, points to Asia (i.e. Asia Minor, where Troy is located), the abode of the Norse gods, Ásgarðr, is explicitly linked with Troy and so on. Ramus ingeniously circumvents this problem by arguing that during his travels Odysseus kept his Greek identity secret and claimed to be a Trojan. Ramus explains: "As much as Odysseus was a Greek, yet, when he arrived from Asia and discovered how celebrated the memory of the Trojans was in the North and, perhaps, conversely how the Greeks were despised because of the destruction of Troy, he preferred to claim that he was Asian and Trojan, so that he would be met with greater goodwill and favor."[28]

Odysseus spent seven years with Calypso on the island of Ogygia, and it was therefore essential for Ramus to identify that island. In his treatise he describes how he tried out various theories before he settled on the island of Hinnøya, in Northern Norway. Ramus then cites a few verses from Hesiod's *Theogony* where Odysseus is said to have sired sons who ruled "very far off in a retreat of holy islands" (1716, 144), and he suggests that these Holy Islands are identical with Helgeland or Hålogaland, which he interprets as 'Holy land' (1716, 145–146). Finally, he equates this with the region from which the earls of Hlaðir, as descendants of Odin, traced their origin—and thus Odysseus became the progenitor of the Norwegian earls.

Ramus presents a story about the arrival of the Æsir, and Odin in particular, in the North that differs markedly from the one found in the Snorronic writings. It is not really necessary to refute his claims, and it is easy to find fault with his reasoning. However, one can marvel at how inventively he not only operates within the paradigm of his times—and in this period Odin *was* commonly held to have migrated to the North, as has been described in the works of Snorri—but also strives to make sense of Norse mythology with the help of the much richer source material of Classical antiquity. Like others before him, he sought a way to write the Norse past into the greater history of civilization by tying it to a canonical narrative of Antiquity. He scrutinized the earlier attempt to link the two mythological worlds that is presented in the prose *Edda* and rejected it in favor of another model in which the cards were shuffled in a different way. The Norse gods did claim that they were Trojans, as described in the prose *Edda*, and they did fool the inhabitants of the North, but this was not the end of the story. The trickery and deceit is more complex than that, and Odysseus lurked behind it all.

Notes

[1] Coumert (2007) thoroughly discusses these and other medieval accounts of origins.

[2] A fundamental treatment of this much-studied theme is Andreas Heusler's *Die gelehrte Urgeschichte im altisländischen Schrifttum* (1908). See also Klingenberg's massive, if slightly bewildering, article "Odin und die Seinen: Gelehrte Urgeschichte in *Snorra Edda* und *Heimskringla*" (1999, 195-313) and Wellendorf (2013).

[3] Curiously *Óðinsdagr* is first attested in the Old Norwegian Law of the Gulathing where one in a discussion of the days of labor and rest in the holy week can read that *Óðinsdagr* (in the Easter week) *er allr heilagr* (eds. Eithun et al. 1994, 42) "All Odin's day [i.e. Ash Wednesday] shall be kept holy."

[4] ... qui apud Romanos Mercurius dicitur et ab universis Germaniae gentibus ut deus adoratur; qui non circa haec tempora, sed longe anterius, nec in Germania, sed in Graecia fuisse perhibetur (ed. Waitz 1878, 53).

[5] 169 Odin *heiti* are listed and discussed by Falk (1924).

[6] Geysi mǫrg heiti hafi þér gefit honum. Ok þat veit trúa mín at þetta mun vera mikill fróðleikr sá er hér kann skyn ok dœmi hverir atburðir hafa orðit sér til hvers þessa nafns (ed. Faulkes 2005, 22).

[7] *Freyja á mǫrg nǫfn, en sú er sǫk til þess at hon gaf sér ýmis heiti er hon fór með ókunnum þjóðum at leita Óðs. Hon heitir Mardǫll ok Hǫrn, Gefn, Sýr* (ed. Faulkes 2005, 29) [Freyja has many names, and the reason for this is that she adopted various names when she was travelling among strange peoples looking for Od. She is called Mardoll and Horn, Gefn, Syr] (transl. Faulkes 1995, 30).

[8] See Wellendorf (2013) and the literature cited there.

[9] The five-book *Nostoi* 'Homecomings', a part of the Epic Cycle, was devoted to this topic. Summaries of this lost work are provided by Proclus and (Pseudo-)Apollodorus. See, most recently, West (2013, 244-287).

[10] As will be seen below, Jonas Ramus interprets these lines differently.

[11] Additional examples of foundational myths in Italy linked with Odysseus are provided by Solmsen (1986, 95-100).

[12] [Q]uae neque confirmare argumentis neque refellere in animo est: ex ingenio suo quisque demat vel addat fidem (Winterbottom and Ogilvie 1975, 39).

[13] The translator was Anders Jenssøn Borch, a chaplain at Akershus Castle.

[14] The third edition carries the slightly modified title: *Tractatus Historico-Geographicus, qvo Ulyssem et Outinum enum eundemque esse ostenditur, et ex collatis inter se Odyssea Homeri & Edda Island. Homerizante, Outini fraudes deteguntur, ac, detractâ larva in lucem protrahitur Ulysses.*

[15] It was first published in 1680 and reached a wide readership and was continually reprinted and read until the 1880s. On Ramus's biography and publications, see Amundsen (2009).

[16] If Ramus is remembered today, it is primarily in the role as the husband of Anna Colbjørnsdatter, one of the few heroines of Norwegian history. On March 28 1716, under the Great Northern War, a troop of 500 Swedish soldiers had arrived at Norderhov, where they demanded food, drink and lodging. According to a widespread legend, Anna, the lady of the farm, complied, but cleverly served her visitors so much food and drink that their military proficiency was severely diminished. At one point she asks the Swedish colonel permission to send a maid to a neighboring farm after sugar. The colonel, whose sound judgment presumably was reduced at this point in time, grants her request. The maid then alarms some Dano-Norwegian troops in the vicinity. They react immediately and take the inebriated Swedes by surprise. Even though the Dano-Norwegian forces were outnumbered three to one, the Swedes lost and many were killed or taken capture (see Eriksen 1991). Many years later after a visit to Norderhov, the Danish Golden Age poet Oehlenschläger composed the poem "Norderhougs Præstegaard" in which he celebrated Anna Colbjørnsdatter and contrasted her brave actions with those of her husband who reputedly hid himself in the basement: 1. I Norderhoug sig hæved en Gaard, | som end den staaer; | Der boede Qvinden med Præsten. | Han frygtsom var i sin geistlige Stand; | Men hun var Mand, | Og ægte Qvinde for Resten. | | 2. Da Svensken kom, han i Kieldren krøb; | Men Blodet løb | Med Kraft i det qvindlige Hierte. | At spildt blev Bøndernes Eiendom, | Naar Fienden kom, | Det skued Anna med Smerte (ed. Liebenberg 1857-1862, 21, 265) [A farm that still stands was situated at Norderhov; the woman lived there with the priest. He was a fearful clergyman, while she was a man and a real woman to boot. He slipped into the basement when the Swedes arrived; but the blood ran hot in the womanly heart. It pained Anna to see that the property of farmers would be destroyed with the arrival of the enemy].

[17] 'Jeg tviler icke paa, at der jo giøres ansøgninger der om, om saa skulle hænde sig [i.e. that Torfæus dies], enten af Jonas Ramus eller saaden en, og vende de da op og ned paa tinget, og skrive noget wisswass, som confuderer semidoctos, og prostituerer væsenet hos de lærde (ed. Kaalund 1920, 373).'

[18] ' . . . mange kløgtige og sindrige, men dog lidet afgiørende Beviser søger at giøre Ulyssem til Odin (Suhm 1771, 39).' See Lassen (2011, 38-39).

[19] The work has now been digitized and is freely available online from various sources including the Royal Library in Copenhagen (http://www.kb.dk/e-mat/dod/130020576716.pdf —the edition of 1702)

and Google Books (http://books.google.com/ —various scans of the edition of 1716).

[20] So by both Holm-Olsen and Lassen.

[21] *libros ejus mihi nondum contigit inspicere* (1702, 162). In the third edition of the work, Ramus made extensive revisions to this part of his text (which deals with the identification of Ogygia, the island of Calypso), and the reference to Rudbeck has been left out.

[22] satis diu sub Outini nomine non soli Polyphemo, sed toti orbi arctoo imposuit Græcus ille Ulysses, qvi ex fraude & fallaciis totus [1702, totos 1716] fuit compositus, qviq; non unus idemq; semper & ubiq; fuit, sed sæpe aliud nomen, sæpe aliam sibi patriam fingendo, Protei instar & Vertumni alias atq; alias visus est formas assumsisse. Jam itaq; tandem detrahenda est impostori larva, sub qva per 29. ferè secula delituit incognitus. Proditur inter alia de Otino, qvod in serpen|tem se transformaverit; verum enimvero e veteri ista serpentis cute, sub qva satis diu fallax & dolosus habitavit Otinus, jam tandem proserpere videbimus Ulyssem (1716, unnumbered, page 3-4 of *Præfatio ad Lectorem*). Here and elsewhere the Ausgabe letzter Hand is cited. Misprints are corrected using the edition of 1702 where possible (all three editions contain numerous misprints).

[23] Οὖτις ἐμοί γ᾽ ὄνομα· Οὖτιν δέ με κικλήσκουσι | μήτηρ ἠδὲ πατὴρ ἠδ᾽ ἄλλοι πάντες ἑταῖροι. (*Odyssey* 9, 366-367, ed. Allen 1917, 160).

[24] Patet itaqve ex his quæ dicta sunt, Ulyssem in peregrinatione sua, ut incognitus pervaderet, Outin appellari voluisse: qvod, cùm ille Græcè in obliqvo casu exprimeret, nostri Græcæ lingvæ ignari etiam in recto casu Outin appellarunt. Qvo nomine cum pleni apud nos sint omnes historiarum libri, uno ore clamitantes Outin quendam Otin vel Odin, qvem Latinè Otinum reddiderunt, ad nos olim ex Asia in septentrionem advenisse, utcunque qvis ille fuerit, nobis hactenus sit incognitum, jam tandem itaque ex nomine virum agnoscimus, & ex ungve [*1702*, unge *1716*] leonem æstimamus (1716, 45-46).

[25] He is also open to entertain the idea that Homer himself misunderstood Odysseus's supposed nickname Οὖτις, and assumed that it was something Odysseus made up in order to fool the Cyclops: fortê Homerus, homo Græcus, cum inveniret Ulyssem se Outin appellasse, ad astutiam hominis

hoc retulit, cogitans ad illudendos peregrinos Ulyssem id nominis sibi finxisse, cum tamen genuinum ipsi esset & proprium (1716, 44) [Perhaps Homer, a Greek, when he heard that Odysseus called himself Outis [acc. *Outin*], ascribed it to the cunning of Odysseus, thinking that Odysseus had invented this name for himself in order to fool foreigners, whereas it actually was authentic and proper to him.]

[26] I have not been able to identify this location, but judging by Ramus's description it is one the cluster of islets due north of Mosken.

[27] Already in Antiquity, Odysseus's travels were by many held to be entirely fictitious (a number of examples of this are given by Rives 1999, 124-125). Yet, the story continues to elicit new attempts at mapping Odysseus's route. Most well known today is perhaps the (controversial) theory of the Italian nuclear engineer Vinci (1995, 5th ed. 2008 and many translations) who locates Odysseus's journey to the Northern part of the Atlantic and the Baltic Sea.

[28] Qvamvis enim Ulysses homo Græcus esset, tamen, cùm ex Asia adveniret, & cum celebrem in septentrione Trojanorum memoriam reperiret, & fortè Græcos contra ob eversam Trojam infames, maluit Asiaticum se & Trojanum profiteri, ut eò majorem sibi gratiam & favorem conciliaret (1716, 49).

“Magical Mooning” and the “Goatskin Twirl”: “Other” Kinds of Female Magical Practices in Early Iceland

Terry Gunnell

For obvious reasons, discussions of magic in the Icelandic sagas have tended to concentrate on the activities involved in *seiðr*.[1] This article, however, will concentrate on two other rather strange types of magical act which are mentioned on several occasions in the sagas but which have so far received comparatively little scholarly attention, largely because the sagas give no explanation of what is taking place, and because, to the best of my knowledge, they have no obvious parallels in classical texts which might explain their origin. The lack of explanation in the texts implies two things: First of all that the saga authors felt the activities needed no explanation for the reading or listening audience, because they, at some point in the process through the oral tradition into the written recording, already knew or understood what was being referred to; and secondly, that if the audience did understand, then the practices in question must have had some basis in actual practice or belief at some point. The idea that the accounts in question must have originated in the oral rather than the written tradition is given further support by the second group of accounts which refer to a practice that will be referred to here as “the goatskin twirl”. These accounts, which are more numerous, vary greatly in wording centering around a basic core, a clear sign that they (if not the tradition behind them) had been passed on in the oral tradition for some time.

The first group of accounts deals with a practice that I have labeled for convenience “magical mooning” (largely because it is difficult to imagine a simpler way to describe it). This practice is described on three occasions. The first example is found in chapter S 180[2] of *Landnámabók* (the Book of Settlements), which has roots in the twelfth century and seems to be based on family oral traditions concerning the first years of the settlement. The event in question takes place in Vatnsdalur in northwest Iceland and involves an encounter between Þorsteinn and Jökull, the sons of Ingimundr inn gamli, and a woman called Ljót (with no patronym), the mother of a difficult man named Hrolleifr whom the brothers are attempting to kill. In the middle of the conflict, Ljót, who is known for her magical powers, is observed leaving her house in what seems to be a state of serious disarray: According to *Landnámabók*: "Þá var Ljót *út komin* ok *gekk ǫfug*; *hon hafði hǫfuðit millum fóta sér*, en *klæðin á baki sér*" [Ljót had *come out* and *was walking backwards*; *she had her head between her legs*, and *her clothes over her back*; my italics]. Jökull's reaction is to throw Hrolleifr's decapitated head at his mother, who announces that she was unfortunately too late; otherwise "nú mundi um *snúazt jǫrðin fyrir sjónum mínum*, en *þér munduð allir ærzt hafa*" ["now *the earth would turn before my eyes*, and *you would all have gone mad*"] (*Landnámabók* 1968, 222; my italics).[3]

The same account is retold in more detail in the late thirteenth-century *Vatnsdæla saga*, chapter 26 (1939, 69-70; my italics), which states concerning Ljót's appearance:

> *hon hafði rekit fǫtin fram yfir hǫfuð sér* ok *fór ǫfug* ok *rétti hǫfuðit aptr milli fótanna*; *ófagrligt var hennar augnabragð*, hversu hon gat þeim *trollsliga skotit*.
>
> [*she had thrown her clothes forward over her head*, and *was walking backwards* and *had stuck her head back between her legs*; she had *an ugly expression in her eyes* with which she seemed to be *shooting magical glances* at them.]

In this version of events, Hrolleifr's head is not thrown at his mother, but her final words are similar enough to suggest a close relationship to the version of the account given in *Landnámabók* (my italics):[4]

> Hún kvaðst hafa *ætlat at snúa þar um landslagi öllu* - "en *þér ærðizk allir* ok *yrðið at gjalti eftir á vegum úti með villidýrum*, ok svá myndi ok gengit hafa, *ef þér hefðið mik eigi fyrr sét en ek yðr.*"
>
> [She said that she had *intended to overturn*[5] *all of the landscape*—"and *you would have all gone mad* and *turned into wild boar out on the tracks with the wild animals*; that is what would have happened *if you hadn't seen me before I saw you.*"]

Worth noting here are the repeated emphases on madness, and on the landscape "turning". It is also important to bear in mind the idea of humans turning into wild animals in this second account.

Another narrative which echoes the previous two accounts closely, but not enough to be a direct literary borrowing, appears in chapter 17 of the fourteenth-century *Þorskfirðinga saga* (also known as *Gull-Þóris saga*), set in the west of Iceland. The account in question focuses on another magically-powerful lady (here named simply "Kerling", or "old woman") who is involved in another attack on a house, and in this case seems to be preventing weapons from biting (much like Þordís spákona [the seeress] does in *Kormáks saga*, chapter 22 [1939, 282-3]). Onlookers observe how "Kerling fór *um völlinn at húsbaki* ok *hafði klæðin á baki sér uppi*, *en niðri höfuðit*, ok *sá svá skýin á milli fóta sér*" [Kerling went *around the grassland at the back of the house* and *had her clothes up on her back*, and *her head down*, so that *she could see the sky between her legs*] (my italics). Kerling is then attacked by another woman called Þuríðr drikkin, who runs out of the house, and:

> þreif í hárit ok reif af aptr hnakkafilluna. Kerling tók í eyra Þuríði báðum höndum ok sleit af henni eyrat ok alla kinnfilluna ofan, ok í því tók at bíta vápn Þóris, ok urðu þá mjök skeinusamir (*Þorskfirðinga saga* 1991, 216-7).
>
> [grabbed her hair and tore off the flesh off the nape of her neck. Kerling then took Þuríðr's ear with

> both hands and ripped off her ear along with all of her cheek. At that moment Þórir's weapons started biting and caused a great deal of physical damage.]

While one can see no mention of madness or turning here, there is nonetheless a strong element of reversal, with a stress on what should be down being up, and vice-versa, and simultaneously the feature of metal temporarily refusing to bite.

As will be stressed later, while generally different in format to the accounts of "magical mooning", the second kind of magic (the "goatskin twirl") nonetheless features certain shared features to "magical mooning", especially in relation to changing laws and conditions, and "turning". While goatskins are only directly mentioned in several of the accounts in question, all of the narratives appear to refer to a similar kind of activity:

The first two narratives again come from *Vatnsdæla saga,* which shows particular interest in magical activities of this kind. The first account (from *Vatnsdæla saga*, ch. 37) deals with yet another powerful lady called Gró (again without a patronym) who is being forcefully encouraged to leave the area. At *sunset* (a timing that is clearly deliberately chosen and worth bearing in mind), someone observes how: "hon *gekk út* ok *gekk andsælis um hús sín ok mælti*: 'Erfitt mun verða at standa í mót giptu Ingimundarsona.'" [She *walked out* and went *widdershins*[6] *around the house and said*: "It will be hard to stand up against the luck of the sons of Ingimundr."] The account then describes how:

> hon *horfði upp í fjallit ok veifði gizka eða dúki, þeim er hon hafði knýtt í gull mikit, er hon átti ok mælti:* "Fari nú hvat sem búit er." Síðan gekk hon inn ok lauk aptr hurðu. Þá hljóp aurskriða á bæinn ok dó allir menn" (*Vatnsdæla saga* 1939, 96; my italics).
>
> [she *looked up at the mountain and waved a goatskin or cloth in which she had knotted a great deal of gold she owned, and said:* "May things go as they have been prepared." She then went in and closed the door.

> Then a mudslide came down on the farm and everybody died.]

The saga adds that "þar þótti reimt jafnan síðan, er byggð Gró hafði verit, ok vildu menn þar eigi búa frá því upp" [after that, people thought the settlement where Gró had been was haunted, and no one wanted to live there from that time onwards], something that would appear to refer to living local beliefs, and a reason for preserving the story.

Another account dealing with the waving of a "gizka" (which some scholars believe to be a shortening of the word "geitskinn" [goatskin] (see the note by Einar Ólafur Sveinsson in *Vatnsdæla saga* 1939, 96)) occurs ten chapters later in the same saga. In this case, however, the magic worker, Bárðr stirfinn, again lacking a patronym, is male, and has been requested to break a spell of bad weather. The account then tells how:

> Hann bað þá *handkrækjask ok gera hring; síðan gekk hann andsælis þrysvar ok mælti írsku; hann bað þá já við kveða. Þeir gerðu svá. Síðan veifði hann gizka til fjalls, ok tók þá af veðrit* (*Vatnsdæla saga* 1939, 127-8; my italics).

> [He asked them to *join arms and form a circle*; *he then walked round widdershins three times and spoke Irish; he asked them to agree to chant their approval. They did so. Then he waved a goatskin towards the mountain and the weather calmed down.*]

As Einar Ólafur Sveinsson comments in his note on this passage, the mention of a group needing to link arms and sing or chant together in a circle brings to mind the *hringr* [circle] that is said to have been "sleginn" [lit. beaten[7]] around the seeress Þorbjörg lítilvölva as she carried out her *seiðr* magic in the famous account in *Eiríks saga rauða* (1935, 206-9). Also worth bearing in mind in this second *Vatnsdæla saga* account are the way the goatskin is waved *towards* the mountain (in other words, towards the wild, or the origin of the weather); and then the rare element of the use of "Irish" language (even though the saga does not state that Bárðr is Irish).

With regard to the latter, it might be said that the key element for the narrative is that the group chant sounded "foreign", another form of overturning (reminiscent perhaps of the use of reversed wording in magical chanting in later times).

A similar account, which lends direct support to the idea that the magical "gizka" in *Vatnsdæla saga* was actually a goatskin, is found in *Njáls saga*, chapter 12, in which another male magic worker called Svanr (once again lacking a patronym) creates a fog. The account again begins by stressing that Svanr walked *out* of his house (once again underlining the apparent necessity for being outside to work this magic) after making a big yawn (he "geispaði mjök": *Brennu-Njáls saga* 1954, 37).[8] The narrative continues as follows:

> *gengu þeir út báðir.* Svanr *tók geitskinn eitt* ok *veifði um hǫfuð sér* ok mælti: "*Verði þoka/ ok verði skrípi/ ok undr* ǫllum þeim/ er eptir þér sækja" (*Brennu-Njáls saga* 1954, 37-8; my italics).
>
> *they both went out.* Svanr *took a goatskin* and *waved/ twirled*[9] *it around his head* and said: "May there be fog / and *may monstrous things come/ and wonders* to all of those/ who are after you."

The account adds that after this "kom þoka mikil í móti" (a great fog came towards those who were attacking), along with a great darkness which caused people to lose their way, and wander off their tracks into the wild, as all direction and order were lost. Worth bearing in mind here is the stress on monsters and wonders.

A very similar activity is described in the later *Víglunda saga*,[10] chapter 12, although now a skin hat (a "kofri") is used instead of a goatskin, along with a raised setting similar to that described as being used in *seiðr* activities. Here, the female magic worker named Kjölvör (as usual with no patronym) is said to climb onto a roof to invoke her powers, which in this case are directed at creating a storm. The saga tells how Kjölvör "fór *upp á hús* ok *veifði kofra sínum í austurætt ok þykknaði skjótt veðrit*" [went *up onto a house* and *waved her skin cap towards the east, and the weather began thickening up*] (*Víglunda saga* 1959, 83; my italics).

Yet another example is found in *Harðar saga*, chapter 25, where a magically-empowered lady named Þorbjörg katla (no patronym) tries to summon up a fog to prevent the Hólmverjar outlaws from attacking her and her family from the sea. The saga tells how: "Hún sækir þá *sveipu sína ok veifði upp yfir höfuð sér*. Þá *gerði myrkr mikið* at þeim Geir" [She fetched *her wrap/ shawl and waved it above her head*. Then *a great darkness* was sent at Geir and the others] (*Harðar saga Grímkelssonar eða Hólmverja saga* 1991, 66; my italics). Once again the action seems to involve a kind of spinning or twirling motion, something perhaps echoed by the use of the word "sveipa" for the garment, which also suggests a kind of encircling movement.[11]

Yet another example relating to a similar sort of twirling or encircling magic being wielded by a female magic user to cause potential hazards at sea occurs in *Hávarðar saga Ísfirðings*, chapter 8. While it is not directly stated what is happening here, the implication is that those present (and most listeners) would have been aware what was implied when the lady in question (Hávarðr's wife who is named Bjargey and has no patronym) is rowed around a boat containing her enemies and "*hafði poka nǫkkurn í hendi ok veifði umhverfis skútuna*. Ok er hon hefir at gert slíkt er hon vildi, þá fleyta þau í árum ok róa í brott, slíkt er þau mega" [had *a bag of some sort in her hand and waved it around the boat*. And when she has done what she wants to do, they put out the oars and row away as fast as they can"] (*Hávarðar saga Ísfirðings* 1943, 316; my italics). Whatever Bjargey has done (related to drawing down punishment on the person who has brought about the death of her son), it is clearly something that makes those in the other boat feel that she deserves to be hunted down and maimed. There seems little question that even though a bag is waved here rather than a skin, the same idea of magical ritual is implied. Indeed, the likelihood is that the bag was also made from skin.

Another parallel is found in a short account of a strong wind which blows away a potential bride in *Reykdæla saga* (ch. 14), and is said to have been caused by yet another powerful woman called

Ísgerðr who has also been engaging in strange activities involving skins: Steinfinnr, a man with similar skills, states that: "Ísgerðr hafði þar komit, frá Bárðartjörn, ok rekit *fótaskinn sitt um höfuð* honum húskarlinum - 'ok *af því varð myrkrit ok svá vindrinn*, sá er henni feykti ofan til naustanna'" [Ísgerðr has come there from Bárðartjörn and thrust her *"foot-skin"*[12] *around the servant's head* - "and *because of that the darkness came and then the wind* which swept her [the bride] down to the boathouse"] (*Reykdæla saga ok Víga-Skúta* 1940, 193; my italics).[13]

That such actions might have once been comparatively widely understood by listeners or readers without any need for further explanation is further supported by the way in which they have come to be reflected in the Icelandic language in the form of expressions referring to the casting of deceptions or illusions, as can be seen in both *Eyrbyggja saga*, chapter 20; and *Grettis saga*, chapter 63. In the former, yet another single, protective mother called Katla, once again with magical powers but no patronym, is shown trying to defend her son, Oddr, from men who have designs on his life. The saga (*Eyrbyggja saga* 1935, 51) tells how Katla "sat á palli ok *spann* garn" [sat on a bench and *span* yarn] (my italics), and by carrying out this *literal* spinning activity, spun an illusion whereby her son Oddr was first mistaken for her distaff (however that was managed), and then her goat (the choice of animal here is interesting). Those searching for Oddr then ask: "*Hvort mun Katla eigi hafa heðni veift um hǫfuð oss*?" [lit. "*Has Katla been waving a skin coat around our heads*?"] (my italics). What is meant is simply "Has Katla been pulling the wool over our eyes", which would be a more fitting way of putting things considering what she is doing. The use of the verb "veifa um" (waving around) and the choice of a skin coat as the main object are particularly interesting in this example, where no such actions appear to have actually taken place.

In *Grettis saga*, chapter 63, the expression appears to have reached a later stage in which direct reference to the activity—and direct sense, if not meaning—have both been lost. Here, the verb *veifa* (to wave) has been replaced by the similar sounding verb *vefja* (to wrap), and the preposition altered from "um" (around) to "at" (at), even though the head (*höfuð*) and the skin (coat) (*heðinn*) are still being referred to. The expression is clearly being used as part of daily language and without any direct connection to magic when a reference is made to how the outlaw Grettir has effectively deceived people: "þótti mǫrgum Grettir *hafa vafit heðin at hǫfði þeim*" [lit. many felt that Grettir had *wrapped the skincoat at their heads*] (*Grettis saga* 1936, 209). There is little question that the expression still means that Grettir had "pulled the wool over people's eyes", but the activity that lies behind the expression seems to have slipped into the background, or faded out of memory.

As noted at the start, the saga writers seem to have felt no need to explain what was actually "going on" in these two types of magical rituals, meaning that they were themselves either bemused by the accounts that had been orally passed down to them, or assumed that their audience knew what was going on. There is little likelihood that they created them out of thin air in a form of polygenesis, and there are no direct models in classical sources. This means that if modern scholars wish to try and understand what is taking place, they need to read the texts very closely (as has been done above) and then place the activities alongside comparative material known elsewhere (ideally material from neighboring countries and a similar period), to see if this provides any possible explanation.

If we begin with the "magical mooning" activity, faint parallels can perhaps be seen in Ibn Faḍlān's tenth-century account of the Rūs boat funeral on the Volga, describing how:

> the deceased's next of kin approached and took hold of a piece of wood and set fire to it. *He walked backwards, with the back of his neck to the ship, his face to the people, with the lighted piece of wood in one hand and the other hand on his anus, being completely naked.* He ignited the wood that had been set up under the ship after they had placed the slave-girl whom they had killed beside her master (Montgomery 2000, 20; my italics).

Here, however, there is no element of threat or physical inversion in spite of the backward-walking and nakedness.

Perhaps a little closer in context is an account written by the late seventeenth-century Scottish clergyman, Robert Kirk, and contained in his *Secret Commonwealth of Elves, Fauns and Fairies.* Kirk writes that someone wanting the gift of Second Sight:

> must run a Tedder of Hair (which bound a Corps to the Bier) in a Helix about his Midle, from End to End; then then bow his Head downwards, as did Elijah, 1 Kings, 18. 42. and look back thorough his Legs untill he sie a Funerall advance till the People cross two Marches; or look thus back thorough a Hole where was a Knot of Fir (Kirk 1893, 26-7).[14]

While this account offers clear parallels to later Nordic legends which suggest that you can see ghosts and spirits by looking though a horse's collar; and devilish beings by standing on or in a priest's shoes,[15] it has little directly to do with the behavior of the female magic workers in the Old Nordic accounts, except for the fact that those referred to appear to be connecting themselves to the "other world" in some way or other. It might nonetheless be kept in mind that Elijah in the Biblical account remained fully clad. The central feature here is that of looking back through the legs, but there is no element of defense or attack involved.

Closer and more intriguing parallels can perhaps be found in other early Icelandic material such as the so-called "Hólmgöngulög" (dueling rules) quoted in in *Kormáks saga*, chapter 10, which are detailed and strange enough to have been genuinely pre-Christian: they clearly have little to do with the church. Most important in the present context is that the passage in question also contains the elements of walking backwards and viewing the sky between your legs:

> Þat váru hólmgǫngulög at feldr skal vera fimm alna í skaut ok lykkjur í hornum; skyldi þar setja niðr hæla þá, er hǫfuð var á ǫðrum enda; þat hétu tjǫsnur; *sá er um bjó, skyldi ganga at tjǫsnunum, svá at sæi himin milli fóta sér ok heldi í eyrasnepla með þeim formála, sem síðan er*

> *eptir hafðr í blóti því, at kallat tjǫsnublót* (*Kormáks saga* 1939, 237; my italics).
>
> [It was the dueling law that there should be a skin/ cloak five ells square, with loops/ holes in the corners; through these should be placed pegs with heads on the end; these were called *tjösnur*; whoever prepared this should *walk towards the tjösnur in such a way that the sky could be seen between his legs, holding his earlobes* with the incantation/ formula/ preamble that is then used in the sacrifice that is called a *tjösnublót* [*tjösnur* sacrifice].]

As with the accounts of "magical mooning", the activity described here is totally unexplained. The account nonetheless suggests that the idea of apparently walking backwards looking at the sky between the legs was seen as invoking some kind of power. Here, however, the figure is male and there is no element of nakedness. The purpose of the ritual is unclear, although, as with Kirk's account noted above, it would seem to involve the supernatural, not least because it is said to be connected to a "blót" (sacrifice).

It seems apparent that one of the key elements of the "magical mooning" ritual seems to be the exposing the female genitalia, which might perhaps find a parallel in one of the woodcuts of witches' Sabbaths by the German artist, Hans Baldung (1485-1545) which includes the image of a naked witch looking back between her legs; and an original illustration accompanying the short story "Le Diable de Papefiguière" (The Devil of Popefingerdom) by Jean de La Fontaine (1621-1695), in which the Devil is frightened off by a woman who exposes herself to him.[16] The latter idea would certainly seem to have ancient roots if it is considered in the context of the much earlier so-called "Sheela-na-gig" images found on the walls of churches in Ireland and Britain which go back to the twelfth century and are exclusively female (see further Freitag 2004 and Anderson 1971 for detailed reviews of all the images in question). These images seem to involve the deliberate exposing of the female genitalia (usually forward-facing, as in the La Fontaine image). Considering their placement often on the outer walls of churches, they would seem to entail some element of apotropaic magical protection against dangerous or evil spirits, similar to the role of the gargoyles found on many medieval English and French churches and the dragons on medieval Norwegian stave churches (and on the prows of Viking boats, a Nordic tradition which seems to go back to the Stone age).[17] Possibly related are other images from the same period found particularly on churches and town walls in Germany (including Köln Town Hall), Switzerland, France and parts of Denmark in which figures (mainly male) seem to be "mooning", in other words exposing their backsides and genitalia, a gesture referring to in German as "Blecker" (lit. "baring"), or "Arschblecker" (lit. "arse-baring"). These activities also appear to serve a apotropaic purpose. A fine example can be found in a miniature contained in the MS Verdun breviary from the early fourteenth century (see further Kroll and Steger 1994; and Schmidt 1953).[18]

The latter images (and their connection to warding off supernatural threats) certainly find a further parallel in a well-known migratory legend known right across the Nordic countries (including Iceland), in which a girl is followed by a ghost in a graveyard who asks "Är mitt öga rött?" ["Is my eye red?"], and then asks back, without turning: "Är min röv svart?" ["Is my arse black?"] (af Klintberg 1972, 202 and 322; and 2010, 63: legend type C 66: "Showing one's backside to a pursuer").[19] According to Bengt af Klintberg (1972, 322), this answer echoes the Swedish expression "Kyss mej i röven" ["Kiss my ass"] which apparently had its original as an apotropaic answer that could be used in Sweden whenever you found yourself under threat from the supernatural.[20]

While such accounts certainly offer vague parallels to the "magical mooning" practices described in the sagas, the key difference in the latter seems to be that while the Nordic female magic practitioners may also be insulting their adversaries, the enemies in question are not supernatural, but human. The approach might thus seem to offer closer parallels to the internationally-known phenomenon of the "evil eye", something which could be perhaps reflected in Ljót's mention of her sight ("sjón mín":

Landnámabók), and "seeing" her enemies, with a magical expression in her eyes ("trollslig" "augnabragð": *Vatnsdæla saga*).[21] The "eye" is nonetheless only part of what is going on here. Indeed, considering they are in a threatening battle situation, the women in question would appear to be increasing their personal vulnerability. The implications of all three accounts of "magical mooning" are that the women's activities are supposed to have *magical* efficacy particularly in the context of battle. Rather than placing any emphasis on the element of exhibitionism, the key features of the accounts seem to be those of a woman coming outside a house (all three accounts); moving backwards (*Landnámabók*; and *Vatnsdæla saga*);[22] having her lower clothing thrown over her back (in other words "downside-up" [all three accounts]);[23] having her head between the legs in an "upside-down" position (all three accounts; also reflected in *Kormáks saga*) and seeing the sky from below (*Þorskfirðinga saga*, as well as *Kormáks saga*); and the element of "turning" (að "snúazt"/ "snúa") (*Landnámabók*; and *Vatnsdæla saga*), both in the sense of turning wits and inducing madness in people (*Landnámabók*; and *Vatnsdæla saga* (which adds the element of animal traits), and "turning" the landscape (*Landnámabók*). In the *Landnámabók* account, Ljót says: "nú mundi *um snúazt jǫrðin* fyrir sjónum mínum, en *þér munduð allir ærzt hafa*" [now *the earth would turn before my eyes*, and *you would all have gone mad*"], while *Vatnsdæla saga* states "Hún kvaðst hafa ætlat at *snúa þar um* landslagi öllu—"en *þér ærðizk allir* ok *yrðið at gjalti eftir* á vegum úti með villidýrum" [She said that she had *intended to overturn all of the landscape*—"and *you would have all gone mad* and *turned into wild boar out on the tracks with the wild animals*;](my italics).

The elements of madness and environmental overturning are strongly reminiscent of Þorleifr jarlsskáld's "Jarlsníð" curse (and so-called "þokuvísur" [lit. "fog-verses"]) performed against Jarl Hákon in Þrándheimr, in *Þorleifs þáttr jarlsskálds*,[24] the wording reflecting most particularly the curses that accompany Egill Skallagrímsson's raising of the *níðstöng* [scorn pole] against King Eiríkr blóðöx in *Egils saga*, and the formula that forms part of the so-called "Buslubæn" directed at King Hringr in the later *fornaldar saga*, *Bósa saga og Herrauðs*. The latter two accounts both seem to center around nature spirits being caused to lose their way in the natural environments they control: Egill says, again with a stress of "turning":

> "*sný ek* þessu níði á landvættir þær, er land þetta byggva, svá at allar *fari þær villar vega, engi hendi né hitti sitt inni* fyrr en þær reka Eirík konung ok Gunnhildi ór landi" (*Egils saga* 1933, 171 [ch. 57]; my italics).
>
> ["*I turn* this curse on the land spirits that populate this land, so that all of them *will lose their way, and not reach or find their home* until they have driven King Eiríkr and Gunnhildr from the land."]

Precisely the same idea is given in the wording of the "Buslubæn", which goes even further in explaining *why* the spirits should lose their way: "Villist vættir,/ verði ódæmi,/ hristist hamrar,/ heimr sturlist,/ versni veðrátta;/ verði óðæmi" ["May the spirits lose their way,/ may terrible things take place [lit. may there be matchlessness],/ the cliffs shake,/ the world go mad,/ the weather worsen;/ may terrible things take place"] (*Bósa saga ok Herrauðs* 1954, 291-2). A further parallel would seem to be the description in *Völuspá*, st. 48 (*Eddadigte* 1964, 12), of how "stynia dvergar/ fyr steindurom,/ veggbergs vísir" [the dwarves groan/ before stone doors/ the cliff face princes] as brothers battle and rocks growl and collapse at the time of *ragnarök*. What seems to be being involved in all of these magical verses is the idea of a form of environmental confusion in which light becomes dark, solid rock shakes, the weather turns stormy, and both men and the world go mad, as even nature spirits lose all sense of direction (one notes that the dwarves are associated with cardinal directions in *Gylfaginning*, chapter 8 (Faulkes 2005, 12)).

One wonders whether there is a possibility that the elements of inversion, walking backwards and looking upwards with clothes thrown over the back in the accounts of "magical mooning" might reflect a similar idea of overturning conventional order, but here in the form of action rather than words, in other words that it might be seen as a kind of "sympathetic magic" (van Gennep 1960, 7-9 and 14). In short, is it possible, considering Ljót's suggestion in

Vatnsdæla saga and *Landnámabók* that she had aimed literally to overturn the landscape and drive men mad, that by looking upwards at the sky from below and walking backwards, she was attempting by magical gesture to symbolically break down the barriers between the world above and the looking-glass "upside-down" world of Hel below, a world of rock and darkness which is ruled by a woman, and where *women* (the *valkyrjur*) are the ones who wear armor, ride on horses, and make the decisions (on the nature of Hel, see further Ellis 1968; and Abram 2003)?[25] Such a temporary opening of the supernatural gates and blending of worlds would naturally introduce a state of chaotic liminality in which all direction, all sense, and all control would be temporarily lost, as the wild took over the civilized, night became day, rock ceased to be solid, and the known became the unknown, just as seems to occur during Þorleifr's performance of the "Jarlsníð".

Returning to the "goatskin twirl" which similarly brings about changes in the weather and visibility, as well as mud-slides, it may be remembered that this too involves the element of "turning", most obviously in the form of skins, cloths, hats or blankets being twirled or spun (in all but two cases by women) deliberately *outside* the house (in all cases except for *Eyrbyggja saga*, where the action seems to have become primarily an expression).[26] It is noteworthy that both of the examples from *Vatnsdæla saga* suggest that the magic worker should walk "andsælis" [widdershins], literally against the movement of the sun, a common feature of witchcraft all over the world, and something that reflects the backward walking of the "mooning" accounts. Both *Vatnsdæla saga* accounts also mention that the twirling of the skin is directed towards the mountains, which, while it might be viewed as the home of bad weather (see above), also represented the beginning of the wilderness, in other words, the "other side". Another account (*Víglunda saga*) stipulates that the twirling is directed towards east (towards Jötunheimar, or once again, against the sun?). In terms of function, one ritual produces a rock slide (*Vatnsdæla saga*, ch. 37); another calms a storm (*Vatnsdæla saga*, ch. 47); two cause bad weather (*Víglunda saga* and *Reykdæla saga*) while three others bring about fog or darkness in daytime (*Njáls saga*, *Reykdæla saga* and *Harðar saga*).

There are obvious parallels to other saga accounts of storms being created by magical ritual, such as those in *Gísla saga*, chapter 13 (1943, 43); *Laxdæla saga*, chapter 35 (1934: 99); *Fóstbræðra saga*, chapter 10 (1943, 169), and *Friðþjófs saga*, chapter 3 (1954, IV, 87-8 and 92) (see further Strömbäck 2000); and perhaps also in the curse invoked by Steinunn mother of Skáld-Refr when she called up a storm against the missionary Þangbrandr in *Kristni saga*, chapter 6 (2003, 16).[27] Similarly, one might consider the accounts of how Sámi *noaider* magicians were believed to control winds, using knots among other things (see further Perkins 2001, 11-12; Price 2002, 263 and 275; and Heide 2006, 196-221 and 245-9); or even those concerning "veðrbelgar" [lit. "weather bags"] like that mentioned in *Þorsteins saga Víkingssonar*, chapter 11 (1954, IV, 28). Indeed, it could well be such "belgar" [bags] which are used by Möndull in his conflict with Grímr Ægir recounted in *Göngu-Hrólfs saga*, chapter 33 (1954, III, 258); and in the narrative from *Hávarðar saga* noted above. The examples from *Þorsteins saga* and *Göngu-Hrólfs saga*, however, would appear to be slightly different in that both tell how the magical practitioner "hristi" [shook] the bags to bring about winds (which issue from the bags), rather than waving them. As regards the accounts of *seiðr*, although they stress that the activity occurs outside in a raised position above the earth (as in *Víglunda saga* when Kjölvör climbs up on a house), nothing is ever said about the waving or twirling of skins.

The recurring element of twirling or spinning in most of the accounts in question nonetheless underlines that what is involved is another form of sympathetic magic (see above; and Heide 2006, 245-9), whereby the practitioner magically simulates what she/he desires (in the form of raising winds, bringing down fog, or changing weather in some other way). The direct relationship between the ritual and the landslide that occurs in *Vatnsdæla saga* is nonetheless less clear, unless one considers the possibility that the two rituals of reversed "mooning" and "twirling" have something in common with each other. The shared elements would be those of reversal and/or inversion (considering the widdershins movement noted in some of the "twirling" accounts); of turning, spinning, or twirling; and the resulting invocation of chaos whereby natural rules are broken, the wild (darkness or storm) takes over, up goes down, down goes up, light becomes dark, and the landscape changes shape. In short, there would seem to be good reason to consider the possibility that both rituals might refer back to some kind of shared concept. As has been noted above, both rituals seem to be essentially associated with women (like *seiðr*), and involve an outdoor setting amidst natural surroundings and natural forces which seem to be called on in one form or another.[28]

It would nonetheless seem that the accounts of magical twirling also reflect a development over time from more detailed accounts (those reflected in *Vatnsdæla saga*) to the form of a comparatively unexplained motif to the final unexplained expressions used in *Eyrbyggja saga* and *Grettis saga* (where there is no longer any association with magic). The same kind of development might be reflected in the development of the object waved from a "gizka"/ "geitskinn" (goatskin: *Vatnsdæla saga*, where in one case [chapter 37], the author is not sure if it is a "gizka" or a "dúkr" [cloth]) to a "kofri" [hat], "sveipa" [wrap], "poki" [bag], "fótaskinn" [foot-skin] and "heðinn" [skin], in which the idea of skin or leather seems to be a common denominator.

Whether the choice of animal in connection with the skin is important is open to question. Þórr (most closely associated with goats) certainly appears to have been invoked by Icelanders when at sea because he seems to have power over the waves and storms (see *Landnámabók* 1968, 250-253 [S 218; H 184: Helgi hinn magri], and 55 [H 15: Kollr]; see also Perkins 2001). Þórr is also shown in both the Poetic and Prose Edda as being the only god to freely wade though water and go fishing (see Faulkes 1998, 25 [ch. 18], and 2005, 17 and 48 [chs. 15 and 50]; see also *Grímnismál*, st. 29, and *Hymiskviða*, as well as other accounts of Þórr's fishing trip). Adam of Bremen, meanwhile, associates him with weather, fertility and thunder and lightning (Adam of Bremen 1917, 259-60; 1959, 208). Furthermore, as noted above, it might be borne in mind that in *Kristni saga*, when Steinunn, mother of Skáld-Refr, wants to wreck a boat at sea, she invokes Þórr; a god who, in *Rögnvalds þáttr og Rauðs* (in *Flateyjarbók*), is said to cause a storm by blowing out his cheeks and into his whiskers (*Flateyjarbók* 1860-8, I, 296). Indeed, Richard Perkins has raised the possibility that various Nordic images depicting men pulling or twisting their beards might reflect Þórr in this capacity (Perkins 2001, 151-2). Nonetheless, as has been noted above, only a few of the accounts in question relate to water and/or the sea. Another possibility is that a goatskin is used because goats are more closely associated with the mountains, or because of their horns (commonly used as a sign of power). One should not forget that goatskins also offered one of the most common forms of disguise throughout the Nordic countries in the Christmas mumming activities that go back to the Middle Ages (see Gunnell 2005).

All in all, while it is difficult to draw any certain conclusions with regard to the background of the two types of magic ritual described in this article, it does seem clear that they both had a background in memories that were passed on in the oral tradition, involving "actual" pre-Christian activities. Both, it would seem, involved the temporary evocation of chaos via an overturning of natural rules, something that temporarily broke down the barriers between worlds.

Notes

[1] See further Strömbäck 2000; Price 2002, 92-232; Dillmann 2006; and Tolley 2009. For other types of magic, see also Mitchell 2011.

[2] Chapters in *Landnámabók* are identified with an S (those coming from the version known *Sturlubók*) and H (those coming from the version contained in *Hauksbók*).

[3] Unless otherwise stated, all translations in this article are those of the author.

[4] Whether this is a textual borrowing is open to question. If it is, the author has made a deliberate decision to alter both the wording and the course of events slightly.

[5] The verb "snúa um"/ "umsnúa" means literally to turn upside-down or revolve.

[6] "Widdershins" means "anti-clockwise"

[7] The verb "slá" is commonly used with dance in later times. It would appear to refer to movement and perhaps some kind of stamping to emphasise a beat. There is little evidence of drums being used in Iceland in the sagas or Eddic poetry: see, nonetheless, *Lokasenna*, st. 24: *Eddadigte* 1971, 51.

[8] The idea of "yawning" ("geispa"/ "blása við") in connection with magic or shamanic activities also occurs in *Hrólfs saga kraka* 1954, 8 (Heiðr) and 10 (Böðvar Bjarki).

[9] Although the verb "veifa" does not have to mean any more than "wave", here the additional information that it was waved "um" [around] Svanr's head gives reason to believe that the waving in this case involved more of a swirling or twirling motion.

[10] The saga is preserved in two manuscripts from the fifteenth century.

[11] A little later in the saga, it is stated that Þorbjörg "skók … enn sveipu sína" [shook her wrap/ shawl again] for a similar purpose, although the verb describing the action here is slightly different: *Harðar saga Grímkelssonar eða Hólmverja saga* 1991, 66. It nonetheless offers parallels to the shaking of so-called "veðrbelgar" [weather bags] noted below.

[12] There is some uncertainty about the meaning of "fótaskinn" which could refer to a carpet or some sort of foot-bag. Whatever the meaning, it is likely that is was something made of skin designed to keep feet warm (in a boat).

[13] Another example which could perhaps be related is a sentence from *Bárðar saga*, chapter 18, stating how King Ólafur Tryggvason gave Gestr Bárðarson a cloth which would protect him when he broke into a grave mound. The sentence in question runs: "… dúk gaf hann honum ok bað hann *vefja honum um sik* áðr en hann gengi í hauginn" [he gave him a cloth which he told him to *wrap around himself* before entering the mound] (my

italics). Both the wording and the present context nonetheless appear to be quite different from the other examples given above.

[14] I am grateful to Jacqueline Simpson for pointing out this reference to me.

[15] See, for example, af Klintberg 2010, 216 (legend type L6: "Parson's maid sees the Devil from outside"; see also af Klintberg 1972, 264), and 56 (legend type C22: "Horses are made to pull").

[16] I am grateful to Stephen Mitchell for pointing out these two images as possible parallels.

[17] On the idea that figureheads ("gapandi höfðunum eða gínandi trjónum" [lit. gaping heads or reaching muzzles]) should be removed from ships approaching land because they might frighten the "landvættir" [land spirits] of Iceland, see *Landnámabók* 1968, 313 (H 268); and also *Hauksbók* 1892-6, 503. *Ulfljótslög*, believed by many to be the earliest Icelandic law (possibly going back, in part, to around 930) is also contained in *Þorsteins þáttr uxafóts* (in *Flateyjarbók* 1860-68, I, 249); and *Brot af Þórðar sögu hreðu* 1959, 231-2. On the dating of *Úlfljótslög*, see further Jón Hnefill Aðalsteinsson 1998, 44-50. Regarding the use of figureheads on boats in northern Norway in the late Stone Age, see further Helskog 1988.

[18] I am grateful to Rudolf Simek for providing me with references about these German images.

[19] An Icelandic version of this story can be found in the folk legend, "Horfðu í glóðaraugað mitt, Gunna," in Jón Þorkelsson 1956, 31.

[20] Another parallel might be found in Swedish legend type H44: "Maid makes farm spirit move" (af Klintberg 2010, 145), in which a girl frightens a farm spirit into leaving the farm by entering the barn bent over backwards, making the spirit think she is a monster.

[21] See further Dundes 1992; and Feilberg 1901.

[22] The element of "backwards" movement is perhaps retained in the *Þorskfirðinga saga* wording that Kerling has her clothes "á baki sér" [on her back] and is "að húsbaki" [at the back of the house].

[23] *Þorskfirðinga saga* underlines this element in the wording "klæðin á baki sér *uppi*, en *niðri* höfuðit" [had her clothes *up* on her back, and her head *down*].

[24] See *Þorleifs þáttr jarlsskálds* 1956, 218-23 (chs. 4-5).

[25] Another faint possibility is that the world below might be *Jötunheimar*, if we consider the first part of *Völuspá*, in which, according to st. 2, the *jötnar* seem not only to be "fyr mold neðan" [below the earth], but also closely associated with powerful women (st. 8, which talks of "ámátkar meyiar" [powerful women], the first females in the poem coming from "iǫtunheimom"): see *Eddadigte* 1964, 1-2.

[26] The idea that the item spun is a goatskin is based largely on the use of the word "gizka" in both *Vatnsdæla saga* accounts, and the direct mention of goatskin in *Njáls saga* (see above).

[27] See also *Kristni saga* (ch. 6), p. 24; and *Brennu-Njáls saga*, 1954, 265-7. The idea of magic being used to calm storms is also mentioned as a skill in *Hávamál*, st. 154: "Vind ek kyrri/ vági á/ ok svæfik allan sæ" [I can calm winds in the bay, and put all seas to sleep]. Here, however, the method is not explained.

[28] In very general terms, one might consider that women seem to have had a more central role in religious activities related to sites on the periphery in earlier times. On such sites, see further, for example, Fredengren 2011; and Monikander 2010.

Archaeology and the Cosmos

Reading Cult and Mythology in Society and Landscape: The Toponymic Evidence

Stefan Brink

Across all cultures, myths have been used to explain phenomena and events beyond people's comprehension. Our focus in research on Scandinavian mythology has, to a large extent, been to describe, uncover, and critically assess these myths, examining the characteristics and acts not only of gods and goddesses, but also of the minor deities found in the poems, sagas, Snorra *Edda*, and Saxo. All this research is and has been conducted to fathom, as far as possible, the cosmology, the cosmogony, and eschatology—in short, the mythology—of pagan Scandinavia. An early branch of scholarship focused on extracting knowledge of this kind from later collections of folklore. This approach was heavily criticized and placed in the poison cabinet for decades, but seems to have come back into fashion, brought once again into the light by younger scholars who are possibly unaware of the total dismissal of the approach in the 1920s and 30s. Another productive area of the research has been the examination of the cults and rituals among pre-Christian Scandinavians as described and indicated by written sources, iconography, archaeology, and toponymy.

When preparing for this paper I planned to do two things: First, to paint, with broad strokes, the toponymic research history of the study of sacral and cultic place names. The goal here is to provide a broad picture of the current state of research in this field, hopefully revealing how toponymists work and think today. Second, I aimed to look at the myths not descriptively—retelling and analyzing the stories in the written sources—but rather *instrumentally*. The focus would be on a preliminary exploration of how societies in early

Scandinavia *used* myths for societal and political purposes. I will not be able to accomplish this task here, but will postpone that analysis for another occasion.

The development of toponymic research can best be described by identifying three notable phases during the last two centuries that took place after the founding of the discipline.

The Founding Fathers – The Romantic Search for the Soul of the Nation and for the Soul of the People in the Nation, as well as Their Religious Beliefs in Ancient Times

The historian and philologist Peter Andreas (PA) Munch (b. 1810 d. 1863) had broad interests, and his scholarly production was immense, especially when one considers that he died at the relatively young age of fifty-three. His impact on research and society, and in the nation-building project of a free Norway, was fundamental. He published the still readable *Det norske Folks Historie* (in 8 volumes, 1852-63) and, more related to our concerns here, a handbook of Old Norse Mythology, *Nordens gamle Gude- og Helte-Sagn*, which first appeared in 1840. It was originally written as a supplementary volume to a didactic book on the history of Norway, Sweden, and Denmark. As a book for students and as a work of general reference, it has maintained its popularity. The third edition of the mythology book (1922) was prepared by Professor Magnus Olsen, who we will discuss shortly; this edition is still an important read—however with the critical glasses firmly on the nose—for any student working on Pagan Scandinavian religion. This book was translated into English in 1926 as *Norse Mythology. Legends of Gods and Heroes.*

Four more scholars were also of great importance. The German Konrad (von) Maurer produced the particularly important *Die Bekehrung des Norwegischen Stammes zum Christenthume* II (München 1856 pp. 188-238). In Denmark, Henry Petersen's *Om Nordboernes Gudedyrkelse og Gudetro i Hedenold* (Copenhagen 1876) and Johannes Steenstrup's *Nogle Undersøgelser om Guders Navne i de nordiske Stedsnavne* (1896) were of great significance. In Sweden, Magnus

Frederik Lundgren published the influential *Språkliga intyg om hednisk gudatro i Sverige* (1878).

Petersen's book is a remarkable overview of Old Norse cult and mythology, and is still worth reading. Of course it contains many things we do not agree with today and many aspects of Petersen's discussions we now find uncritical. But reading the book from the standpoint of when it was written in the 1870s, one cannot help but be impressed. Typical of scholarship at the time was a focus on the King, conceptualized as the ultimate cult leader (*Rigets ypperste Hovgode*), who resided at the main communal cult site (*et for hele Riget fælles Hovedoffersted*) (Petersen 1876, 7). Petersen, like Munch, introduces place names as a source for understanding the myths and cultic practices in Denmark. Admittedly his use of toponyms is uncritical for our time, but pioneering for his. Johannes Steenstrup's article, which I believe is the first systematic analysis of cultic and sacral place names in Scandinavia, is an impressive piece of research for its time, and Steenstrup is able to sift nuggets from Fool's Gold.

Hans Hildebrand (1898–1903, 6), the National Antiquarian in Sweden during the latter part of the nineteenth century, developed the idea that names, such as *Härnevi*, actually contained in the first element the name of a pagan god or goddess. In the case of *Härnevi*, for instance, he hypothesizes a goddess *Härn*, a proposal that was taken up by Magnus Olsen (1908) in modified form.[1] Olsen connected the name with ON *Hǫrn*. This type of information concerning gods and goddesses both known and unknown from the Old Norse literature, appeared again and again in the scholarship during the decades around the turn of the twentieth century.

Phase One: The Uncritical and Merry – 'Everything-Seems-Possible' – Phase

During these years scholars believed that they could reconstruct the existence of numerous gods and goddesses from place names as well as identify various cult sites. So, for example, Erik Noreen proposed that the name *Kåvö* (OSw *Quadowi*) in Närke contained the words *kvadha* 'resin' and *vi* 'cult site', explaining it as a site where a fertility cult had taken place (Noreen 1914). Decomposed in this manner, Noreen took the name to suggest that the cultic participants had offered 'resin' (*kåda*) to a fertility god or goddess, and used, as supporting evidence, archaeological finds of obviously offered cakes of resin from the Bronze Age (*sic*!), while also describing the importance of resin in folk culture and folk medicine (cf. Edlund 2012, 63).

Oscar Lundberg (1913) proposed that the name *Vrinnevid* (OSw *Wrindawi*) was related to the Old Icelandic name of a goddess, *Rindr*, whom he proposed was a fertility goddess. Furthermore, he proposed that it was also related to the word *rind* 'ivy', found in Gotlandic dialects, allowing him to connect the name to ivy which, in German and English folklore, is on some level related to fertility. Consequently, Lundberg proposed that this goddess *Vrind* was made of or represented by ivy, and who had a cult at this *vi* or 'cult site'.[2]

This phase in toponymic scholarship is epitomized by two scholars, Magnus Olsen and Elias Wessén who are, without doubt, two of our most philologically sound but also imaginative and creative scholars. The former, the successor to Sophus Bugge in the chair in 'Gammalnorsk og islandsk språk og litteratur',[3] was also an utterly daring (some would say uncritical) scholar. The latter, Wessén, was Professor of Scandinavian languages (nordiska språk) in Stockholm, with—I have been told—a crackling dry personality. He was a fellow of the Swedish Academy, in chair sixteen, for thirty-four years.[4] Both were unbelievably productive, and both laid the foundations for future research in several fields. Olsen, for example, laid the groundwork for future scholarship in Norwegian runology by publishing the Norwegian runic corpus, with one volume dedicated to inscriptions in the older futharc, and five volumes to inscriptions in the younger futharc. He wrote the still most readable and influential book in Norwegian toponymy, *Ættegård og helligdom. Norske stedsnavn sosialt og religionshistorisk* belyst (1926), translated into English as *Farms and fanes of ancient Norway* (1928). This work is still cited by scholars in toponymy, philology, archaeology and the history of religions as if it were state-of-the-art, and then criticized for being wrong and obsolete. This criticism is absolutely astonishing since the book is nearly one hundred years old, and Olsen wrote it within the theoretical frameworks of the disciplines current at the time in which he worked. At the time of its publication, it was an absolute sensation given its deep knowledge of sources, its overarching scope, and its theoretical rigor. By way of analogy, one cannot seriously compare a Model-T Ford with a modern Ferrari or Lamborghini, any more than one can compare Olsen's early work with contemporary scholarship. But this is what some scholars do today. I find this critique utterly unfair. Olsen's doctoral thesis, *Hedenske kultminder i norske stedsnavne* (1915), was more extensive yet uncritical. In it, he collects and discusses all the sacral and cultic place names he was able to find in Norway. This is still an important work, but one has to use it cautiously.[5]

For certain names in Norway and Sweden beginning with *Elg-* and *Äll-*, Olsen came up with a most ingenious, and admittedly hazardous, explanation. He saw here the reminiscence of a male pair of gods, to be compared with the *Alci* who, according to Tacitus's *Germania* (chap. 43), were a pair of twin male gods amongst the *Nah(a)rvali*, a Germanic tribe. According to Tacitus, their worship took place in a cultic grove, led by a female cult leader (or at least a cult leader dressed in a female outfit, which is the actual wording). The main argument used by Olsen was the place name *Elgjartún*, attested approximately a dozen times in Norway, which he combines with the Latin *alcis*. Here, the Latin stem was *alk-*, which, according to Grimm's Law or the First Germanic sound shift, would result in PGmc **alh-*. Olsen has to assume that Verner's Law was in operation here, resulting in a further sound shift to **alg-*. In principle, this derivation is not at all astonishing. Olsen then assumed a feminine *i*-stem, **algi*, resulting with *i*-umlaut in ON **elgr* f., with a genitive in the singular **elgjar-*. Both Sophus Bugge and Magnus Olsen thought that this reconstructed word (**elgr* f.) from a linguistic point of view was a close relative to the reconstructed word **al*, which in turn goes back to a PGmc **alh-*, found in Gothic as *alhs* 'temple' (Feist 1939, 36; Hellquist 1948, 10). This word is obviously found in several Scandinavian place names, which can then be placed in a sacral or cultic context, such as *Ulleràl*, *Gutnal*, *Fröjel* etc.[6]

Already in an early article discussing the name *Njarðarlog* (1905), Olsen developed the tenacious idea of a cultic name pair. From the names *Njarðarlog* and *Tysnes* he believes he can identify a pair of interconnected deities: the goddess (*sic*!) *Njorð* and the god *Týr*. He develops this idea later on in the article *Hærnavi* (1908), where he suggests a pair of names, one a male and one a female deity, which were to be seen in context as a linked combination: *Hærn* and *Þórr*, *Freyr* and *Freyja*, *Ullr* and *Niærþer* etc. Olsen sees here an example of a fertility cult in the landscape, with name pairs found close to one another (within a couple of kilometers), where two deities had been worshipped together. How this combined fertility cult may have been practiced over these distances, no one has been able to explain—at least not yet.

Elias Wessén had an even greater publication list, laying the foundations for Swedish runology, producing several volumes in the series *Sveriges runinskrifter*. He also contributed to legal history by translating and commenting all of the Swedish medieval laws, and to etymology by publishing an etymological dictionary for the Swedish language. He also wrote several grammars for Old Swedish and Old Norse. For our purposes here, he authored several early works on pagan religion, particularly emphasizing toponymic evidence. Foremost among these works are *Forntida gudsdyrkan i Östergötland* 1-2 (1921-22), *Minnen av forntida gudsdyrkan i Mellan-Sveriges ortnamn* (1923) and *Studier till Sveriges hedna mytologi och fornhistoria* (1924).

Wessén worked in the same vein as Magnus Olsen. He thought, for example, that he could identify certain cult sites in the landscape based on name elements such as *sked*, *skede*, *skeid*, and *lek*, *leik*. He found the name *Hästskede* particularly important, suggesting that these sites had been ones used not only for games and horse races, but also potentially as sites for the sacrificial slaughter and offering of horses. He adopted and further developed Olsen's idea of the godly name pair, with a male and a female deity worshipped in combination.

At this same time, Hugo Jungner wrote his doctoral thesis, *Gudinnan Frigg och Als härad* (1922), in which he extended these speculative analyses and combinations, going one step further than Wessén, and analyzing the sacral and cultic place names of

Västergötland. The book was more or less immediately placed in the toponymic poison cabinet, thanks to some devastating reviews. In particular, rejection of the work by an up-and-coming young scholar in Lund, who later on would make a name of himself, namely Jöran Sahlgren, was a considerable blow. Sahlgren in contrast was to dramatically change the discourse in Scandinavian toponymy, particularly in regards to sacral and cultic names.

Phase Two: Hypercritical Reaction – The Clean-Up Phase

With his review of Jungner's thesis, Sahlgren had started a clean-up operation in the discipline. This clean-up had begun somewhat earlier with his critical examination of the *vi*-names; in that work, Sahlgren aimed to show that many of these names were not cultic, but denoted forests, based on the OSw *viper*. He singled out three scholars for criticism: Jungner, Olsen and Wessén. The most programmatic criticism came in 1950 in his article, *Hednisk gudalära och nordiska ortnamn. Kritiska inlägg* (The study of the pagan gods and Scandinavian place names. A critical contribution).

Before we discuss the article, it is productive to spend some time pondering why Sahlgren was the one who started this obviously necessary clean-up operation. At the same time in Lund there was another young very active Docent, the folklorist Carl Wilhelm von Sydow.[7] von Sydow was fiercely engaged in chiseling out a discipline for himself, *Folkloristik* (Folklore). Consequently, his actions were drastic and his polemic was sharp: he did not shy away from calling a stance by a venerated Professor as stupidity or idiocy. Describing the pugnacious, young von Sydow, Alan Dundes has both eloquently and mildly written: "Von Sydow had the reputation of being a contentious personality, and he engaged in heated polemics with various individuals during his career" (1999, 139). von Sydow was obviously a close friend of Sahlgren and I imagine that von Sydow's polemic nature made an impact on Sahlgren. Sahlgren's article on *mytosofi* should probably be seen in this context (Sahlgren 1923a).

In an early article from 1923 and in a later article from 1950, Sahlgren dismisses proposals such as Noreen's resin-cult site,

Quadovi, and Lundberg's fertility goddess *Vrind* etc.[8] Instead he offers profane explanations for all these names: *Quadovi*, 'the forest where they took resin from', and *Vrindevid*, 'the forest where there was ivy' (Sahlgren 1923b, Sahlgren 1950).

Concerning Magnus Olsen's ingenious and thought-provoking combination and etymological exercise regarding the names in *Elgjar-*, *Älle-*, Sahlgren's verdict was swift and harsh: The etymology was invalid, and the analysis of the medieval name forms are mis- or rather over-interpreted. The sound, and most obvious, explanation was that the fist element in all these names was *elk*, ON *elgr*. The names *Elgjartún* should be interpreted as 'enclosure or catch device for moose, and names such as *Ällevi* as 'moose forest'.

Concerning Wessén's *leik* and *skeid*-names, Sahlgren's verdict is even harsher. He starts his evaluation of the theory by writing (Sahlgren 1950, 4):

> Wesséns lärda utredning… verkar fängslande och till att börja med bestickande. Den reser sig som ett forntida stavbyggt temple högt over vardagslivets id. Men om hörnstavarna murkna, skall hela templet falla.
>
> [Wesséns learned investigation... seems compelling and initially plausible. It rises like an ancient stave-built temple high over everyday life struggle. But if the corner staves are rotten, the whole temple will fall.]

Of course Sahlgren identifies the rotten corner staves. The *Hästskede* names, he concludes, have the meaning 'border or neck of land where horses are', the *leik*-names are to be understood as places where forest birds, especially wood-grouse (*tjäder*), play during early spring. The name *Lekvall*, *Leikvoll*, was the third rotten stave. According to Sahlgren, the name meant 'places where the Nordic youth used to play, wrestle' etc. And finally, the fourth and last rotten corner in Wessén's 'stave-built temple' was something Sahlgren condescendingly called the Kilometer Method (*kilometermetoden*). "With the help of this method", Sahlgren banters, "you can prove practically any place-name hypothesis" (Med hjälp av denna metod kan man för övrigt bevisa praktiskt taget vilken ortnamnshypotes som helst).

The end of Sahlgren's critical review of the field is devastating (Sahlgren 1950, 20):

> Min granskning av de fyra hörnstavarna ha visat att tre äro helt murkna och att den återstående dvs. *Lekvall* ej har dimensioner, som behövs för ett Ullstempel. Den duger emellertid till timmer i en lekstuga, där ungdomen driver sina profana danser och lekar.
>
> [My review of the four corner staves have shown that three are completely rotten and that the remaining, ie. *Lekvall*, does not have the necessary dimensions for an Ullr's temple. It is good enough, however, for timber in a play house, where young people pursue their secular dances and games.]

This damning indictment was written by the only Professor in Place-Name studies (in the world) at the time and the director of the Place-Name Archive and hence by far the most influential scholar in the field in Scandinavia. The punch line was a real knock-out blow; the opponents, i.e. Elias Wessén, Magnus Olsen and anyone cultivating the field of sacral and cultic place names, was flat on the mat for the full ten count. It was impossible to get up after such a knockout punch. And this was also the result. The field of research—which Sahlgren had given the pejorative and by theology infested epithet *mytosofi* (mythosophy)—was put to rest. It lay fallow for more than thirty years. No sound scholar and certainly no one with aspirations of becoming an academic place-name scholar, touched this contaminated field of research for decades.

It is interesting to note that some scholars have recently worked in this same vein, with others believing that it is important to minimize the damage that (especially younger) scholars cause when analyzing these types of names. In Iceland, the former director of Örnefnasofnun, Professor Þórhallur Vilmundarson, took, one could argue, as his toponymic mission to show that there are no—or utterly few—theophoric names in Iceland. All the proposed names of this kind have better, profane explanations, according to Þórhallur. He has even taken his method to Scandinavia proper, desacralizing many of the place names there. Þórhallur made an effortless clean-up operation, but one gets the impression that sometimes the new profane meanings look somewhat far-fetched, and that this clean-up operation has become more of a mission than a balanced analysis.[9] His Norwegian counterpart, Eivind Vågslid (1963–84), tried in the same way to desacralize most Norwegian place names.

The most important scholar today working in this tradition is Professor Lennart Elmevik in Uppsala. He has, for example, dismissed the idea that the goddess *Freyja* can be found in Scandinavian place-names, and has de-sacralized several especially Swedish place names, which had been given a theophoric, sacral or cultic interpretation in earlier research. In some cases Elmevik is probably right, but sometimes one gets the impression that contemporary colleagues think Elmevik is going perhaps a bit too far with his clean-up efforts.[10] The future will tell.

In a way we are faced here with a clash of theoretical stances or starting-points. Elmevik once stated, with a sigh of relief, after being able to, in his opinion, desacralize a supposed cultic or sacral place name, in this case dismissing the goddess Frigg in a place name *Friggeråker*, that his operation had lifted a the heavy burden from the shoulders of the toponymists. They no longer were responsible for defending something that had been used as a witness to pagan Scandinavian religion. Elmevik (1995, 74) writes:

> Ortnamnsforskningen påtar sig ett stort ansvar om den inför vetenskaper som betjänar sig av dess resultat, i föreliggande fall i främsta rummet religionshistorien, ställer sig som garant för att *Friggeråker* vittnar om Friggkult.
>
> [Toponymy assumes a huge responsibility if, for subjects which are served by its results, in the present case primarily history of religions, it stands as guarantor for *Friggeråker* as a witness to a cult of Frigg.]

Life obviously felt easier if one could transfer an assumed sacral name to the profane sphere. Such a stance mirrors a theoretical position where one tries to establish facts or a solid foundation upon which to build research. Such a position is, of course, a totally acceptable position one to take, whereas someone like Magnus Olsen, discussing the same place name, *Friggeråker*, can be said to be an advocate for a likewise totally acceptable but more assaying theoretical position. Olsen (1915, 207) in a cautious way assumes: "hvis dette, som det synes rimeligt, er sammensat med gudindenavnet Frigg" [if this, which seems reasonable, is compounded with the name of the goddess Frigg].

Phase Three: The Balanced (?), Middle-of-the-Road Phase

No one dared to touch this field of research for more than thirty years. The toponymists found safer grounds to cultivate during this period. However, one scholar, who had achieved great insights into the field already during the early 1940s, and had built up knowledge unsurpassed by earlier and later scholars, was Professor Lars Hellberg in Uppsala. Already in 1942, he had realized that the cultic and sacral place names had to be seen in a social and societal context. Taken in that light, the toponyms became a vital aspect of the theoretical model he developed. He labeled this model *Den förhistoriska Sveastaten* (The prehistoric Svea-State). In the 1970s and 1980s, he was aware of the fact that this position was not only controversial but also out-of-touch with the current research agenda of most of his colleagues. It was, in a way, set in a theoretical framework that was in fashion in the 1930s and 40s. Consequently, he never presented the entire theory in print; rather he gave some hints in articles and in fairly obscure Festschrifts. A more consistent glimpse of his theory was presented in a local history of the town of Kalmar in 1979; and also in a duplicated paper for a Norna conference in 1975. These papers provided a skeleton of his theory. Today, the research discourse is starting to catch up to Hellberg's theories, and we are now able to recognize how important his model was, even though it was dressed in obsolete clothes.

Lars Hellberg was the first to finally end the deadlock in the field of sacral toponymy. As a retired Professor, he dared, in 1986, to publish his paper, *Hedendomens spår i uppländska ortnamn* (Traces of heathendom in Upplandic place names). This work opened the floodgates and ushered in a new interest in the field. Within a relatively short period, the paper was followed by a Nordic conference *Sakrale Navne* (Sacral names) in 1990. Hellberg had been irritated by a new exhibition at the Historical Museum (Historiska museet) in Stockholm in 1983, *Myter* (Myths), which had become a public success. He criticized the exhibition texts and the glaring lack of contributions from disciplines other than Archaeology. Most irritating for him was the fact that:

> Expositionens rambeskrivningar gav ingen övertygande undervisning om att hednisk tro och kult en gång var en levande kraft i det svenska samhället. Att vi i Sverige har mängder av ortnamn som vittnar härom nämndes ingestädes. De kultiska ortnamnen och deras i sin detaljrikedom helt unika information hade utställningen alldeles glömt bort eller också medvetet ställt åt sidan. Man måste fråga sig hur detta kunde vara möjligt (Hellberg 1986, 46).
>
> [The exposition's descriptions of its framework provided no convincing teaching that paganism and cult were once living forces in Swedish society. Nowhere was it mentioned that we in Sweden have lots of place names that testify to this. The exhibition had either forgotten to mention, or deliberately set aside, the cultic place names and their wealth of detailed, unique information. You have to wonder how this could be possible.]

Hellberg gives the answer by, in short, retelling the research history that I have described above, how the study of sacral and cultic place names had become a 'dangerous' field in which to venture after Jöran Sahlgren's programmatic criticism.

This tragic situation obviously forced Lars Hellberg to finally speak out. He did this by giving an exposé of the sacral and cultic place names from the province of Uppland in Sweden, presenting his knowledge, chiseled out over decades more or less in secret, discussing cultic names in *vi*, *vé* and *væ*, *åker* and *aker*, *harg* and *hǫrgr*, *eke* and **al*, theophoric place names containing the major gods and goddesses. He finally dared to present, in an academic journal, his elaborate theory on the prehistoric *Svea* state, where the sacral and cultic place names played a vital part. His theory included not only cultic and theophoric names, but also names containing the terminology of pagan cult leaders (or cult priests as he calls them), such a **vivil* and **lytir*. He also identified their residential farms, which he identified with the element *bolstaþer*. He even dared to bring up the contested cultic name-pairs with which Olsen and Wessén had experimented, and that Sahlgren had so sharply dismissed. For Hellberg, these name-pairs indicated prehistoric, administrative districts that had a common cult and served a political purpose. Hellberg's article is an eloquent evocation for the restart of research in this field. He was not to be let down.

During the 1990s articles started to appear by scholars such as Jørn Sandnes, John Kousgård Sørensen, Thorsten Andersson, Bente Holmberg and myself. This new revival was crowned by Per Vikstrand's doctoral thesis, *Gudarnas platser. Förkristna sakrala ortnamn i Mälarlandskapen*. This study provides an excellent and balanced analysis, and offers a new update on the status of the field for us to work from.

Looking to the Future

Today we find incredible interest in the sacral and cultic place-name material, an interest emanating mainly from the field of archaeology. Consequently, we have remarkable material that we dare address again. After the last two decades of transformation in the discipline, we can share this interest with neighboring disciplines. Archaeologists now dig up fascinating finds at sites with names such as *Lunda*, *Ullevi*, *Uppåkra*, *Götavi* etc. Modern archaeology has revealed new information, which makes yesterday's truths look less obvious than once believed.

Take the case of Noreen's *Kåvö*, OSw *Quadovi*. According to Noreen, it was to be understood as a place for some type of 'resin cult', through association with an assumed resin cult during the Bronze Age as well as the importance of resin in folk culture and folk medicine. He became a sitting duck for Sahlgren when the latter went hunting. In Sahlgren's polemic writings, Noreen's stance was described as so incredibly naïve and out of touch with historic and archaeological reality that Noreen became a laughing stock. Sahlgren was hailed as a solid academic hero. This case is still used as a warning example, illustrating just how bad things can turn out if you do not have the proper linguistic and contextual knowledge, as well as a sound, critical mind. Yet I wonder what Sahlgren would say if he were to be confronted with the new results from the recent excavation of an obvious cult site at Lunda in Sörmland. The site is most compelling and thought-provoking. Along with its name *Lunda*, there are several phases of an obvious prestigious hall building, and finds of gold-plated silver figurines, the physical attributes of which cannot be described in a text aimed at sensitive people or family gatherings. Most important in this connection is a hillock with trees (obviously the old *lund* 'grove') that had been sprinkled by thousands of small beads or drops of resin, obviously for some cultic purpose.[11] Should this presage a nervous little twitch in the corner of his eye, or perhaps even press him to reassess his position and soften his criticism of Noreen? Probably not. But this case shows us that a portion of humility is always useful when working with this type of elusive material.

The criticism Sahlgren aimed at Magnus Olsen—or rather the criticism with which he ridiculed him—which at that time appeared to be both obvious and devastating, namely that regarding the *Elgjartún* etc. names, is again worth reevaluating. At the time, no one undertook either a landscape or historical contextual analysis of the names. As a result, no one looked at how these names were found in a landscape setting. It is easy to see that these names are found in central locations in ancient settlement districts (*bygder*), such as *Elgetun* in Eidsberg, Akershus; *Elton* in Vestre Toten, Oppland; *Elton* in Nordre Land, Oppland; and *Elton* in Nannestad, Romerike. Neither Sahlgren, nor any other scholar at that time, asked themselves: why would there be 'enclosures for moose' or even 'traps' (fenced-in pits), or other catch devices for moose in these geographic locations? Are we aware of any enclosures or traps for moose *in the center of settlements* at any time in Scandinavian history or prehistory? Personally, I have never read about, heard of, or seen anything of that sort. Or do we know of moose being fenced in and kept in enclosures in settlements? Not to my knowledge. Someone should have raised that question. No one did. So, do I think that Magnus Olsen was right? Well, I do not know. The lesson for me is rather not to take anything for granted, to work contextually within the discipline of toponymy and to have an open mind when we are working with this kind of long-gone, complex material.

The archaeological activities during the last three decades have produced so much new material in this field, which must be seen in an Old Norse cultic and mythological context, that it is necessary to reassess old ideas and to challenge the "obvious truths" of disciplinary orthodoxy. It also shows that it is advisable to approach this field with humility, with an open-mind and with an interdisciplinary approach. The real problem that confronts us today is that there are essentially no active researchers working in toponymy. But I will spare you my reader the reason for this.

Notes

[1] Inge Særheim has summarized the different suggestions explaining the first element in the name *Härnevi*, which has oscillated from being a goddess, to a profane object, back to a deity again, this time a god (2012, 183 and 192).

[2] Of course, Jöran Sahlgen dismissed this interpretation by Lundberg and instead proposed a profane **Vrindaviþi* 'the ivy forest'. Later research has been less dogmatic, without taking a definite position (see Moberg 1965, 63; Vikstrand 2001, 91; Edlund 2012, 63).

[3] Later renamed 'Norrøn Filologi' in Oslo, from 1908.

[4] For some reason, he was always looked upon as a rather unreliable scholar by my former teachers in Uppsala. Why I have never understood.

[5] I have discussed this work in my article in the Festschrift to Margaret Clunies Ross (Brink 2007).

[6] See i.a. Brink 1992; Elmevik 2004.

[7] Perhaps best known today for being the father of the Hollywood actor Max von Sydow.

[8] In Swedish we have the vivid expression *lustmord* (murder of passion) to describe this type of polemic.

[9] Þórhallur published most of these analyses in his own journal *Grímnir*; see also Þórhallur Vilmundarson 1992.

[10] See the long list of publications by Elmevik on these issues at: http://katalog.uu.se/empInfo/?languageId=1&id=XX518.

[11] This important excavation, led by Gunnar Andersson, has seen many interesting publications, e.g. G. Andersson 2006 and G. Andersson 2008.

Is It Possible to Date a Fornaldarsaga? The Case of *Star-Oddi's Dream*

Anders Andrén[1]

Dating Icelandic texts has been an issue for a long time, and is still a focus in Old Norse scholarship. Above all linguistic, genealogical and stemmatic evidence has been used to date manuscripts and texts (Mundal 2013). Historical contexts, however, have seldom been used since most Icelandic texts are set in the past or in the distant past. Although most scholars agree that the texts reflect the time when they were composed rather the time that they portray, little has been done to use this perspective in trying to date the texts. In this article, I explore the possibility of linking motifs in a legendary tale with certain known events and places as a means for dating a text.

My example is *Star-Oddi's dream* [*Stjörnu-Odda draumur*], which is a short story set in Gotland in a distant "Viking Age" past. The story is known from several manuscripts from the seventeenth and eighteenth centuries, but they all go back to a copy made in 1686 by Árni Magnússon of the major saga codex *Vatnshyrna*. This codex is mentioned for the first time in 1609. It later belonged to the collection of Peder Resen and was transferred to the university library of Copenhagen in 1675. *Vatnshyrna* was destroyed in 1728 in the Copenhagen fire, and its contents only survived because of the copy made by Árni Magnússon in 1686 (McKinnell 1993). Although *Vatnshyrna* no longer exists, several attempts have been made to date the codex. Genealogies in two of the sagas in the codex end in the 1390s, thereby giving a date to the late fourteenth century (Heizmann 1993; McKinnell 1993) or, as Sveinsson suggest, "about or little before 1400" (1958:13). However, a related codex, the so-called *Pseudo-Vatnshyrna*, is preserved in fragments, and these are written with different hands from about 1390 to about 1410 (McKinnell 1993). Consequently, it is possible that also *Vatnshyrna* was written by several hands, meaning that the genealogies in the two saga only help date these two texts and not the entire codex. Other parts of the codex, therefore, may have been older or younger, including *Star-Oddi's dream.*

Star-Oddi's Dream

Star-Oddi's Dream is an amusing story told straightforwardly without any extraordinary elegance, although it ends with some unusual stanzas in *dróttkvætt.* The frame of the story is that a certain Star-Oddi, living in northern Iceland, dreamt that a man visited his home and began to tell a story about Gotland (Hreinsson 1997:448–459).

According to the storytelling guest, Gotland was ruled by a king, called Hrodbjart, who was married to Hildigunn, and had a son called Geirvid. One third of the kingdom was ruled by the Earl Hjorvard, who was married to Hjorunn, and they had a daughter called Hlegunn. While Geirvid was "promising, intelligent, and more mature than other boys of his age", Hlegunn was a difficult child, since she "has no intentions of cultivating ladylike pastimes". Instead, "it was her habit always to wear battle clothes and carry weapons, and those who crossed her path ended up seriously wounded or dead if she was displeased". To get rid of his difficult daughter, earl Hjorvard equipped her with three longships, while Hlegunn promised never to raid Gotland as long as her father lived. Instead she left home and "began to carry out viking raids on land and sea, and won fame and fortune".

In the meantime, King Hrodbjart died and a funeral banquet was held to which everyone "inside or outside the country" was invited "so that no one should come uninvited". After the banquet, "the king was interred in a mound according to the old tradition then current among the nobility". After the funeral, "all the wisest men and closest friends of the king" decided to elect Geirvid as king, to rule under the guidance of his mother because he was only eight years old. However, because of the young age of the king, many followers left the royal court, and "went on viking raids" or "travelled to different countries to trade".

When Geirvid was twelve years old he wanted to accomplish a great deed, in order to gain honor and fame. He chose to fight with two outlaws, Garp and Gny, who had plagued the Gotlandic population for a long time, killing people for their money. The young king was advised not to approach the two outlaws, and no-one wanted to follow him. Only a young man called Dagfinn finally joined him on his way into Joruskog (Strifewood), where the two outlaws lived. Deep in the forest the king and his companion found "a very high hill, which was steep on all sides". Looking out from this hill they spotted the two robbers, and the king went down the hill alone and eventually killed them both. Afterwards, the king and his follower found the robbers' house in a large clearing in the forest. It was "well furnished and full of all kinds of riches". King Geirvid returned from the forest with much honor and ordered a meeting, where he announced the good news that the two outlaws had been killed. He asked the inhabitants to retrieve what had been stolen from them in the forest, but they all gave their money to the king, who they thought "had fully earned it". The king now ordered a mound to be built, where he could sit on a throne. When it was finished, Dagfinn recited a poem in praise of the king.

In the meantime Earl Hjorvard's wife Hjorgunn died, and "was borne out and honored as was customary at that time for powerful women". After grieving for some time the earl remarried the widowed Queen Hildigunn, who "was then no more than forty years and seemed to be an excellent match in every respect". Their "married life was happy, and before long they had a daughter", who was called Hladreid. However, soon after the birth of Hladreid, Earl Hjorvard died, and King Geirvid placed his own men in the third of the island that Earl Hjorvard had ruled.

This news travelled fast and far, reaching Earl Hjorvard's daughter Hlegunn, who was now freed from her promise not to plunder Gotland. She sent shield-maidens as messengers to King Geirvid, telling him that he should either grant her half his kingdom or meet her in battle at Sildasund. The king answered Hlegunn's ultimatum by gathering an army, with men bearing shields and spears, at a promontory called Hofshofdi by Sildasund. Both sides met in longships in the sound, and "casualties were soon heavy on both sides, but it was not long before the losses began to eat into the king's troop strength and his ships became much emptier". With the help of Dagfinn, the king could finally see that Hlegunn was using sorcery and fighting in the guise of a she-wolf. However, after the she-wolf was killed with a sword, Hlegunn's warriors surrendered.

After the battle King Geirvid brought peace to his kingdom, and prepared a "sumptuous banquet", which was followed by a well-attended meeting, where the king once again was elevated on the mound. Dagfinn composed a *drápa* of thirty stanzas in honor of the king, and the king gave his sister Hladreid to Dagfinn. She was "of marriageable age, though still very young, but the fairest and most beautiful of women and very capable in all things". At the following marriage a "most elegant banquet was held" with "the most prominent people in the land". After these events the dream was finished and Star-Oddi woke up, thinking that he had actually been Dagfinn, marrying the princess Hladreid. Of the thirty stanzas Star-Oddi was able to remember eleven, which he then recited in *dróttkvætt*. The saga ends with the comment that "the saga may seem strange or unusual, but most people think that Oddi must have told what he actually seemed to experience in the dream, because he was considered both wise and truthful. Nor need it surprise anyone if the poetry is somewhat wooden, since it was composed in Oddi's sleep".

People and places

Star-Oddi's Dream is clearly fiction, but some of the "facts" are nevertheless of interest. The anonymous author of *Star-Oddi's Dream* mixed the fictional story with some concrete knowledge of Gotland, its organization, landscape, and historical persons (Andrén 2008). The hero of the saga was clearly King Geirvid, but no king can be found on the island. Gotland was not a kingdom in the high Middle Ages, but a society ruled by a handful of dominant families that controlled the legal assemblies. There were twenty assemblies, each of them led by a *senior* or a judge. The twenty *seniores* or judges ruled the island through the general assembly Gutnalthing at Roma. At the general assembly the twenty *seniores* elected a *landsdomare*

Fig. 1. The medieval remains of Lauks consist of a masonry storehouse from the thirteenth century and a farm cross. The stone foundation of the cross is medieval, whereas the wooden cross has been renewed several times. Apart from the storehouse, another medieval stone house, with four floors, still existed in the mid eighteenth century (Qviström 1995). This building was probably the residence of the farmstead (photograph by the author).

("judge of the land"), who ruled Gutnalthing and represented the island in negotiations with foreign powers (Yrwing 1978:80 ff., Lerbom 2003). A few of these men are known by name. A certain Aivar Strabein negotiated in the distant past with the Swedish king according to the mythological *Guta saga* from the thirteenth century (Holmbäck & Wessén 1943:292). In 1161, a certain Licnatus, probably from Stenstu in Stenkyrka, signed a trade treaty with the Saxon duke Henry the Lion (Myrberg 2008:157). And in 1305 a certain Gairvat from Gothem negotiated with the Swedish king and archbishop (Snædal 2002:142). The first man who is known to have held the title "judge of the land" was Gervid Lauk, who died in 1380 (Lundmark 1929:351ff.). He lived on the large farm of Lauks, where a storehouse of stone from the thirteenth century and a medieval farm cross are still preserved (fig. 1). The farm is mentioned indirectly for the first time in 1370, and in 1511 it still was owned by one of the judges on the island (Andrén 2011). Gervid Lauk was buried in the parish church of Lokrume, where his gravestone is still preserved (fig. 2).

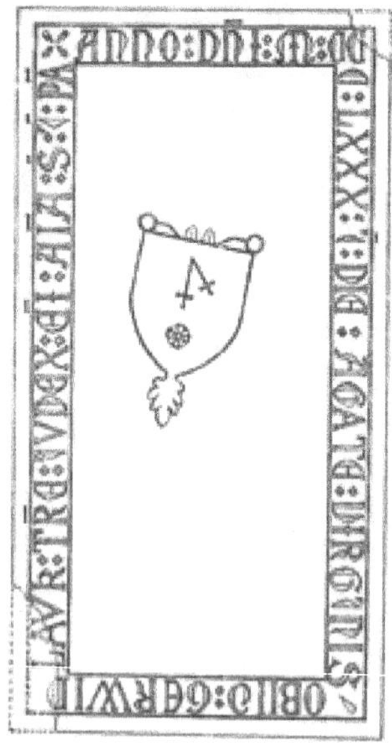

Fig. 2. The gravestone of Gervid Lauk in the church of Lokrume. According to the Latin inscription he was *terre ivdex* ("judge of the land") and died on 5 February 1380 (after Lundmark 1929 fig. 417).

Apart from the gravestone, nothing is known about Gervid Lauk, but his name and political position on Gotland indicate that he actually was the model for King Geirvid in *Star-Oddi's Dream*. The expression in the saga that he was elected by "all the wisest men" may reflect the procedure at the Gutnalthing, when a "judge of the land" was elected. No other name in the saga can be connected to a known person, but the two deeds of King Geirvid may be discussed in relation to events in the late fourteenth and early fifteenth centuries.

In 1361, Gotland was conquered by a Danish army led by the Danish king Valdemar. For several decades after this conquest the political situation on Gotland was very unclear (Thordeman 1944; Westholm 2007). However, in 1394 Gotland was conquered by Swedish and German knights supporting the deposed Swedish king Albrekt of Mecklenburg. These so-called Vitalian Knights plundered the island, terrorized the Baltic Sea, and were generally regarded as outlaws. They built three small castles on Gotland and, in one of them, Landescone (Vivesholm), their leader Erik of Mecklenburg, the son of King Albrekt, died in 1397 (fig. 3).

Fig. 3. The gravestone of Duke Erik of Mecklenburg in St Mary's in Visby (photo by the author).

Finally, the knights were expelled from the island in 1398 by the Teutonic Order that conquered Gotland in 1398 (Yrwing 1978:51ff.). These plundering and outlawed knights might be viewed as the model for the outlaws in the saga who plagued the Gotlandic population for a long time, killing people for their money.

The second deed of King Geirvid is the victory over the shield maiden Hlegunn at a promontory by Sildasund. Judging by the name Sildasund, this story might be a reflection of the siege and battle at Slite in 1404. The battle was fought around the castle of Slite (Nilsson 1995), that was situated on a narrow promontory between the Baltic Sea and the Bay of Boge on the east coast of Gotland (fig. 4).

Fig. 4. The ruins of Slite castle. On the small "Castle Hill", in the south-western part of Slite, the foundations of a square stone tower and an outer wall are still preserved. A small test excavation was made in 1994, and German stoneware and an arrowhead of a crossbow were found (photograph by the author). Only a few hundred meters south-west of the castle ruin is a narrow strait between the Baltic Sea and the Bay of Boge, which may represent Sildasund in the saga.

The background of the conflict was that the Danish Queen Margarete tried to reconquer Gotland from the Teutonic Order by sending an army of 2000 men to the island in the autumn of 1403. The Danish army landed at Slite in November 1403, and marched to the west coast, where it began to besiege the city of Visby in January 1404. The Teutonic Order responded by sending an army of 2200 men and 1500 sailors that landed at Visby in early March that same year. They forced the Danish army back, part of which retreated to the castle of Slite. In the middle of March, the Teutonic Order began a long and bloody siege of the castle of Slite. Only in the middle of May did the Danish garrison surrender due to a lack of supplies (Yrwing 1978:51ff.; Öhrman 1983:34ff.).

If this identification of the battle by Sildasund with the battle at Slite is correct, some further aspects of the saga can be discussed. First, the shield maiden Hlegunn must be identical with the Danish Queen Margarete. According to the saga, Hlegunn claimed her rights to the island through her inheritance form her father Earl Hjorvard. This claim in the saga is in accordance with real events, where Queen Margarete claimed her hereditary rights to Gotland from her father King Valdemar who had conquered the island in 1361 (Yrwing 1978:50). Second, in the battle of Sildasund the Gotlanders were the victors whereas, in the battle of Slite, the Teutonic Order was the conqueror. This contrast might be partly reconciled if the Teutonic Order was supported by the local population on Gotland. It is well-known that the Gotlanders strongly opposed the Danish invasion in 1361, although the locals were finally defeated in a bloody battle outside Visby (Thordeman 1944; Westholm 2007). After the turbulent years of the Vitalian Knights in 1394–98, it seems as if the Gotlanders supported the Teutonic Order, since the Teutonic Knights restored law and order on the island. In 1407, the Gotlanders actually pleaded with the Teutonic Order not to sell the island to Denmark, since negotiations about a purchase of Gotland had begun (Yrwing 1978:51ff.). Because of this pledge, it is quite possible that the Gotlanders supported the Teutonic Order at the battle of Slite in 1404, although this is not mentioned in the few surviving documents.

Between myth and reality

The possible links between an Icelandic *fornaldarsaga* and political events in Scandinavia make it possible to understand how these legendary narratives were created. *Star-Oddi's Dream* was based on a few real events and persons in the second half of the fourteenth century and the first years of the fifteenth century, and it must have been composed after the battle of Slite in 1404. Typical of the genre was that the events and persons were not necessarily contemporary (Heinzle 2003). Geirvid Lauk had been dead for over two decades when the battle of Slite took place. Instead, a few real elements were moulded into a legendary context. One of the most interesting cases of this remoulding is, of course, the shield maiden Hlegunn. The extraordinary case of Queen Margarete as a female sovereign of the Scandinavian union from 1397 to her death in 1412 (fig. 5) was transformed in the saga into the mythological

Fig. 5. A tomb for a shield maiden? The tomb of Queen Margarete in the cathedral of Roskilde (photograph by the author).

figure of a shield maiden, capable of using sorcery and fighting in the shape of a she-wolf. The only real facts that are left after these mythological transformations are a few names of persons and places. These parallels between motifs in the text and events and places indicate that *Star-Oddi's dream* must have been composed and written directly for the codex *Vatnshyrna*. But the parallels also indicate that parts of this destroyed codex must have been written as late as the early fifthteenth century.

Notes

[1] Many thanks to Tarrin Wills, who directed my attention to *Star-Oddi's Dream*, and to Alan Crozier, who checked my English.

Snorri's Edda: The Sky Described in Mythological Terms

Gísli Sigurðsson

Mythologies from around the world all have an astronomical aspect to them in the sense that they reflect detailed knowledge and observation of the sky above. All over the world people have used mythological language to talk about and share astronomical knowledge among the learned elites of all cultures; knowledge about the movements of the sun, the moon and the planets within the ever revolving firmament around the fixed points in the extreme north and south.

It can be demonstrated, from celestial observations in nineteenth century Icelandic tradition, that certain ideas in Old Norse mythology referred directly to peculiar celestial phenomena, beyond the obvious idea of the bridge Bifröst being a mythological interpretation of the rainbow. In view of the actual proof from the nineteenth century it should be worth discussing the possibility of taking that idea a step further and read the entire Snorri's Edda as a mythological interpretation of the world as it appears to the naked eye: The earth below and the sky above where the stars and other heavenly bodies move around, as well as up and down, some in a clearly regular pattern and others less so, day and night. This approach changes radically all our discussion about systematic thought behind the individual myths as well as about their source value as reflections of pre-Christian ideas in the north.

I think therefore that we should be open to the possibility that Gylfaginning (Gylfi's Illusion) should be read as a general introduction to what can literally be observed in the sky where, as Snorri tells us eighty-two times, we should be looking for the gods. Gylfi's illusion in the frame-story is therefore to think that he is observing what he is being told about the gods and their dwellings and the world tree in the sky when, in fact, all he sees with his mortal eyes is the stars, the planets, the sun and the moon, and the Milky Way; with occasional celestial phenomena such as the rainbow, sun-/moon haloes and eclipses, all of which have their mythological equivalent and "can be seen from Earth" as Gylfaginning (ch. 11) puts it when explaining the children Bil and Hiuki, well known as moondogs in English. At the end of the illusion, Gylfi is left alone out in the wilderness, without the mythological scene around him, much like the theatre-audience when the curtain falls.

For us it should not be such a strange idea to interpret much of what we read in the Norse myths (as well as myths from other cultures) as representing a sensible worldview by people who observe what is around them with their bare eyes: We stand on the earth which slopes down into the ocean in some or all directions, depending on the location, but the heaven is always above with the gods' dwellings—and the divinities moving around, either regularly or in a more irregular way, providing plenty of room for speculation and interpretation as to what they might be up to. At the very end of the horizon, beyond where we can actually see or travel in our mortal life, the heaven meets the earth and the ocean. That is where the underworld must be with plenty of space for monsters and evil creatures reaching out for us—but which the good divine forces of the heavens are constantly battling to keep away from our inhabitable earth. We are of course, what is called modern people, and we know that this is a "wrong" understanding of what we see. Modern science has figured out that the earth revolves around itself and the sun in the solar system. The history of science traces how the correct ideas (that is modern ideas) developed and gradually replaced the older, wrong ideas (cf. Þorsteinn Vilhjálmsson 1986/1987 and Hoskin 1997). We rarely stop in order to contemplate how the overall system must have worked from the perspective of the "wrong" ideas which people had when all they could do was observe what was going on around them with their own eyes, and then tell stories and recite poetry about it in order to fathom the experience, share it, and transmit it along with the lasting marks which they could make in the rocks and stones around them in order to figure out the system of the majestic movements they could observe in the sky.

A person who had his or her eyes open in Norway before it became customary to sail across the ocean to the British Isles, the Faroe Islands, Iceland, Greenland and ultimately to Vinland, would have been perfectly right to assume that the ocean, big and round as it clearly was, would eventually catch up with the heaven in the west. In the east however, it must have been well known that the further one traveled, the more the earth was inhabited by strange people and eventually creatures. In the north, everybody knew that the sea ended in frozen ice, whereas those who travelled south could report that everything grew warmer in that direction, thus probably ending in the warmest known condition: fire. No one could be certain how far they would have to travel in order to be enflamed, but this worldview, which the ancients could build up from information and individual experiences/stories from travellers, is logical, even for the modern person, living in Scandinavia and with a reasonable sense of geography.

The same does not apply to another but no less important part of the ancient world view, a part which has now more or less disappeared from the eyes and consciousness of the enlightened modern man: The heavens. Before modern light-pollution, the stars enveloped the earthly world of man every evening when it turned dark and the clouds were not in between, so close but yet beyond reach. The sky was (and is) partly stable, with a highly systematic daily and annual movement of the sun, the moon and the firmament, revolving around the polar star in the high north, as seen from the northern countries. On the horizon, the parts do not always rise at the same time or in the same place but, by systematic observation, this would be one of the first things that homo sapiens figured out in terms of scientific knowledge—even though most modern people have hardly any understanding of it. Inside this regularly moving scene, a few planets moved back and forth or up and down, sometimes meeting each other but more often roaming randomly around the fixed stars here and there, admittedly very slowly but always in the general vicinity of the path on the firmament which the sun travelled through the sky each and every year. Long-term, accumulated observation, accompanied by some registration lasting more than a few lifetimes, led to the knowledge that the sun, regular as it seemed to be, was not always at exactly the same point on its path at the same time of year. It took the sun roughly two thousand years to move one twelfth of the horizon, thus marking different long-term ages in human history. According to our culture's time reckoning, Christ was born at the beginning of the Age of Fish, as reflected in the fishing metaphors in Christianity, and we are now at the dawn of the Age of Aquarius—as many are familiar with from the musical Hair. On the move and in some special relation to the sun, people could and can observe the moon, sometimes hidden and sometimes not. It cannot have taken as long to figure out the system there: The moon starts a new cycle twelve times a year (thirteen times once in a blue moon), but always in a new spot on the sun's path and thereby dividing the solar year into twelve spaces which moved and move slowly but regularly each and every year until, after nineteen years, the moon repeats the same pattern, thereby defining a moon age of nineteen years.

This accumulated understanding of the movements of the heavenly bodies within the firmament can be called the heritage from the oldest systematic observation of the world, built partly on repeated measurements and registration, year after year, and age or century after century, of what could be observed with the bare eyes at a time when the heaven was still an enchanting and mysterious phenomenon or space, inhabited by gods who could from there observe the swollen womb-like earth below. The system was clear and regarded as one of the first law-enforcements carried out by the gods, as we know from stanzas 5 and 6 of Völuspá (Gísli Sigurðsson 1998: 4). At their first assembly, the gods regulated the chaos in the world by adjusting the movements of the sun, the stars, and the moon, thereby making it possible to keep track of time.

This oldest scientific knowledge of mankind is no longer part of general education in Western cultures, not even among the university educated elite which specializes in understanding texts of old: We no longer understand how the world looks with the eyes of an observing individual who stands with both feet on the ground and can be quite certain that he or she is absolutely correct in saying that the sun rises in the east and goes down in the west—which we now know is only an illusion. The continuous transmission of this knowledge from generation to generation must have been expressed in what we call mythological terms and it was no doubt gradually discontinued among the different population groups that now make up Western civilization. In northwestern Europe, it is likely to have begun with the spread of Christianity which also brought with it classical astronomy in books. Only later did the now accepted worldview of science take shape, describing the big picture as it might be observed from space rather than by earthly eyes only. We now know that the explanations that the ancients came up with to account for what was going on in the heavens were "incorrect". There are, for example, no twelve dwellings of equally many gods in the sky, as we are told in Grímnismál (Gísli Sigurðsson 1988: 70-83), no more so than there are twelve dwellings of the apostles up there, as Julius Schiller tried to argue in *Coelum Stellatum Christianum* in 1627, aided by the best astronomers of his time: Tycho Brahe, Johannes Bayer and Johannes Kepler (cf. G.S. Snyder 1984: 96). Schiller tried to present this idea because he desperately wanted to Christianize the heavens (as many human cultures had been Christianized ages earlier) and finally get rid of the well-established pagan figures from classical mythology that dominated all maps of the heavens in his day. We know that this attempt failed and the terminology from classical mythology is still in use in Western cultures—rather than the terms of Christianity, which we are told has been the dominating religion in these cultures for the duration of most of the Age of Fish. We are also confident that the sun is not drawn through the sky in a wagon, and it is not haunted or surrounded by wolves; the rainbow is not a divine bridge between heaven and earth; and the Milky Way is a galaxy of stars which our solar system is a part of, and has nothing to do with the River Nile and the pyramids trying to capture the image of Orion and the Milky Way in the sky (cf. Bauval & Gilbert 1995:124-5; 148 ff.). Nor is the Milky Way any type of a beam, supporting the heavens above—as some people might be tempted to think when they observe it in the north on a clear night, far away in time and space from the electrically lit culture of modern times. And even though Snorra Edda speaks of the world tree, the ash of Yggdrasill, as being in heaven (see later) very few people take that literally because we all know that there are no trees there. Rather, most scholars who have tried to understand the world view of Snorra Edda have built up some sort of social structure or fantasy (cf. Hastrup 1981; Bæksted 1986: 53) without any clear reference to the world we live in and which is free for all to see when and if we only turn off the lights.

In the last decades, the question has been raised if it might not have serious consequences to continue our studies with this big gap amongst us in what should be the accumulated knowledge of Western civilization, a gap which is particularly problematic for modern scholars trying to understand texts that were written by people who thought that this knowledge was self-evident as a basic foundation when learned people think and speak about the world.

Interest in the astronomical knowledge of ancient peoples was revived during the seventh and eighth decades of the last century, in connection with theories about erected stones and rows of stones of the kind that most recognize from Stonehenge in England. The first conference of what was called archaeoastronomy was held in Oxford in 1981 and, two years later, in September 1983, the Center of Archaeoastronomy and National Air and Space Museum held the first international conference on ethnoastronomy at the Smithsonian Institution in Washington D.C. More conferences and publications followed, leading to a professorship in archaeoastronomy at the University of Leicester in the year 2000 (cf. Campion, N. 2004: xvii-xx). Proceedings from the first Smithsonian conference did not appear until 2005, under the title *Songs From the Sky: Indigenous Astronomical and Cosmological Traditions of the World* (Chamberlain et al. 2005) but visible results from the conference had appeared in the year 2000 as the volume: *Astronomy across Cultures: The History of Non-Western Astronomy* (Selin 2000). At the first Smithsonian conference, the Icelandic medical doctor, Björn Jónsson from Swan River, Manitoba, was among the presenters. The previous winter Björn had presented his, to put it mildly, very innovative ideas with a series of lectures in the planetarium of the University of Manitoba, by the invitation of Professor Haraldur Bessason. A few years later Björn published his book *Stjarnvísi í Eddum* (1989), which he then translated as *Star Myths of the Vikings* (1994?)—still available from his son in Swan River. Björn's main idea was that Nordic myths were, as has now become more and more apparent that the myths of peoples around the world generally are, interpretations of phenomena that could be and had been observed in the sky with the bare eyes. The general world-view was a description of the firmament with the mythological vocabulary, the world tree itself with branches that "standa yfir himni" [stand above heaven] (Heimir Pálsson 1988: 29) were a mythological interpretation of the Milky Way, and the individual stories/myths outline the various remarkable journeys undertaken by the planets, from one star sign to the next, where the audience should recognize major mythic characters, events, and dwellings of mythological figures. Björn based his ideas among other things on a similar theory about myths, introduced in the book *Hamlet's Mill* by Giorgio Santillana and Hertha von Dechend in 1969 (updated and rewritten in German by von Dechend in 1994) as well as the ideas and writings of the Icelander Einar Pálsson (1978: 119). Einar had suggested that the gods' twelve dwellings in Grímnismál should be interpreted as the Norse equivalent to the signs of the Zodiac.

The theories, ideas, and research by Björn and of those who inspired him are far-reaching and it is no easy matter to confirm if and how they might be relevant for the study of Norse myths. I am only familiar with a handful of academic attempts where scholars have tried to use the theories in Björn's book. The book was both praised and criticized favorably in *Journal for the History of Astronomy* (1997, 28/4: 353), two years after Björn died. In 2002 James Ogier gave a talk in Kalamazoo about "Eddic Constellations" and Andres Kuperjanov, an Estonian folklorist, has used Björn's idea about the world tree and the Milky Way in connection with his work. Kuperjanov thinks that the idea is so self-evident that he cites it with these words: "Bjorn Jonsson has started with interpreting constellations in the Milky Way area, which owing to its peculiarity can be used as a key. The Milky Way represents, of course, the world tree Yggdrasill." (2006: 56)

Ogier brought forth several general arguments in order to demonstrate that research into myth with an eye on the sky might be effective. He pointed out that Linda Schele (cf. Freidel, D., Schele, L. and Parker, J. 1993: 75-107) had interpreted the Mayan world tree as the Milky Way, mentioned the parallel names of the Norse weekdays with the star names of the classical gods in the Latin-derived languages—who are seen as roaming around in the sky; and not least did Ogier point to the seventeenth century picture of the Norse world tree in the manuscript AM 738 4to (printed in Jónas Kristjánsson 1993: 31). Ogier argues that whoever made the picture was still aware of the astronomical interpretation of the mythological worldview and that he had expressed that in his picture. Ogier was also fascinated by Björn's argument that the description in st. 10 of Grímnismál of how to find the door to Valhalla with a wolf hanging west from the door and an eagle bending over it (that is "Mjög er auðkennt / þeim er til Óðins koma / salkynni að sjá: / Vargur hangir / fyr vestan dyr / og drúpir örn yfir." (Gísli Sigurðsson 1998: 72)). Ogier agreed that this should be understood as a reference to the star signs Aquila and Lupus (Lupus cannot however be seen from Iceland, cf. www.stjornuskodun.is). Between these, there is the sign Ophiucus, sometimes referred to as the thirteenth sign of the Zodiac because it is on the Sun's path without being counted as one the official twelve signs. One need not stretch the imagination at all to describe Ophiucus as a door (cf. http://www.stjornuskodun.is/nadurvaldi). Shortly after this, in Grímnismál, st. 24, there is the famous count of doors and the warriors (*einherjar*) in Valhalla: adding up to a significant number from Babylonia and the Rig Vedas in India (as many have pointed out). This, Ogier feels, shows "the poet of the Edda as knowledgeable in astronomical lore and the Edda itself as part of an ancient astronomic tradition" (2002: 6). Ogier has since that given another paper at the SASS conference in 2011 in a similar vein and published an article in the same year that demonstrates the possibilities of this line of thought. Recently, Christian Etheridge submitted his MA thesis in Aarhus, which provides us with the most up-to-date assessment of the advent of learned astronomy in Iceland in the twelfth and thirteenth centuries and how it was received by the culture (by translating the names of stars with gods' names).

The relationship between classical myths and the stars in the heaven are clear to all (cf. McDonald 1996 and Condos 1997) from the planets who bear the names of the gods like the days of the week—in the Latin derived languages it is the names of the Roman gods but in the Germanic languages we have the equivalent names of the Norse deities (Sunna, Máni, Týr, Óðinn, Þór, Freyr/Freyja). It is more difficult to confirm directly that the connection between the myths and the starry sky was a living knowledge in the minds of Northern Europeans in the middle ages. From the days of Charlemagne in Northern France, however, we can point to such knowledge being present as is confirmed by a manuscript that was written there, and then illuminated with colored pictures of starsigns from a classical source with a poem by Germanicus Caesar. He had composed this poem on the basis of Phainomena by Aratos of Soloi, containing the basic idea that myths described celestial phenomena (cf. Bischoff et al. 1987/89). In spite of this well-known connection, scholars of Classical texts seem to be able to go ahead with most of their analysis without contemplating the implications this might have—as if the astronomical lore were in another dimension.

The comparison with ethnoastronomy from cultures outside the Euro-affected zone, which has now been accumulated and made accessible as a result of the Smithsonian initiative (cf. Chamberlain et al. 2005, and Selin 2000 above) makes it generally likely that Norse myths should in many fundamental ways be read as similar to myths from other parts of the world, in the sense that they, among other things, refer to celestial phenomena. It remains problematic to find evidence to confirm that idea and then to develop some understanding of how the possibility of such an astronomical dimension to the myths might affect our overall interpretation and assessment of the mythology as a whole—as we know it from the eddas.

In Snorra Edda and Grímnismál we are again and again reminded that the phenomena described in the text are to be seen in the heaven—as Björn Jónsson points out in the introduction to his work: "The connection of the Eddas to the sky is further strengthened by noting that the Gylfaginning in just 50 pages contains 77 obvious celestial references. The Poem Grimnismal contains a numerical listing of 'the celestial lodgings of the gods' (bustadir goda a himni)" (1994: 11). One may say that it only requires taking the text literally in order to start contemplating the sky while reading it. Such an understanding should even be strengthened by the frame story in Gylfaginning where the earthly king, Gylfi, goes to meet the gods. They then generate the illusions (ch. 2 of Gylfaginning) so that what Gylfi (or Gangleri as he chooses to call himself) sees with his bare eyes is transformed through the magic of the stories and godly explanations of the celestial phenomena that are really in front and above him. Finally, Gangleri hears some noise and suddenly everything vanishes where before he had seen a hall and a borough through the illusions perpetrated by Hár, Jafnhár and Þriðji. Gangleri stands alone on the flat ground, in the world as it appears without any mythological illusion. Gylfaginning's references to the heaven have never been taken seriously by scholars—but rather understood in a similarly unclear sense as when the Christian God is said to be in heaven. But what if the text is taken seriously at face value and the real sky is observed with Gylfaginning as a guidebook?

A short, almost in passing, explanatory note in the nineteenth century folklore collection of Jón Árnason might contain the confirmation needed in order for us to be able to prove that people in Iceland actually spoke of real and visible phenomena in the sky with mythological vocabulary in the nineteenth century. In the chapter on Nature legends in the first volume of Íslenzkar þjóðsögur og Æfintýri (1862), it says under the heading "Airvisions and Moontales" (Loptsjónir og Túnglsögur):

> Sundogs or extra suns are points of light around the sun, not uncommon in the South. If two sundogs are seen at the same time, on each side of the sun, one in front and the other behind, it is said that the sun is "í úlfakreppu", or that "it runs both in front and behind the sun" and both sayings are derived from the wolves Sköll, that was thought to swallow the Sun, and Hati who was to take the Moon. Sometimes this is called "gílaferð", and the sun-dog

> in front of the sun "gíll". He is thought of as a bad omen for weather, if one is not running behind too, but that sun-dog is called wolf too, and from that the saying is derived: "Seldom a "gíll" means good unless a wolf comes running after" (Jón 658-9).

In a footnote Jón himself refers to ch. 12 of Gylfaginning in Snorra Edda and st. 39 of Grímnismál in order to explain these wolves. In Snorra Edda it says about the sun and the wolves:

> Then High replied: "It is not surprising that she [i.e. the sun] goes at great speed, he comes close who is after her. And she has no escape except to run away." Then spoke Gangleri: "Who is it that inflicts this unpleasantness on her?" High said: "It is two wolves, and the one that is going after her is called Skoll. She is afraid of him and he will catch her, and the one that is running ahead of her is called Hati Hrodvitnisson, and he is trying to catch the moon, and that will happen." (Faulkes 1987: 14-15)

If it were not for the chapter in the Þjóðsögur of Jón Árnason no one would ever contemplate the possibility that the episode in Snorra Edda was explaining sundogs that can sometimes be observed on each side of the sun-halo that surrounds the sun in such conditions. The same can be said about the moon-halo which Björn (1989: 111-13) thinks is referred to in the previous chapter in Snorra Edda, where the characters Bil and Hiuki are said to be "carrying between them on their shoulders a tub called Sæg; their carrying-pole was called Simul. Their father's name is Vidfinn. These children go with Moon, as can be seen from earth." (Faulkes 1987: 14) Björn suggests that the carrying-pole should be understood as the light beam that stretches between the moondogs —and the tub itself must then be the moon— "as can be seen from earth" which is a very straight-forward statement encouraging this kind of interpretation. Before Björn, Richard Allen (1899: 267) had pointed this out and suggested a parallel in Jack and Jill (i.e. Hiuki and Bil) which native speakers of English know from the nursery rhyme: "Jack and Jill went up the hill / to fetch a pail of water, /

Jack fell down and broke his crown / and Jill came tumbling after." This little verse, according to Björn (1994?; 186), describes how the moon-halo dissolves—as seen from earth of course.

The vocabulary used by Jón Árnason about the sundogs on the halo around the sun can hardly be understood as anything but evidence for a continuous tradition from much earlier times about how myths are used to describe real phenomena in the sky. If that were not the case we would have to conclude that Jón Árnason, or someone else before him, had come up with this interpretation of the mythology—and thus preceded both Richard Allen and Björn Jónsson in putting forth the theory that is under discussion here. Of these two possibilities, the former is much more likely to say the least. It is not easy to come up with any alternative explanation. So, for once, it looks as if we have something in our field that amounts to scientific proof.

This conclusion has far-reaching effects on the entire modern scholarly approach to Norse Mythology. Even though it only provides one firm point of evidence, it is so solid that it would be unreasonable to try to doubt that it should not also be applied to other aspects of the mythology. Having said that, it must also be acknowledged that it is no easy matter to find the clue to such an interpretation in any detail. The basic idea nevertheless alters our approach in many fundamental ways. First, the idea can explain how it was possible, for centuries, to keep alive and share among people in a large geographical area the manifold and complex system which the Norse myths and their world view in the Eddas reflect—and which resembles in many ways the myths of other Indo-European peoples, of course. The "script", so to speak, was always in the heavens and kept the ideas and the stories alive as long the tradition was continuous. In an oral tradition, there is always plenty of room for creativity and reinterpretation, as we know, and no one can ignore that the individual myths must also have played a manifold ideological and socio-cultural role—in addition to keeping track of and sharing astronomical knowledge. Second, it makes it highly unlikely that Snorri or some group of people around him were making up a system out of chaotic myths, or even making up stories from scattered and fragmented "sources"—as seems to be an accepted mode by some to understand Snorri's method. Third, this would not allow for any speculation about a "mythographer" in Iceland transferring the systematic thoughts from Greco-Roman mythologies into a Norse context—even though some influence and inspiration is of course very likely, both at the oral and written level, down to such a basic idea as assembling it all into a book, not entirely dissimilar to Ovid's Metamorphoses. Indeed the relationship between the heaven and mythologies around the world is so strong and well confirmed that there is no need to suggest that Norse myths were not already an integral part of such a systematic knowledge long before awareness of the Mediterranean astronomy started to spread into northern Europe with the book-culture of the Church. The system, in other words, must have been there long before the days of Snorri. And as with all systematic knowledge, it is safe to assume that the overall understanding of the system was only kept alive among a learned elite in the oral studies of their culture, such as poets, lawmen and magicians, perhaps even the Norse *goðar* and their closest collaborators, that is oral scholars of the kind who are likely to have cherished wisdom poetry, like Alvíssmál and the *þulur* of Snorra Edda for ages.

The idea of an astronomical aspect of the myths has the potential to revolutionize the foundation of our discussions about why and how the so-called "pagan" myths and ideas could live on for so long after the official Christianization of the religious culture. If the sky was indeed the scene or storehouse for the mythology, it must in many ways have been equally stable as the place names of the mountains on the horizon. The religious and/or ritualistic function of the myths would only be part of their function. The stories could then be interpreted as a straight-forward description of what can be seen on a starry winter night—exactly as Gylfi's illusion sets it up. What appears first to be stars and a white path across the dome, going down under in two places on the horizon, should rather be imagined to be the home of divine figures, with different dwellings and with individual characters visible and moving around in both a regular pattern (as the sun and the moon do), and in a very individualistic way when it comes to the planets Mars, Mercury, Jupiter, Venus and Saturnus—traditionally translated as Týr, Óðinn, Þór, Freyr/Freyja—and perhaps Loki (Ogier,

Misinterpretatio...). Far away (and below the horizon most of the time), the forces of evil are kept at bay by the ever-moving Þórr who travels the outskirts of the encircled cultured zone constantly. A worldview of this kind is unlikely to disappear from the minds of people with the coming of Christianity—as we can see from star maps of the heaven down to the present day. In Western cultures they have always been drawn with characters from classical mythology (cf. Snyder 1984; see also the web resources atlascoelestis and celestia), which has dominated the culture after the spread of Christianity and Mediterranean book-culture—with a few exceptions such as the previously mentioned attempt by Schiller to Christianize the sky in the early seventeenth century. The "pagan" world view has lived a good life long after it has lost all its religious references, perhaps partly because knowing classical mythology has been essential for the learned elite in order to understand the old literature and pictorial arts—not altogether dissimilar to the function of the mythology for skaldic poetry which would have been meaningless for an audience who did not know the Norse mythology.

Even though the basic idea about star myths in the Eddas is accepted in the most general terms, as I think I have demonstrated that we must, it remains difficult to interpret individual myths and to figure out exactly what is referred to, especially because we are so desperately lacking in the basic knowledge and understanding of how the sky moves and works if we do not apply the explanatory model of modern science. As a starting point, the theories and suggestions of Einar Pálsson and Björn Jónsson can help us to lift the veil from our eyes. More importantly, I think we can go ahead with comparative studies of ethnoastronomy. In many parts of the world, people still have a living knowledge of the sky that is mediated through mythological language. The study of such cultures should be helpful in trying to understand the knowledge that used to be commonplace among the learned peoples of all the cultures that came before us—but which has now mostly been lost out of our modern school systems, thanks to the scientific revolution. The reason being of course that the learned of old were wrong: What we see in the sky is not gods going about their business but planets in the solar system. But even though the road has not been paved in front of us, and we have to cover lots of rough territory, it should be regarded as a comfort that we can confirm the connection between Norse myths and the sky with the reference in the nineteenth century Þjóðsögur of Jón Árnason. Thereby we can reject in one sweeping move most of the doubts and speculations whether the mythology of Snorra Edda can be built on an old tradition or whether it should be read as a learned construction from the time of Snorri Sturluson. The tradition behind Snorra Edda can be traced as far back as man has thought in a systematic fashion about his surroundings. That tradition must have changed, adapted to different times, and ideas through the ages and millennia. At the same time, it cannot but remain stable up to a point, because it is always trying to understand the same sky above, which has served as a storehouse for the memory of all generations from time immemorial. The idea of the Star Myths of the Eddas thus marks a new starting point for the study of Old Norse mythology, a starting point that I fail to understand how we can avoid for much longer to assemble on.

Underneath the Self-Same Sky: Comparative Perspectives on Sámi, Finnish, and Medieval Scandinavian Astral Lore

Thomas A. DuBois

The night sky occupied an important place in the lives and religious concepts of Nordic peoples. It served as a device for keeping track of the passage of time and the seasons. It provided a means of reliable navigation on both land and sea. And it acted as a key repository for myths, ideas of the cosmos, and sacred history. Even with the coming of Christianity, the sky was imbued with supernatural significance: in Nordic languages, the same word denotes both the visible sky and the royal residence of God, his angels, and his fortunate friends. In this paper, I compare the astral lore of medieval Scandinavians with that of pre-modern Finns and Sámi, with the aim of ascertaining the extent to which such comparison gives evidence of a common underlying view of the cosmos. As I hope to demonstrate, despite considerable surface variation in terms of cosmogonic and eschatological myths, as well as the naming and formation of specific constellations, the three linguistic populations of the Nordic region do indeed seem to have shared some basic ideas of the sky, its denizens, and the activities pictured there. But crucially, I suggest, they regarded the relation of the beings they saw there to each other and to the human community in different ways. I posit that an examination of these differences may shed light on the mythologies of the region but more importantly, helps delineate the main lines of interethnic relations within the Nordic region during many centuries of productive and sometimes antagonistic coexistence.

Scholars of ethnoastronomy and archaeoastronomy have pointed out that the celestial bodies and astral phenomena observed by viewers in different cultures are by no means random. Certain phenomena, such as changes in the position of the rising and setting sun, the phases of the moon, and the seasonal positions of certain constellations are readily observable with very little special equipment aside from a good vantage point from which to observe the sky and clear, dark nights (Fabian 2001). Within the sea of stars visible to observers equipped with these simple advantages, certain celestial bodies stand out as notable due to their brightness, contiguity to other stars in a manner that creates a noteworthy constellation, or behavior. In the Northern hemisphere, the stars Sirius, Arcturus, Vega, Capella and Procyon are among the most visible in the night sky and typically attract names among observers cross culturally. Constellations like the seven-plus tightly clustered stars of the Pleiades, Orion (the square created by bright stars Betelgeuse, Bellatrix, Rigel and Saiph, enclosing the three stars of Orion's belt Alnitak, Alnilam, and Mintaka), the seeming "twin stars" Castor and Pollux, and the Big Dipper (the handle stars Alkaid, Mizar, and Alioth, and the four corners of the dipper Megrez, Dubhe, Merak, and Phecda) are each easily identified by viewers and readily pointed out to others surveying the same sky. The planets (from the Greek meaning "wanderer") are notable because they do not march in step with other stars but go their own way, showing up in unusual places over time. Particularly intriguing cross culturally is Venus, bright at sunrise and sunset, Jupiter, and Saturn. Also striking in terms of behavior is Polaris, the North Star, which does not appear to move across the sky in the manner of other stars but rather holds fast, like an anchor or pivot. These constancies of astral phenomena lend star maps a certain degree of regularity cross culturally, regardless of whether cultures are in close contact with each other or not. In the Nordic region, where the different linguistic populations have lived side by side for millennia, many concepts have been shared over time.

Archaeologists have amply demonstrated the astronomical interests and expertise of ancient Europeans, stretching back to widely disseminated constellations like the Ursa Major (so widespread that it appears to predate the movement of ancient peoples into North America), massive Paleolithic monuments like

Stonehenge, as well as intriguing items of Bronze Age ritual paraphernalia like the Trundholm sun chariot or the Nebra sky disc (Baity 1973, Mellor 2004, Gurshstein 2005). Scholars studying the ancient and pre-modern cultures of the Nordic-Baltic region have aimed at documenting the astronomical lore of the cultures of the area and/or interpreting extant verbal or material culture as reflective of astral concepts or phenomena (Haavio 1952, rept. 1991, Kuusi 1963, Gibbons 1972, Lundmark 1982, Valonen 1984, Sommarström 1991, Rydving 1992, Jónsson 1994, Pentikäinen 1995, Ogier 2002, Siikala 2002, Kuperjanov 2006, Svonni 2006, Sammallahti 2012, Turi 2012). Approaches have varied widely according to the culture examined. Studies of Sámi ethnoastronomy have relied largely on firsthand reports of knowledgeable tradition bearers describing the stars and constellations they know from local oral tradition. Finnish scholarship has examined astral lore largely as a means of shedding further light on the ancient folk songs of Finnish and Karelian cultures and their possible meanings. And at the most conjectural, scholars working on Old Norse materials have attempted to recognize astral lore within preserved medieval texts, the production of which occurred well into the Christian era and in a framework of awareness of continental astrology and astronomy. Although comparison across these different bodies of evidence and within differing methodological frameworks presents considerable challenges, I believe it is possible to point to at least some enduring elements of astral lore in each area that prove useful points of comparison with adjacent cultures. The following survey is by no means exhaustive, and I leave many important topics, such as Nordic understandings of the Milky Way or of features like the Aurora Borealis, for other works. Nonetheless, I believe the following examination provides a good basis for demonstrating the usefulness of cross-cultural examination of the topic of astral lore within the Nordic region.

Creation of heavens and earth

All three Nordic linguistic groups possessed cosmogonic myths accounting for the creation of the earth and skies and the eventual establishment of humans and/or gods within them. In at least the

Norse and Sámi cases, these myths also contain predictions of the ways in which the cosmos will come to an end as well.

In the *Gylfaginning,* Snorri Sturluson details the beginning of the cosmos out of the formless void known as Ginnungagap (Holtsmark and Helgason 1950, ch. 4-6, pp. 4-9; Faulkes 1987, 9-12). The gap, which according to Snorri's reading of *Völuspá* contains the space eventually occupied by both earth and the heavens, is situated between two poles: the frigid spring of Hvergelmir, located in Niflheim—out of which flow various rivers, known collectively as the Elivágar—and the fire-filled southern region of Muspell, inhabited by a people suited to that environment and typified in particular by the guardian figure Surtr. The earth and its first denizens—the frost giants—are formed when the cold rivers of the Elivágar meet with the sparks emanating from Muspell and form the core upon which layer after layer of rime accumulates. This rime eventually produces Ymir or Aurgelmir, the primordial frost giant, and through parthenogenesis, the various other frost giants descended from him. The rime also produces a primordial cow named Auðhumla, who helps unearth and enliven the giant or man Buri, who marries the giant maiden Bestla to give birth to the gods Óðinn, Vili, and Vé. Óðinn and his brothers kill Ymir, along with all but one of the frost giants, Bergelmir, who manages to escape and become the progenitor of all present frost giants. Ymir's body in turn becomes the basis of the terrestrial world, while his skull becomes the sky. Scholars of mythology have long recognized the parallels here with the Greco-Roman Titanomachy, in which Zeus and his Olympian siblings overthrow the Titan gods to take over control of the cosmos in their stead. Such a myth finds reflection in other Indo-European traditions (e.g, Celtic) and may represent an ancient Indo-European borrowing from Near Eastern mythologies (Grimm 1882, vol. 2, 518-57). Of course, the Norse version is distinctively colder than its Middle Eastern or Mediterranean counterparts, drawing on the environmental experiences of Nordic life in imagining the beginning of the world.

Of the sun, moon, and stars, Snorri writes:

> Þá tóku þeir síur ok gneista þá er lausir fóru ok kastaði hafði ór Muspellzheimi, ok settu á miðian Ginningahimin, bæði ofan ok neðan, til at lýsa himin ok iörð. Þeir gáfu staðar öllum elldingum, sumum á himni, sumar fóru lausar undir himne, ok settu þó þeim stað ok sköpuðu göngu þeim. Svá er sagt í fornum (Holtsmark and Helgason 1950, ch. 7, p. 9).
>
> [Then they took molten particles and sparks that were flying uncontrolled and had shot out of the world of Muspell and set them in the middle of the firmament of the sky both above and below to illuminate heaven and earth. They fixed all the lights, some in the sky, some moved in a wandering course beneath the sky, but they appointed them positions and ordained their courses. (Faulkes 1987, 12)]

The sun and the moon, created from Muspell's sparks, are in turn, somewhat quizzically, associated with the astralized humans Máni/Moon (a boy) and Sol/Sun (a girl), who are placed in the sky by the gods in punishment of their father's arrogance. Drawing from the Eddaic poem *Vafþrúðnismál* as well as various skaldic kennings, Snorri states that their father Mundilfœri has dared to name them after the heavenly sparks that have already been ordained to travel through the sky during the day and night. Two further humans, Bil and Hiúki, offspring of Viðfinnr, can also be seen traveling with Moon along with their carrying pole Símul, as Snorri notes "Svá sem siá má af iörðu" [as can be seen from earth] (Holtsmark and Helgason 1950, 12; trans. Faulkes 1987, 14). It is not clear whether Bil, Hiúki, and Simul represent figures visible on the moon itself (the man-in-the-moon concept) or are heavenly bodies that travel along with the moon, such as the planets Jupiter and Venus, which can often be seen in close association with the moon in the late winter sky.

Beyond this set of stirring cosmogonic myths, the reversing eschatological account of the final battle and destruction of this temporary stasis—Ragnarökr—is alluded to in a number of the Eddaic poems as well as in Snorri's *Prose Edda.* A protracted winter—three times longer than normal—will usher in the end, while the sun proves of little use. After numerous crimes and warfare on earth, the wolves that pursue the sun and moon will finally catch and destroy them. The stars will disappear and a great earthquake will shake trees and other structures to the ground. An ensuing battle will pit the Æsir and their allies against the sons of Muspell, various monstrous animals, Loki and all the frost giants. Mutual destruction on both sides will lead ultimately to the rising again of the earth from the sea, the reestablishment of Æsir control in the persons of the sons of Óðinn and Þórr, and the birth of a new sun equally as beautiful as her murdered mother (Holtsmark and Helgason 1950, ch. 51-2 68-75; Faulkes 1987, 52—7; for discussion, see Lindow 1997, 164-175; Lindow 1997). Intriguingly, Bo Gräslund has argued that cataclysmic climatic events around 536-7 CE may lie behind many of the details of this imagined ending: the prolonged winter, loss of the sun, and the resulting destruction of all levels of society (Gräslund 2007). Gräslund marshals not only Old Norse materials to his aid but also Finnish folk song evidence to demonstrate a pan-European climate crisis as a vivid historical experience that colored the ways in which poets thought of the end of the world ever after.

Although we do not possess any Sámi myths of comparable detail regarding the beginning of the world, we do have an intriguing account of the wedding between the daughter of the sun and the sons of Gállá (see below) which seems to be an example of the broadly disseminated myth of the release of the sun merged with an indigenous Sámi account of Sámi ethnogenesis. In the epic poem *Biejjie-baernien sååangoe,* (song of the son of the Sun), composed by the nineteenth-century Sámi minister Anders Fjellner, a Sámi progenitor travels to the land of the sun to woo a wife (Fjellner 2003). With the help of the sun maiden, the suitor is able to trick the sun, portrayed as a cannibalistic ogre, into consenting to the marriage. The new couple is pursued by the bride's angry brothers but manages to reach earth nonetheless, where the bride becomes the mother of subsequent Sámi. In other legends, this same bride is said to have brought the reindeer with her from the sky, supplying the Sámi with one of their chief tools and companions in the Nordic environment. In Sámi star maps, generated through interviewing Sámi elders about their understandings of the sky during the nineteenth and twentieth centuries, Gállá often figures as the star Sirius, with the stars of Orion's belt possibly representing his sons, Gállábartnit.

As Lundmark (1979) has shown, Fjellner's poem is the self-conscious attempt of a Sámi intellectual of the nineteenth century to provide his people with a sense of their cultural history, much in keeping with the antiquarian writers of the eastern Baltic (Kuperjanov 2006). At the same time, there is little to doubt that Fjellner based his poem on some lore that he heard during his childhood in the South Sámi area or during his adult career in North Sámi communities, as Gaski points out (Fjellner 2003). Indeed, Fjellner's movements between these two areas seems to have heightened his sense of a shared Sámi tradition, and inspired him to gather materials that he sought to put into a poetic form that borrowed from both North and South Sámi languages.

Another key source of insight into Sámi astral lore is Johan Turi, whose 1910 compendium of Sámi traditional knowledge *Muitalus Sámiid birra* was the first book ever written in a Sámi language (Turi 2010). Turi includes two star maps in his book and notes in brief the details of an eschatological myth. In depicting the figure Fávdna (the star Arcturus) using his bow (the handle stars of the Big Dipper—Alkaid, Mizar, and Alioth) to hunt an astral moose/reindeer (see below), Turi writes next to his depiction of Polaris: "Of Boahjenásti [the Base Star = Polaris], there is a little story. Boahjenásti holds the heavens up, and when, on the last day, Fávdna will shoot Boahjenásti with his bow, the sky will fall, and then the earth will be crushed and the whole world will catch on fire and everything will end" (Turi 2012, 188). Turi's account signals a view of the sky as a roof held up by pole, a concept found in many Siberian cosmologies. When the pole is broken, the sky roof collapses, leading to the destruction of the earth below. Turi was an observant Christian, and his view of the "last day" included details of the Christian Last Judgment, heaven, and hell. Yet alongside this view, we can glimpse an older understanding of the end-time, one based on traditional Sámi views of the cosmos and its structure.

Finnish mythology has been reconstructed largely on the basis of folk songs collected in the nineteenth and early twentieth centuries. Scholars have correlated details of these archaic songs with nineteenth-century astral lore concerning constellations to suggest the main lines of a primordial Finnish cosmology (Haavio 1952, rept. 1991; Hautala 1954; Pentikäinen 1989; Siikala 2002). One important cosmological song within this corpus deals with the creation of the cosmos from a broken egg (Kuusi, Bosley et al. 1977-92). In the Estonian and Ingrian cultural areas, a swallow or waterfowl lays an egg on an island in the primordial sea. The egg topples into the sea, breaks, and creates the earth, present sea, sky, and celestial bodies (Pentikäinen 1989, 131-40; Valk 2000). The same myth seems to have been known, with some variations, among other Finno-Ugric peoples, including (as Valk details), Sámi, Mordvins, and Komi. Among Karelians, the myth undergoes an important transformation, in which the waterfowl, or some other migratory bird, lays her eggs on the knee or elbow of the culture hero/deity Väinämöinen (see below). The hero then moves his body part, causing the eggs to topple and transform as generally detailed. Nineteenth-century evidence indicates that Karelians performed this myth as a kind of seasonal ritual song, in conjunction with spring planting (DuBois 2001). In this sense, as Finnish scholars have pointed out, the Karelian and Finnish tradition seems to have incorporated aspects of the Scandinavian Ymir myth while still retaining the core of the earth-egg tradition. As with Fjellner's poems, modern scholars may doubt the antiquity of such a myth, given that it was collected only in the nineteenth century. Yet, as the minister Jacob Fellman discovered when he collected the song from a singer in 1828, Karelians viewed the song as a piece of common knowledge, not as a novel or improbable imaginative innovation. Fellman records his informant's remarks: "Well, good brother, we have the same belief as you. The eagle flew from the north, set an egg on Väinämöinen's knee, and created the world from it. And that's what you believe too" (Pentikäinen 1989, 140). In this respect, and given the existence of Paleolithic petroglyphs in the region that seem to depict the myth's events (Valk 153), there seems little grounds to suggest that the song does not reflect on some level ancient Balto-Finnic cosmology.

Other astral myths found in Balto-Finnic song traditions include accounts of a Smith Ilmarinen, involved in the fashioning of the sky (Kuusi et al. 1977, 98), the temporary blotting out of the sun due to the growth of a giant oak (Kuusi et al. 1977, 263-7), the quest of a culture hero (Lemminkäinen) to a land of the sun (Päivölä) (Pentikäinen 1989, 35-39), and the capture and release of the sun by an enemy (Kuusi et al. 1977, 195-204). The Lemminkäinen poems combine the journey to the sun's kingdom with a bridal quest in a manner reminiscent of Fjellner's Sámi poem. Many of the references to these mythic events occur in Finnish and Karelian incantations, and are brief mentions of otherwise unexplained mythic narratives. Yet they seem to indicate a set of ancient beliefs that are distinctively Finno-Ugric, albeit with an admixture of the champion narratives described below.

Heavenly Endeavors

If Norse and Finno-Ugric astral myths seem to describe very distinctive understandings of the sky, they show a surprising degree of similarity in the beings and activities found there. In both, the sky is home to giants and gods, and occasional displaced humans, all of whom engage particularly in hunting and fishing, sometimes with a secondary, potentially conflicting admixture of agricultural details. We shall examine the activities that take place in the sky first and then the actors involved.

From the astral lore of Sámi elders like Johan Turi (Turi 2010; Turi 2012), Iŋggá Lemet (Klemeth S Helander) (Sammallahti 2012), and other knowledgeable informants (Lundmark 1982), we know that the night sky was dominated by a massive constellation called in North Sámi *Stuorra sarvva* (the great bull moose or reindeer). In Iŋggá Lemet's description (collected by Pekka Sammallahti in the winter time as the two men stood beneath the same starry sky), this animal's horns include the stars of the Western constellations Cassiopeia, Perseus, and Aries. For Lemet, the bull's prominent nose was made up of the Pleiades, while its tail end and back leg included the Gemini stars Castor and Pollux, and the Orion star Betelgeuse. This massive deer seems to have had little distinct personality or significance except as the object of an intense hunting competition engaged in by a number of other stars, representing the culture hero Gállá (Sirius), Gállá's sons (Gállábartnit—the belt stars of Orion Alnitak, Alnilam, and Mintaka), the demon Fávdna (Arcturus), the giant Riihmagállis (Capella), and another hunter Bážá (portions of the constellation Leo). To these may be added two further hunters, Čuoiggaheaddjit (skiers) depicted in Johan Turi's star maps in a position that suggests that they may have corresponded to the bright stars Castor and Pollux (Turi 2012, 184). The demonic Fávdna in particular uses a bow that corresponds to the handle of the Big Dipper, while Gállá is often accompanied by dogs or a staff indicated by nearby stars. As Turi and other authorities show, the exact attribution of particular names to particular stars seems to have varied somewhat, and sometimes the same constellation could have multiple names and meanings, as with belt of Orion: in various Sámi accounts, these same stars could be understood as the sons of Gállá, a group of fishermen, a group of skiers, a fishing hook, or a pole for hanging a pot over a fire (Sammallahti 28; Haavio 220-3). The Pleiades, too, had multiple names: they were also viewed as an old woman with a pack of dogs or a group of reindeer calves (Turi 2012, 184; Sammallahti 2013, 27). In any case, the idea of roving hunters and fishermen in the sky is clear in all these accounts, as are details related to deer hunting and reindeer husbandry.

In Finnish astral lore, hunting and fishing activities also predominate in the night sky, albeit with occasional overlay of agricultural images. The belt stars of Orion could be seen as a fish hook (Koukku-otava) (Haavio 223), while the seven stars of the Big Dipper were recognized as a fish net (Otava). Finnish incantations as well as epic songs seem to place both the bear and the moose in the sky as quarry of heroic hunts (Kuusi et al. 1977, 262 and 271-5), details that appear to tie in with Finno-Ugric astral lore more broadly (Hautala 1954; Pentikäinen 1989; Kuusi and Anttonen 1999; Csepregi 2005; Pentikäinen 2005; Miettinen 2006; Piludu 2006; Rebourcet 2006; Pentikäinen 2007). Scholars have tended to emphasize these hunting associations, particularly in connection with the constellation Ursa Major, which (in addition to being a fishing net) was also sometimes seen as a great bear, as in the astral lore of many cultures in the northern hemisphere. The pursuit of a great moose by the hero Lemminkäinen (or in some versions by a hero identified as a Sámi; Lundmark 1982, 99), has also been interpreted as a narrative that probably formerly found depiction in the skies. Prominent constellations like Orion could also be viewed as agricultural images, however, such as a reaper (Väinämöinen) with a scythe (Haavio 223).

As we shall see below, the Norse sky often serves as the site of similar activities, although these are undertaken by characters decidedly less favored by their human and divine viewers.

Champions in the Sky: Karl, Kaleva, Gállá

In the Scandinavian languages the Big Dipper is known as *Karlavagnen*—the wagon of the men—a name that parallels the English term Charles's Wain. Scholars beginning with Jacob Grimm have noted the two-fold meaning of *karl* as both a term for a man of status in ancient Germanic society and a name eventually associated with the Charlemagne of medieval European legends (Grimm 1882 vol. 1, 151). The Norse root *karl* (OE *ceorl)*, as placename scholars Lars Hellberg and Stefan Brink have pointed out, seems to have had a particular meaning in the medieval period as a designation for a free land-owning farmer, a member of the *comitatus* of a king or chieftain, and possibly one of the leader's military supporters. Placenames using the term are found in Sweden, Swedish Finland, Denmark, Norway, and Scandinavian England. As Hellberg points out, placenames in Finland seem to map well with early stages of the Swedish medieval colonization of the east coast of the Baltic, indicating perhaps the term's military significance (Hellberg 1984, Brink 1999, Brink 2012). So the presence of *karl* in the sky, in association with one of the most easily recognized and prominent constellations, is probably related to the idea of a dominant champion or group of champions visible in the sky. Other Scandinavian names for various constellations seem to reinforce this notion: stars of the Orion constellation, for instance, were sometimes called Kiempens Sverd ("the sword of the champion") (Haavio 224).

Among Finns, the word or name *karl* becomes borrowed phonetically as Kalevi or Kaleva, a name familiar to the international audience through Lönnrot's use of it in the title of his epic *Kalevala*, "the lands of Kaleva." According to Lönnrot, Kaleva and his sons Kalevan pojat were in origin prominent settlers in Finland, eventually remembered as giants (Lönnrot 1963, 368; Lönnrot 1993, 176-78). Lönnrot's theory reflects the prominence of the name in Finnish legendry of the nineteenth century. In such narratives, Kaleva or his sons are associated with the creation of large topographic features such as mountains or great stones, a feature shared by the Estonian Kalevipoeg, the figure raised as an epic hero in Friedrich Reinhold Kreutzwald's 1853 epic *Kalevipoeg*. In both cultures, these figures are sometimes heroic, sometimes dangerous, and Lönnrot notes that they seem to have been eclipsed in Finnish lore by the more familiar figures that he celebrated in the core of his epic: Väinämöinen, Ilmarinen, and Lemminkäinen. Such a statement comes close to the Titanomachy seen in the Norse material, and aligns Kaleva and the Kalevan pojat with the population of powerful beings eventually displaced by later gods. In such a parallel, as we shall see, Väinämöinen becomes the counterpart of Óðinn. The evidence seems to indicate, however, that Väinämöinen and Kaleva are not so much adversaries as synonyms, or that Kaleva's sons eventually figure as supporters of the god Väinämöinen rather than enemies. Such ambiguity obtains of course in the Greco-Roman Titanomachy, in which some Titans allied with the Olympian gods while others stood in opposition.

Just as the Norse *karl* root appears in the name for the Big Dipper, the Finnish Kaleva finds mention in the swirls in the Milky Way known as *Kalevan porras* (Kaleva's step) or *Kalevan kynnys* (Kaleva's threshold) (Valonen 1984, 16). Orion's belt—the same constellation known at times by Scandinavians as Kiempens sverd—was sometimes known as *Kalevan miekka,* (Kaleva's sword), a term that also referred to sheet lightning (i.e, bright flashes in the sky without a recognizable bolt) (Haavio 224). So too, the star Sirius was called *Kalevan tähti* (Kaleva's star) (Valonen 1984, 17), a term exactly paralleled by the Sámi name for the same star Gállá, also a loanword from the Norse *karl*. Jan Puhvel notes that the figure of Kaleva seems to have been impressive enough to the Finns' Slavic neighbors that they came to describe one of the Russian epic champions Svjatogor Kolyvanovič, in which the hero's patronym precisely matches the Finnish Kalevanpoika or Estonian Kalevipoeg (Puhvel 1987, 236).

Sky Gods: Óðinn and Väinämöinen

In the *comitatus*-based warrior society of the Nordic "heroic age," champions needed lords, and the champions of the sky often become dominated, or replaced, by sky gods. Thus, Karlavagnen seems to become associated with Óðinn, to judge from Dutch names for the constellation, as well as various of the god's poetic epithets (Grimm 1882 vol. 1, 151). Grimm also notes that other gods are associated with wagons, including Þórr and Freyr (vol. 1, 329). Ogier (2002), drawing on Tacitus, suggests that certain of the planets may have been worshipped as gods, as in Roman practice. Þórr, equated with Jupiter, would thus be represented in the sky by the bright roaming planet Jupiter, while Tyr would be represented by the murkier red Mars and Óðinn by the wily Mercury. We do not have clear evidence that the medieval Scandinavians shared this contintental Germanic view, but it is likely that they would have had some name for at least the brightest planets (Jupiter, Venus and Saturn) as do astral traditions in general.

In a parallel fashion, the Finnish hero/god Väinämöinen—already present, as we have seen, in Karelian versions of the creation myth—becomes associated with various astral bodies. In addition to being called *Kalevan miekka,* for instance, the stars of Orion's belt were also sometimes known as *Väinämöisen miekka,* (Väinämöinen's sword). The Pleiades were known sometimes as *Väinämöisen virsu* (Väinämöinen's slipper) or by the plural form *Väinämöiset* (also as *Seulaset,* or the "sieve") (Haavio 223). An agricultural image obtains in Väinämöinen wielding a harvester's scythe in the name for Orion *Väinämöisen viikate* (Väinämöinen's scythe). More typical of Väinämöinen's associations, however, are those related to water and fishing: a calm patch on the surface of a lake or river could be called *Väinämöisen tie* or *kulku* or *lahti* (Väinämöinen's road, path, or bay) (Haavio 226). A synonymous byname in many songs about Väinämöinen is *Uvantolainen,* based on the root *uva-* meaning, sluggish, calm water. Songs tell of Väinämöinen's magical creation of boats (Kuusi et al. 1977, 183-90), his procurement of fire out of the stomach of a fish (Kuusi et al. 1977, 99-101), and his adventures capturing a giant pike, the jaw of which he uses to create the first harp, or *kantele* (Kuusi et al. 1977,167-73). In this light, the description of the Big Dipper as a fish net (reflected in the modern name for the constellation, *Otava)* may also relate to Väinämöinen and his activities. It appears in comparative perspective that Väinämöinen, perhaps originally exclusively a god of water and fishing, becomes elevated to the status of chieftain god under the influence of the hierarchical mythology of the Scandinavians. That the Finns adapted their god of fishing to this new role reflects in turn the lack of a hierarchical kingship in ancient Balto-Finnic societies and the prominence of fishing as a source of sustenance and wealth.

In contrast, among Sámi, such mythic hierarchizing and displacement does not seem to have occurred. Gállá and his sons remain both the champions of the astral hunt and the progenitors of the Sámi people, and none of the gods mentioned in eighteenth-century missionary accounts of Sámi religion—including gods thunder or wind—find depiction in the stars. Gállá is a figure of status in a Sámi sense: a good hunter, the father of able sons, and the owner of worthy dogs and skis.

Enemies in the Sky

Although the term *karl-* appears associated with the Sámi culture hero Gállá and his sons, the Sámi employed the root in their names for threatening astral figures as well. It is found, for instance, in the name of the powerful ogre Riihmagállis, a character described at some length by Turi (2012, 146-7) as a kind of Stállu, a class of beings that appear in Sámi legendry as usurpers of land and women, given to violent tempers and cannibalistic tendencies (for discussion, see Turi 2011, 141-8; Laestadius 2002, 237-53). As noted above, Riihmagállis corresponded to the star Capella, which is located across from Gállá and his sons on the other side of the Stuorra Sarvva constellation. Scholars and often Sámi themselves have generally regarded Stállu figures as legendary renderings of Norse colonists, as the notes of both Turi and Læstadius indicate. Pekka Sammallahti also points out that the name for the demonic figure Fávdna derives from a Sámi adoption and abbreviation for the Norse name for the Big Dipper, *karlavagnen* (27), with which Fávdna is associated. As mentioned above, the handle of the Big Dipper becomes the bow of the demon, with which he will someday, intentionally or inadvertently, destroy the world. Johan Turi also describes another star connected with Fávdna in one of his star maps. The star appears at the opposite side of the sky from Fávdna and is described as "the one who races Fávdna: it disappears at the same time as Fávdna and comes into sight at the same time" (Turi 2012, 184). Given the likely stars of intensity in the night sky and their placement in relation to Arcturus, this Fávnna gilpa-násti (Fávdna's competing star) may correspond to Vega.

In Finnish and Karelian tradition, in which, as we have noted, Väinämöinen has become incorporated in the earth egg myth, it is noteworthy that most songs describe Väinämöinen's floating on the primordial waters as the result of his having been shot by a Sámi enemy. As Arhippa Perttunen's version of the song puts it at its opening:

> Lappalainen kyyttösilmä
> Piti viikosta vihoa
> Kaukausta ylenkatsetta
> Päälle vanhan Väinämöisen:
> Vuotti illoin, vuotti aamuin
> Tulovakse Väinämöista (Kuusi et al. 1977, 110)
>
> [The slit-eyed Sámi
> for ages held enmity
> long felt contempt
> for old Väinämöinen:
> he waited in the evenings, he waited in the mornings
> for Väinämöinen to come]

When he finally does see Väinämöinen, the unnamed Sámi shoots an arrow that gravely injures his opponent and topples him from his boat or from the moose he is riding, so that he is left to float upon the sea, becoming eventually the resting place of the nesting bird and a prime mover in this way of the creation of the earth.

Thus the Sámi were there before the beginning of the earth, or perhaps, a specifically astral Sámi was the being responsible for the attack. It is also notable that, as Kaarle Krohn notes (quoted by Lundmark 1982, 99), the hunter of the astral moose in Finnish epic songs is most often described as a Sámi, going by such names as "kaunis Kauppi lappalainen" [the handsome Sámi Kauppi], or the Lapin Lauri [Sámi Lauri]. Not all Finnish scholars have accepted this aspect of the moose hunt songs as ancient, preferring instead to attribute the story of the hunter to a Finnish hero like Lemminkäinen. Yet the astral lore seems to indicate, at least at some level of antiquity, a narrative of competitive or antagonistic relations between Sámi and Finns, in which at least some of the figures in the night sky were equated with Sámi adversaries.

In addition to his story about placing the human Sol and Máni in the sky as a punishment for their father's presumption, Snorri includes further tales of sky enemies, described particularly as giants. In his *Gylfaginning* account of the building of the wall around the sky fortress Ásgarðr, Snorri tells of a giant smith and his horse Svaðilfari that enter into a wager with the Æsir that they can complete a wall around the gods' dwelling in the space of one year, a feat that would gain them as a result the sun and moon as well as the goddess Freyja (Faulkes 35—36). Loki must find a way to prevent the team from completing the wall in time, while Þórr, the perennial enemy of giants, comes in at the end of the story to dispatch the defeated smith. In his *Skaldskaparmál* (Faulkes 1998, 1-2; Faulkes 1987, 60-61), Snorri tells of a giant Þjazi and his daughter Skaði, who are often described in a manner reminiscent of depictions of Sámi (Kusmenko 2006). With Loki's coerced assistance, Þjazi steals the goddess Iðunn, whose apples ensure the gods immortal life. As a result, they grow old, but send Loki to recover Iðunn while Þjazi is off fishing. Þjazi catches sight of Loki in falcon form flying home with Iðunn and transforms himself into an eagle to catch him. The other gods start a fire that burns the feathers of Þjazi, causing him to crash and die. In recompense for this killing, the gods award a settlement to Þjazi's daughter Skaði in which she is allowed to marry one of the gods. She chooses Njörðr, the Vanir god of fishing, sea, wind, and fire, who is living among the Æsir, while Loki performs a painful trick with his testicles to make her laugh. As a further compensation, Snorri writes:

> Svá er sagt at Óðinn gerði þat til yfirbóta við hana at hann tók augu Þiaza ok kastaði upp á himin ok gerði af stiörnur tvær. (Faulkes 1998, 2)
>
> [It is said that Óðinn made further compensation to her by taking the eyes of Þiazi and casting them up into the sky, making of them two stars]

In the Eddaic poem *Hárbarðsljóð,* on the other hand, it is the god Þórr who is said to have hurled the eyes of Þjazi into the sky(str. 19):

> Ek drap Þiaza,
> enn þrúðmóðga iötun,
> upp ek varp augom
> Allvalda sonar
> á þann inn heiða himin;
> þau ero merki mest
> minna verka,
> þau er allir menn síðan um sé.
> (Jón Helgason 1971, 33)
>
> [I killed Þjazi
> the fierce giant
> I threw the eyes
> of the monarch's son
> upward to the bright sky;
> they are the greatest mark
> of my works
> they stand ever after for all men to see.]

Here Þórr's act seems not a gesture of conciliation but a menacing warning to the enemies of the Æsir. In looking up at the sky, ill-willed giants, their affiliated Sámi neighbors, or any other resisting humans are warned of the superior strength and belligerence of the

Norse god. Largely on the basis of the fact that the eyes are two in number and described as prominent in the night sky, scholars have conjectured that they may have corresponded to the stars Castor and Pollux (e.g., Grimm 1882, vol. 2, 724).

In another astral myth, again contained in Snorri's *Skaldskaparmál* (Faulkes 1998, 22; Faulkes 1987, 79-81), the god Þórr visits a healer *(völva)* named Gróa in order to remove a fragment of a whetstone that has become lodged in his head after a battle with the giant Hrungnir, who had been invited to Ásgarðr in Þórr's absence and made himself a nuisance. Þórr means to thank Gróa for her efforts to remove the whetstone by recounting the story of how he met with Gróa's husband Aurvandil when crossing the Elivágar. He had carried Aurvandil in a basket on his back, but one of Aurvandil's toes had stuck out and become frozen. Þórr broke it off and "kastaði upp á himin ok gerði af stjörnu þá heitir Aurvandilstá" [threw it up into the sky where it became the star known as "Aurvandil's Toe"] (Faulkes 1998, 22). Snorri cites and quotes the skaldic poem *Haustlöng* as his source for this account, although the poem itself makes no mention of the toe incident or of the constellation. The story of the star is, in other words, an addition to the account of the battle between Þórr and Hrungnir that Snorri has learned from another source and included at this juncture. Scholars have suggested the resultant star may have been the planet Venus, which, in Old English Christian texts, is called *Earendel* and employed as an image of Christ (Grimm 1882, vol. 2, 723; Turville-Petre 1964, 78).

It is noteworthy that this same depiction of champions and enemies seems to continue into Christianity in Scandinavian astral lore. In a list of Icelandic glosses for Latin and Greek star names appended to a twelfth-century Icelandic ecclesiastical calendar / almanac (Gml. kgl. sml. 1812 4to), the V-shaped Hyades are glossed as *ulfs keptr* (wolf's jaw), while the star Auriga is described as *ásar bardage* (god's battlefield), terms reflective of a sky viewed as a field of martial or mortal combat (Beckman and Kålund 1914-16, 72-75). A now demonized Óðinn and his band of faithful warriors lives on in the image of the fearful *Oskorei,* nightriders condemned to ride through the night sky during the dark season around Christmas.

The sky is the place in which the enmities between rival groups become eternally enacted, a mythic canvas for the conflicts of the terrestrial and divine world.

Similarities amidst differences

What this overview of Sámi, Finnish, and Norse astral lore seems to indicate is that, beneath all the surface variation regarding the names of particular constellations or the correlation of particular astral bodies with particular heroes, gods, or demons, a certain shared understanding seems to have existed. The sky was the imagistic site occasionally of agricultural tools and activities, but more often of the ancient harvesting traditions conveyed by the North Sámi term *bivdit,* to hunt or fish. These activities are carried on by champions described by terms derived from the Norse *karl.* In the Norse and Finnish cases, they are also sometimes presided over by gods, Óðinn and Väinämöinen, if not also possibly Þórr and Ilmarinen. In the Sámi case, in keeping with the less hierarchical, more egalitarian social system of a hunter-gatherer people, Gállá is not a chieftain but rather a head of a household and an ancestor. Enemies also occur in the skies: in the Sámi case, the struggle between Gállá, Fávdna, and Riihmagállis concerning who will succeed in capturing Stuorra Sarvva is not yet resolved, while Fávdna and Fávnna gilpa-násti similarly circle the sky in perpetual competition. In the Norse and Finnish cases, in the manner of the Titanomachy, the struggles between the enemies and the gods are largely over, having ended to the advantage of the gods but sometimes—as the Norse star myths show—entailing small acts of compensation from the Æsir to their former enemies, ranging from the gifting of a marriage partner (Skaði's marriage to Njörðr) to the installation of defunct body parts (eyes, a toe) as constellations in the sky.

It is striking in closing to notice which constellations become associated with which parts of this overall drama: in the Norse case, it is one of the most prominent constellations—the Big Dipper—that becomes associated with the triumphant *karlar* and/or their leader Óðinn, riding a wagon through the conquered cosmos. The Big Dipper is always found high in the sky and is visible throughout the year, even if the summer sky was largely unknown to Nordic peoples. It is little wonder, in this respect, that Christian Europeans would have eventually associated the constellation with Charlemagne, the quintessential conqueror-hero of medieval legendry and history. Finns, on the other hand, saw this same constellation as either a fish trap associated with the fishing deity Väinämöinen or a portion of the Great Bear constellation, both symbols of the older hunter-gatherer way of life that was still of importance to Finns even after the adoption of agriculture. Väinämöinen may have dominion over the astral fishing net, but he also ranges across the sky, being found in the Pleiades, Orion, and the Milky Way. Orion's Belt is also a prominent constellation, but is not always so visible and often hovers more on the horizon, except in the height of winter (December, January, February), when it climbs to a height equal to that of the Big Dipper. Here, Finns and Sámi alike placed their adaptations of the Norse *karl* figure, making them champions, a god, or a part of the community's ancestry. The Star Sirius, which generally stays close to the horizon and never occupies as prominent a spot as the Big Dipper, becomes seen in Sámi astral lore as the great hero Gállá, while the somewhat dimmer star Arcturus, associated with the focus of the Norse narrative of hegemony (the Big Dipper), becomes viewed as a demon. Fávdna competes not only with Gállá, but also with another star which appears at the other end of the sky and refuses to ever come closer to its enemy. For the Norse and Finns, the war is over and its results are visible in the twinkling lights of Þjazi's Eyes or Aurvandil's Toe, or in the memory of Väinämöinen's successful creation of the earth despite the attempted assassination by a Sámi. For the Sámi, as we have noted, the astral war continues unchanged, until the inevitable moment comes when Fávdna, the embodiment of the Norse threat, will destroy the entire earth. In the meantime, however, the Sámi culture heroes remain at the margins, practicing their ancient ways and biding their time.

In the above overview of Norse, Finnish, and Sámi astral lore, it is easy to lose the forest for the trees. The three linguistic groups called the same stars by different names and saw different constellations in the spaces between the stars that most often figure in a culture's ethnoastronomy. If one approaches astral lore from the viewpoint of a list of recognized constellations and planets, the three linguistic groups of the Nordic region appear to have possessed quite distinct and mutually exclusive bodies of lore. Yet by looking at the actors and activities described in the skies, we can recognize a shared view of the cosmos. The fact that these activities corresponded to the traditional livelihoods of the Finno-Ugric peoples rather than the cultural and economic innovations of the farming, raiding, trading Norse, and the fact that many of the Norse figures associated with stars (such as Þjazi) bear Sámi imagery, reflects perhaps a worldview in which the Norse saw themselves as colonizers rather than as indigenous to the region. Such a conjecture correlates well with Snorri's various attempts to explain the "arrival" of the Norse in the Nordic region and their relation to ancient great civilizations of the south and east such as Troy. The fact that the Titanomachy seems to be an ancient characteristic of Indo-European mythologies offers an alternative explanation for this tendency, however: narratives of a past struggle may simply reflect an Indo-European mythic heritage among Norse settlers. Yet the striking oneness of the night sky and its denizens with both Finnish and Sámi denizens of the North bespeaks cultures with no such conscious notion of ancient migration. Finnish myths of conflict between Väinämöinen and Sámi may reflect a process of internal colonization indicated well in the archaeological record, in which the agricultural Balto-Finns began to expand their settlements, displacing their fellow Finno-Ugrians who had not adopted agriculture, i.e., the Sámi. This process seems to have begun at least with the development of the Kiukainen culture in southwestern Finland sometime after c. 1200 BCE, but continued right into the nineteenth century in remote areas of northern and eastern Finland, meaning that enmity and resentment between Finns and displaced Sámi was a familiar part of the lives of many stargazers and singers at the time when the ancient folk songs were committed to writing in the nineteenth and twentieth centuries. That the Sámi saw Fávdna as a source of danger and destruction, and that they identified with Gállá, a star that often stayed on the horizon rather than usurping the center of the sky, is also perhaps indicative of a Sámi understanding of interethnic relations, in the ancient past and in the present day of knowledgeable men like Johan Turi and Iŋggá Lemet. Ultimately, perhaps, the imbalances perceptible in the cosmic relations of these key groups within the astral lore of the region—the various ways in which Norse, Finns, and Sámi portrayed themselves and their neighbors through the images they saw in the skies—may reflect social, economic and cultural conflicts that endured in some ways from the medieval era down to today. The sky is not a foreign or remote world but rather a telling reflection of the conflicts and characteristics of the earth below.

Virtual Mythology

Eternal Myths in Digital Shape: Computer Games as Ritual Arenas

Ulf Palmenfelt

> *The web of culture used to be spun from the stories a child heard at a grandparent's knee. Today, it derives from that child's experience with interactive multimedia.*
> *(Ohmae 1995. 162).*

We know that huge numbers of people devote considerable amounts of time to playing computer games. Since the beginning of the 1990's, more than 700 million game consoles have been sold. In 2010, 63 million PC and console games were sold in the UK, which is more than one per person. In 2010, computer games were sold for 25 billion US dollars worldwide. The leading online game, World of Warcraft, is played by some 10 million persons. One of the most popular single player games, Grand Theft Auto, sold 12 million copies in the first four months, when the third part of the trilogy was released in 2004. In the United Kingdom, one in sixty people bought this game within nine days of its release (Miller 2008, 258). According to a Swedish survey from 2010, 92% of the children in the age range 9-16 years play computer games (Ungar & Medier 2010). My question is why? Being a folklorist, I will suggest that computer games might meet similar needs that myths, fairy tales, folk legends, and other genres of folklore did one hundred to one hundred and fifty years ago.

Folklore as a tool for handling life

One possible approach to folklore is to regard it as a set of cultural tools that allow people to interpret their experiences, to handle social tensions, to negotiate moral questions, and to understand the eternal existential mysteries of life and death.

Myths, for example, are usually understood by folklorists as accounts about the origins of the world and its inhabitants, of societies and cultures. Generally, the function of myth is to explain not only how some Supreme Being created man in the beginning, but also that this creator put man on top of the hierarchical ladder, above all other living creatures. Myths also teach us about the eternal truths of mankind, what is right and wrong, what is good and evil, and how to understand the mystery of life and death.

Folk legends often handle man's relation to the supernatural forces in the present. They can be expected to exemplify the kinds of supernormal situations we are likely to encounter and how to act if and when we do. Many folk legends illustrate the boundaries between known and unknown territories, both geographically and symbolically.

Proverbs summarize universal human experiences and knowledge, often seen from the point of view of the established groups in society.

Jokes and anecdotes negotiate the limits of normality and credibility by stretching or shifting the perspectives from which we regard reality. On the surface, jokes and anecdotes often demonstrate a democratic quality as they let the underdog win over the oppressor. However, since they make us laugh at this breach of the social rules, we might as well argue that their function is to demonstrate how ridiculous any deviation from the status quo would be.

There is no doubt that computer game creators have borrowed elements from myths, folk legends, and proverbs as well as from jokes and anecdotes.

Fairy Tales

The traditional folklore genre that shows the most and the closest similarities to contemporary computer games, however, is the fairy tale, at least from the point of view that I want to try here. Both fairy tales and computer games offer playful arenas for testing the limits of the physical reality, of social and cultural norms, and of moral values. When we listen to a fairy tale, it belongs to the unwritten agreement between teller and audience that both parties pretend to believe that invisibility hoods, seven league boots, talking animals, singing trees and dragons with seven heads exist. The fairy tale telling situation creates a (day)dreamlike playground, where we are invited to consider the boundaries of reality. What would it be like if you could hear the princess breathing in the giant's subterranean cave or if you could see a fly on the church tower in the next parish?

If we regard the fairy tale telling situation from the point of view of ritual theory, we could assume that it takes place inside a liminal state, where "normal" moral and ethical standards are temporarily made invalid or even reversed. What would living be like if you always got what you wished for, if you had a table that was filled with food at your command, or if the gooseherd was allowed to marry the princess? The ritual arena of the fairy tale telling session allows for bold and maybe even subversive intellectual leaps. Returning to everyday reality, on the otherhand, reveals that the visit to the taleworld was not a *rite de passage* but only a temporary stroll in the land of the daydreams.

Dragon Age: Origins

To compare these ideas about fairy tale listening to what happens to a computer game player, I want to use my own experiences from playing the game *Dragon Age: Origins*, produced in 2009 by the Canadian company BioWare.

Dragon Age: Origins could be regarded as a free adaptation of Peter Jackson's *The Lord of the Rings* (2001-2003) film trilogy to a computer game format. It is at least safe to say that the game creators have been strongly inspired by some features of the films. The humanoids consist of three races: men, dwarves and elves; the temporal setting is vaguely medieval; clothes, weapons, and landscapes are similar in the game and the film. There are dragons and giant spiders to fight, there are wizards to trust or distrust, there are beacons to be lit, old treaties to revive, and spooky tunnels to explore. The overall assignment is to build an alliance between the good forces to oppose the representatives of evil.

"Origins" in the game's title might lead our thoughts in the direction of myth, but I believe that we should sooner interpret it as an expression of the producers' hope that this would be the first in a long row of profitable games.

The producers have created an extensive history of the game's world, including mythology, religion, culture, literature and folklore. All this fictive knowledge is gathered in a Codex, of which the player can pick up chapters and fragments during the game. The philosophical explanations for evil given in this documentation are of a quasi religious nature: seven Old Gods ruled over the ancient world. They were responsible for the original sin consisting in turning humanity away from the Maker. As a result of this, the Maker, in his turn, has turned away from humanity, transformed the seven Old Gods to arch demons and locked them up in eternal prisons beneath the earth.

Similarities and Differences between Fairy Tales and Computer Games

When you start the game, you are symbolically transported into the ritual arena of Dragon Age. Just as in the story telling situation, you are invited to play according to other moral and ethical values as well as different laws of nature than those to which you are accustomed. According to Victor Turner, the ritual arena of computer games should be defined as liminoid instead of liminal, since game playing cannot be regarded as a *rite de passage* that changes the social status of the player (Turner 1982, 58; Dovey & Kennedy 2006, 34ff.) Game researchers Jon Dovey and Helen Kennedy develop Turner's idea:

> … games serve as a kind of ritualized 'condensed realm of order', a temporary space with constraints and opportunities unlike those operating in the everyday world. Particular rule-bound spaces (for Turner, liminal ritual spaces or liminoid leisure spaces) ritually license otherwise taboo activities, like

> murder and mayhem (Dovey & Kennedy 2006, 100).

Game researchers Katie Salen and Eric Zimmerman (2004, 94) argue that game players not only enter the famous "magic circle" of Johan Huizinga but also adopt "a particular frame of mind or 'lusory attitude', or what child culture scholar Brian Sutton-Smith called a "subjunctive mood", or a sense of "what if?" (Sutton-Smith 2001:4).

One of the two crucial differences between listening to a fairy tale and playing a computer game concerns the agency of the player (cf. Dovey & Kennedy 2006, 7). The fairy tale teller will continue narrating whether you are listening or not, whereas the computer game stops the second you stop entering your commands via the keyboard. The player has to be active to keep the game going. This does not imply that computer game playing is an interactive enterprise as it is sometimes argued. As a player you are not able to perform any actions that fall outside what the game creators have allowed the game engine to permit. Basically, you are only allowed to turn the game on and off, move your avatar along the preset paths, and complete the stipulated quests more or less in a fixed order. But, on the other hand, if you do not do this, nothing at all happens.

The other vital difference has to do with the mode of communication. The fairy tale, whether orally told or read from a printed text, is a narrative with epic qualities. It has chronology and causality; it is communicated through the mediation of a narrator (sometimes both the performer and the supposed creator of the text) and, since it is a completed story, it is told in the past tense.

Computer games certainly have epic elements, too. Within the specific quests, one often finds clear causal connections, while the order between the separate episodes often appears to be random. We could compare games with the classical epics (or with many fairy tales for that matter), where the story line is limited to following the main character travelling from place to place, performing one heroic deed after the other (cf Manovich 2001: 246f).

Computer games show a closer kinship to the literary form of drama, where we as audience watch the events in real time as they unfold; we hear the actors say their lines without the mediation of a narrator, and we see the environment where the action is taking place. However, computer games take us one step further than the theater. We are actually invited to step up onto the stage and share the feelings, reactions and experiences of our PC, playable character, who is not only passively present in the here and now, but also actively taking part in the action as it evolves.

It is no coincidence that computer games have been used pedagogically to train airplane pilots, test drivers, and soldiers (Haraway 1991). In front of the computer screen, the trainee can practice accurate reactions in complicated situations that would be too expensive or too dangerous to carry out in real life. Playing entertainment computer games puts the player in the same situation of simulation (cf. Aarseth 2003, 52). Over and over again, the player has to react to similar situations appearing on the screen, analyze potential risks and possibilities, settle on the appropriate tactics, select and group the most efficient allies and take action. The game forces you to learn certain patterns of action and repeat them until they almost become reflexes. And this rehearsal takes place in a ritual arena where we face challenges different to those we are used to in ordinary life and where we are allowed to, or even expected to, try different patterns of action governed by different moral values than usually govern our actions.

What does the world of Dragon Age: Origins *look like?*

The story line of *Dragon Age: Origins* is simple. The player is assigned the task to unite all good forces against a threatening attack from the evil powers, led by the fifth arch demon. (Four earlier "blights" have all been defeated by the good side.) To accomplish this task, the player has to fulfill quite a few side quests before being ready to face the final onslaught. Above all, it is necessary to engage in the inner politics of several societies, choosing one party to side with and consequently to defeat others.

Playing the game involves meeting **a never-ending row of quests**, each of which must be completed before you are allowed to go on to the next one. True, there are resting points between many of the quests, where you can gather your allies in camp or watch the filmed cut scene that introduces the next quest. Whenever you are not in the middle of a fight, you are able to leave active playing and take care of your characters' equipment, change their fighting tactics, check statistics, or read the Codex entries.

Most of the quests are built around **acute or latent conflicts.** The hostile forces may attack you unexpectedly or the game may urge you to seek them out and attack them. In the first case, you will be surprised, startled or scared, as the attack is often accompanied by a loud or frightening sound. The enemies you have to face are violent, cruel and bloodthirsty. You are seldom given any logical reason why they want to kill you. You are not even given a reason why the darkspawn necessarily have to stage a huge blight every four hundred years, as noted in the game's Codex:

> No one knows what it is that drives the darkspawn in their relentless search for the sleeping Old Gods. Perhaps it is instinct, as moths will fly into torch flames. Perhaps there is some remnant of desire for vengeance upon the ones who goaded the magisters to assault heaven. (Codex Entry: Archdemon).

Did the game creators made their own task so easy that they invented all kinds of Evil creatures just because the Good ones per definition need an enemy? Did their imagination stop at the outward shape of the evil beings, their terrifying sounds and their cruel killing methods? Did they forget to explain the origins of their evil? Was it too difficult or too uninteresting? Of course not. The lack of explanation, the vagueness, and the ambiguity are exactly that which qualifies the evil in Dragon Age to be apprehended as eternal. Mythical evil stands outside time and space.

The dramatic peaks of the game are the recurring fights. The game takes roughly eighty hours to play through and during that time you have to kill approximately one thousand seven hundred times to reach the end. Between the fights there are relatively long transport distances. Consequently, you have to learn to **orientate** in unknown three-dimensional landscapes. You are often put down in unknown areas, where you get a similar feeling as when you come out on street level from a subway station in an unknown city. Large parts of the transport involve moving in subterranean tunnels, where you might experience the feeling of being caught in a labyrinth. During the game, some of the environments change due to warfare, so when close to the end of the game you return to the city of Denerim, where you have spent a lot of time earlier, well-known buildings are ruined, burning, or simply wiped out.

Although the master narrative of the game concerns the metaphysical fight between good and evil, the **materialistic elements** are remarkably strong. All objects that the game characters are able to handle have a fixed price and can be bought and sold. Between fights, you are supposed to sell the items you have looted from killed enemies and buy better equipment for your allies. Immaterial features are measured in points and percent. The qualities, skills, knowledge, and experiences of the playable characters, and even their relations with one another, are quantified in numerical terms. You can collect approval and disapproval points, which give you more or less influence over your fellow characters, and all these numbers are accumulated in the game statistics. It is also possible to loose points. Like a stock exchange speculator who has invested in the wrong papers, your accumulated values may evaporate. Of course, the only way a digital game engine can handle matters like these is in terms of mathematical calculations, but it would not be necessary to make these operations part of the gaming situation.

The game invites you to explore your own **emotional reactions**. During the game you experience what it feels like to become small as a mouse, strong as a Golem, to walk through fire, and move between parallel universes. You get caught in a nightmare where you constantly return to the same places and see no point of escape. Many times you experience how you react when you become scared and what it feels like to have to execute innocent people, including women and children, for the sake of the higher good.

What Does Dragon Age: Origins *Train the Player To Do?*

If we accept the metaphor of computer games as simulation machines, what knowledge, then, does *Dragon Age: Origins* train the player to apply? Here are some of my suggestions:

- You have to be constantly alert and prepared to foresee attacks and meet them when they come. Violence is the prime solution to all problems.
- You have to accept that you might have to perform disgusting and horrible acts, including the killing of innocent beings, to defeat a larger evil. A good cause justifies cruel methods.
- You will be trained to do fast categorizations of beings into classes and races, and act according to them. You are supposed to lie, betray, break your promises, abandon your allies or kill them, depending on what will best serve your own purposes. Calculation is more important than empathy.
- Your degree of success in the game is measured in numbers. You are expected to collect experience points, approval points, and money. Accumulation of material values is a supreme driving force.

Why?

Why do we find these features in a computer game produced by a North American company in the post 9/11-world? It would be easy to claim that the bearing elements of *Dragon Age: Origins* reflect some of the dominating myths of today's Western market economies (see e.g. Sutton-Smith 2001: 17). Maybe they do, but rather than making that statement myself, I plan to talk to active players about their motives for playing. From a series of such interviews, it is my ambition to discuss the cultural consequences of moral and ethical values being communicated and negotiated in the ritual arenas of computer games.

References

Aarseth, Espen 2003. Genre Trouble: Narrativism and the Art of Simulation. In *First Person: New Media as Story, Performance, and Game*. Edited by Noah Wardrip-Fruin and Pat Harrrigan. Pp. 45-55. Cambridge MA: MIT Press.

Abram, Christopher. 2003. Representations of the Pagan Afterlife in Medieval Scandinavian Literature. PhD Dissertation, University of Cambridge.

Adam of Bremen: *Gesta Hammaburgensis ecclesiæ pontificum*. See Schmeidler 1917.

Adam of Bremen: *The History of the Archbishops of Hamburg-Bremen*. See Tschan 1959.

Allen, Thomas W., ed. 1917. *Homeri Opera, Tomus III Odysseae libros I-XII continens*. Oxford: Clarendon. 2nd edition.

Amundsen, Arne Bugge. 2009. Jonas Ramus. In *Norsk Biografisk Leksikon*. Accessed June 2, 2014. http://nbl.snl.no/Jonas_Ramus.

Anderson, Jørgen. 1971. *The Witch on the Wall: Medieval Erotic Sculpture in the British Isles*. Copenhagen: Rosenkilde and Bagger.

Andersson, Gunnar. 2006. Among Trees, Bones, and Stones: The Sacred Grove at Lunda. In *Old Norse Religion in Long-term Perspectives: Origins, Changes, and Interactions*. Edited by Anders Andrén et al. Vägar till Midgård 8. Pp. 195-205. Lund: Nordic Academic Press.

Andersson, Gunnar. 2008. Pärlor för svin: Den heliga lunden och rituell praktik i Lunda. In *Gestalter och gestaltningar: Om tid, rum och händelser på Lunda*. Edited by Gunnar Andersson and Eva Skyllberg. Riksantikvarieämbetet. Arkeologiska undersökningar. Skrifter 72. Pp. 65-129. Stockholm: Riksantikvarieämbetet.

Andersson, Theodore M., and Kari Gade, transl. 2000. *Morkinskinna: The Earliest Icelandic Chronicle of the Norwegian Kings (1030-1157)*. Ithaca: Cornell Univ. Press.

Andersson, Thorsten. 1992a. Haupttypen sakraler Ortsnamen Ostskandinaviens. In *Der historische Horizont der Götterbild-Amulette aus der Übergangsepoche von der Spätantike zum Frühmittelalter*. Edited by Karl Hauck. Abhandlungen der Akademie der Wissenschaften in Göttingen. Philol.-Hist. Klasse 3:200. Göttingen: Vandenhoeck und Ruprecht.

Andersson, Thorsten. 1992b. Orts- und Personennamen als Aussagequelle für die altgermanische Religion. In *Germanische Religionsgeschichte. Quellen und Quellenprobleme*. Edited by Heinrich Beck et al. Ergänzungsbände zum Reallexikon der germanischen Altertumskunde 5. Berlin: de Gruyter.

Andersson, Thorsten. 2005. Theophore Namen. In *Reallexikon der Germanischen Altertumskunde* 30: 442-52.

Andrén, Anders. 2008. Lies about Gotland. In *Facets of Archaeology: Essays in Honour of Lotte Hedeager on her 60th Birthday*. Edited by Konstantinos Chilidis, Julie Lund, and Christopher Prescott. Pp. 47-55. Oslo Archaeological Series 10. Oslo: Oslo Academic Press.

Andrén, Anders. 2011. *Det medeltida Gotland: En arkeologisk guidebok*. Lund: Historiska Media.

Anthony, David W. 2007. *The Horse, the Wheel, and Language: How Bronze-age Riders from the Eurasian Steppes Shaped the Modern World.* Princeton NJ: Princeton University Press.

Ármann Jakobsson, and Þórður Ingi Guðjónsson, ed. 2011. *Morkinskinna.* Íslenzk fornrit 23-24. Reykjavík: Hið íslenzka fornritafélag.

Baity, Elizabeth C. 1973. Archaeoastronomy and Ethnoastronomy So Far. *Current Anthropology* 14(4): 389-449.

Bárðar saga Snæfellsáss. 1991. Edited by Þórhallur Vilmundarson and Bjarni Vilhjálmsson. Íslenzk fornrit 13. Pp. 99-172. Reykjavík: Hið íslenzka fornritafélag.

Battista, Simonetta. 2003. Interpretations of the Roman Pantheon in the Old Norse Hagiographical Sagas. In *Old Norse Myths, Literature and Society*. Edited by Margaret Clunies Ross. Pp. 175-97. The Viking Collection 14. Odense: Odense University Press.

Beckman, Natanael and Kristian Kålund, eds. 1914-16. *Alfræði Íslenzk. Islandsk encyklopædisk litteratur. II. Rímtǫl.* Copenhagen: S. L. Møller.

Bellows, Henry Adams, transl. 1923. *The Poetic Edda, with Introduction and Notes*. New York: American-Scandinavian Foundation.

Bergmann, Friedrich Wilhelm. 1874. *Vielgewandts Sprüche und Groa's Zaubersaga.* Strassburg: Trübner.

Bischoff, Bernhard et al. 1987/1989. *Aratea. Nachbildung der Handschrift Ms. Voss. Lat. Q. 79 der Rijksuniversiteit Leiden. Bd. 1 Faksimile. Bd. 2 Kommentar mit Beiträgen von Bernhard Bischoff, Bruce Eastwood, Thomas A. P. Klein, Florentine Mütherich und Pieter F. J. Obbema.* Luzern: Faksimile Verlag Luzern.

Biskupa sögur. 1858. Edited by Jón Sigurðsson and Guðbrandur Vigfússon. Íslenzka bókmentafélag. Copenhagen: S. L. Møller.

Björn Jónsson. 1989. *Stjarnvísi í Eddum.* Reykjavík: Bókaútgáfan Skjaldborg.

Björn Jónsson. 1994. *Star Myths of the Vikings.* Swan River, Manitoba: Hignell Printing.

Böldl, Klaus. 2000. *Der Mythos der Edda: Nordische Mythologie zwischen europäischer Aufklärung und nationaler Romantik.* Tübingen: Francke.

Bósa saga ok Herrauðs. 1954. In *Fornaldar sögur Norðurlanda*. Edited by Guðni Jónsson. 3: 281-322. Akureyri: Íslendingasagnaútgáfa.

Bracciotti, Annalisa, ed. 1998. *Origo gentis langobardorum: Introduzione, testo critico, commento*. Bibliotheca di Cultura Romanobarbarica 2. Rome: Herder.

Brennu-Njáls saga. 1954. Edited by Einar Ól. Sveinsson. Íslenzk fornrit 12. Reykjavík: Hið íslenzka fornritafélag.

Brink, Stefan. 1990. Cult Sites in Northern Sweden. In *Old Norse and Finnish Religions and Cultic Place Names*. Edited by Tore Ahlbäck. Pp. 458-89. Scripta Instituti Donneriania Aboensis 13. Stockholm: Almqvist & Wiksell International.

Brink, Stefan. 1992. Har vi haft ett kultiskt *al i Norden? In *Sakrale navne: Rapport fra NORNAs sekstende symposium i Gilleleje 30.11.-2.12.1990*. Edited by Gillian Fellows-Jensen and Bente Holmberg. NORNA-rapporter 48. Uppsala: Nornaförlaget.

Brink, Stefan. 1999. Social Order in the Early Scandinavian Landscape. In *Settlement and Landscape*. Edited by Charlotte Fabech and Jytte Ringtved. Pp. 87-112. Århus: Århus University Press.

Brink, Stefan. 2006. Mythologizing Landscape: Place and Space of Cult and Myth. In *Kontinuitäten und Brüche in der Religionsgeschichte*. Edited by Michael Stausberg. Pp. 76-112. Ergänzungsband zum Reallexikon der germanischen Altertumskunde 31. Berlin: de Gruyter.

Brink, Stefan. 2007. How Uniform Was the Old Norse Religion? In *Learning and Understanding in the Old Norse World: Essays in Honour of Margaret Clunies Ross*. Edited by Judy Quinn, Kate Heslop, and Tarrin Wills. Pp. 105-36. Turnhout: Brepols.

Brink, Stefan. 2012. *Vikingarnas slavar: Den nordiska träldomen under yngre järnålder och äldsta medeltid*. Stockholm: Atlantis.

Brink, Stefan. 2013. Myth and Ritual in Pre-Christian Scandinavian Landscape. In *Sacred Sites and Holy Places: Exploring the Sacralization of Landscape Through Time and Space*. Edited by Sæbjørg Walaker Nordeide and Stefan Brink. Pp. 33-51. Studies in Early Middle Ages 11. Turnhout: Brepols.

Brot af Þórðar sögu hreðu. 1959. Edited by Jóhannes Halldórsson. Íslenzk fornrit 14. Pp. 227-47. Reykjavík: Hið íslenzka fornritafélag.

Bugge, Sophus. 1856. Untitled remarks in Grundtvig 1856: 667-68.

Bugge, Sophus. 1860. Forbindelsen mellem Grógaldr og Fiölsvinnsmál oplyst ved sammenligning med den dansk-svenske folkevise om Sveidal. *Forhandlinger i vidensk.-selsk. i Christiania 1860*: 123-40.

Bugge, Sophus, ed. 1867 *Norræn fornkvæði. Islandsk samling af folkelige oldtidsdigte om nordens guder og heroer almindelig kaldet Sæmundar Edda hins fróða*. Oslo: Universitetsforlaget, 1965.

Burrows, Hannah. 2013. Enigma Variations: Hervarar saga's Wave-Riddles and Supernatural Women in Old Norse Poetic Tradition. *Journal of English and Germanic Philology* 112: 194-216.

Bæksted, Anders. 1986. *Goð og hetjur í heiðnum sið. Alþýðlegt fræðirit um goðafræði og hetjusögur.* Translated into Icelandic by Eysteinn Þorvaldsson. Reykjavík: Bókaútgáfan Örn og Örlygur hf.

Campion, Nicholas. 2004. Introduction: Cultural Astronomy. In *Astrology and the Academy.* Edited by Nicholas Campion, Patrick Curry and Michael York. Pp. xv-xxx. Bristol: Cinnabar Books.

Cassel, Paulus. 1856. *Eddische Studien. I: Fiölvinnsmál* [sic]. Weimar: Böhlau.

Chadwick, Nora K. 1964. The Russian Giant Svyatogor and the Norse Útgartha-Loki. *Folklore* 75: 243-59.

Chamberlain, Von Del, John B. Carlson, and Jane M. Young, eds. 2005. *Songs From the Sky: Indigenous Astronomical and Cosmological Traditions of the World.* University of Maryland, College Park Center for Archaeoastronomy: Ocarina Books.

Clunies Ross, Margaret et al. eds. 2007-. *Skaldic Poetry of the Scandinavian Middle Ages.* 9 vols. Turnhout: Brepols.

Clunies Ross, Margaret, ed. 2007. *Poetry on Christian Subjects.* 2 vols. Skaldic Poetry of the Scandinavian Middle Ages 7. Turnhout: Brepols.

Clunies Ross, Margaret. 1983. Snorri Sturluson's Use of the Norse Origin Legend of the Sons of Fornjótr in his Edda. *Arkiv för nordisk filologi* 98: 47-66.

Clunies Ross, Margaret. 1994. *Prolonged Echoes: Old Norse Myths in Medieval Northern Society. I. The Myths.* The Viking Collection 7. Odense: Odense University Press.

Colbert, David. 1989. *The Birth of the Ballad: The Scandinavian Medieval Genre.* Stockholm: Svenskt visarkiv.

Colbert, David. 1999. The Birthplace of the Ballad. *Sumlen* 1992-3: 279-84.

Colgrave, Bertram, and Roger A. B. Mynors, eds. 1969. *Bede's Ecclesiastical History of the English People.* Oxford: Clarendon Press.

Condos, Theony. 1997. *Star Myths of the Greeks and Romans: A Sourcebook.* Grand Rapids MI: Phanes Press.

Coumert, Magali. 2007. *Origines des peuples: Les récits du Haut Moyen Âge occidental (550-850).* Collection des Études Augustiniennes—Série Moyen Âge et Temps Modernes 42. Paris: Institut d'Études Augustiniennes.

Csepregi, Márta. 2005. The Elk Myth in Ob-Ugrian Folklore. In *Shamanhood: An Endangered Language.* Edited by Juha Pentikäinen and Peter Simoncsics. Pp. 99-120. Oslo: Novus Forlag.

Detter, Ferdinand and Richard Heinzel, eds. 1903. *Sæmundar Edda mit einem Anhang herausgegeben und erklärt.* 2 vols. Leipzig: Wigand.

Dillmann, Francois-Xavier. 1997. Kring de rituella gästabuden i fornskandinavisk religion. In *Uppsalakulten och Adam af Bremen*. Edited by Anders Hultgård. Pp. 51-73. Uppsala: Bokförlaget Nya Doxa.

Dillmann, Francois-Xavier. 2006. *Les magiciens dans l'Islande ancienne: Etudes sur la representation de la magie islandaise et de ses agents dans les sources littéraires norroises*. Uppsala: Kungl. Gustav Adolfs Akademien för Svensk Folkkultur

Dovey, Jon, and Helen W. Kennedy. 2006. *Game Cultures: Computer Games as New Media*. New York: Open University Press.

Dronke, Peter, and Ursula Dronke. 1997. *Growth of Literature: The Sea and the God of the Sea*. H. M. Chadwick Memorial Lecture 8. Cambridge: Department of Anglo-Saxon, Norse and Celtic.

Dronke, Ursula. 1968. Beowulf and Ragnarǫk. *Saga-Book of the Viking Society* 17: 302-25.

DuBois, Thomas A. 1999. *Nordic Religions in the Viking Age*. Philadelphia: University of Pennsylvania Press.

DuBois, Thomas A. 2001. Narrative Expectations and the Sampo Song. *Scandinavian Studies* 73(3): 457-474.

Duczko, W. 2004. *Viking Rus: Studies on the Presence of Scandinavians in Eastern Europe*. Leiden: Brill.

Dumézil, Georges. 1958. *L'idéologie tripartite des Indo-Européens*. Bruxelles: Latomus.

Dumézil, Georges. 1959. *Les dieux des germains: Essai sur la formation de la religion scandinave*. Paris: PUF.

Dümmler, Ernst, ed. 1895. *Epistolae Karolini Aevi. Tomus II*. Monumenta Germaniae Historica. D. Epistolae. (1.) Epistolarum Tomus IV. Karolini Aevi II. Berlin: Weidmann.

Dundes, Alan, ed. 1992. *The Evil Eye: A Casebook*. Madison: The University of Wisconsin Press.

Dundes, Alan. 1999. *International Folkloristics: Classic Contributions by the Founders of Folklore*. Lanham MD: Rowman & Littlefield.

Edlund, Lars-Erik. 2012. Namn och bygd och språkvetenskapen: Nedslag genom hundra år. *Namn och bygd* 100: 61-83.

Edwards, Paul, and Hermann Pálsson, ed. and transl. 1989. Introduction. In *Vikings in Russia: Yngvar's Saga and Eymund's Saga*. Pp. 1-37. Edinburgh: Edinburgh University Press.

Egils saga Skalla-Grímssonar. 1933. Edited by Sigurður Nordal. Íslenzk fornrit 2. Reykjavík: Hið íslenzka fornritafélag.

Eide, Eldar. 2001. *Gand, seid og åndevind*. PhD Dissertation, Universitetet i Bergen

Einar Ól. Sveinsson. 1958. *Dating the Icelandic Sagas*. London: Viking Society for Northern Research.

Einar Ól. Sveinsson. 1971-73. Svipdag's Long Journey: Some Observations on Grógaldr and Fjölsvinnsmál. In *Hereditas: Essays and Studies presented to Professor Séamus Ó Duilearga, former Honorary Director of the Irish Folklore Commission.* Edited by Bo Almquist, Breandán Mac Aodha, and Gearóid Mac Eoin. Pp. 298-319. Dublin: Folklore of Ireland Society, 1975. [Orig. publ. in Béaloideas 39-41 (1971-73).]

Einar Ól. Sveinsson. 1975. Svipdagur og Menglöð: Athugsemðir um Grógaldur og Fjölsvinnsmál. In *Löng er för: Þrír þættir um írskar og íslenzdar sögur og kvæði.* Pp. 11-116. Studia Islandica 34. Reykjavík: Bókaútgáfa menningarsjóðs.

Einar Pálsson. 1978. *Rammislagur.* Reykjavík: Mímir.

Eiríks saga rauða. 1935. Edited by Einar Ól. Sveinsson and Matthías Þorðarson. Íslensk fornrit 4. Pp. 193-237. Reykjavík: Hið íslenska fornritafélag.

Eithun, Bjørn, Magnus Rindal, and Tor Ulset, eds. 1994. *Den eldre Gulatingslova.* Norrøne tekster 6. Oslo: Riksarkivet.

Ellis, Hilda Roderick. 1968. *The Road to Hel: A Study of the Conception of the Dead in Old Norse Literature.* New York: Greenwood Press.

Ellmers, Detlev. 1972. Zur Ikonographie nordischer Goldbrakteaten. *Jahrbuch des Römisch-Germanischen Zentralmuseums Mainz* 17(1970): 201-293.

Elmevik, Lennart. 1990. Aschw. Lytis- in Ortsnamen: Ein kultisches Element oder ein profanes? In *Old Norse and Finnish Religions and Cultic Place Names.* Edited by Tore Ahlbäck. Pp. 490-507. Scripta Instituti Donneriania Aboensis 13. Stockholm: Almqvist & Wiksell International.

Elmevik, Lennart. 1995a. Härnevi och Friggeråker. *Namn och bygd* 83: 67-77.

Elmevik, Lennart. 1995b. Fornnordiska gudagestalter och svenska ortnamn. *Saga och sed*: 11-19.

Elmevik, Lennart. 1997. Svenska ortnamn med förleden Frö-. In *Ortnamn i språk och samhälle: Hyllningsskrift till Lars Hellberg.* Edited by Svante Strandberg. Pp. 107-15. Nomina Germanica 22. Uppsala: Acta Universitatis Upsaliensis.

Elmevik, Lennart. 1999. Kultiska ortnamn i Sverige: Verkliga och förmenta. In *Kultur och samhälle i språkets spegel.* Edited by Gunilla Gren-Eklund. Pp. 31-38. Uppsala: Uppsala universitet.

Elmevik, Lennart. 2003a. En svensk ortnamnsgrupp och en hednisk prästtitel. *Ortnamnssällskapets i Uppsala årsskrift*: 68-78.

Elmevik, Lennart. 2003b. Kan gudinnenamnet Fröja säkert spåras i norska ortnamn? *Namn och bygd* 91: 142-43.

Elmevik, Lennart. 2003c. Freyr, Freya och Freyfaxi. *Studia anthroponymica Scandinavica* 21: 5-13.

Elmevik, Lennart. 2004. Till diskussionen om ett sakralt *al i nordiska ortnamn. In *Namenwelten: Orts- und Personnamen in historischer Sicht*. Edited by Stefan Brink, Lennart Elmevik and Astrid van Nahl. Pp. 38-56. Ergänzungsbände zum Reallexikon der germanischen Altertumskunde 44. Berlin: de Gruyter.

Elmevik, Lennart. 2007. Den fornnordiska gudavärlden speglad i ortnamnen. *Kungl. Vitterhets historie och antikvitetsakademiens årsbok*: 151-64.

Elmevik, Lennart. 2013a. Fsv. Skædhvi. *Namn och bygd* 101: 210-11.

Elmevik, Lennart. 2013b. Svedvi och Nedervi. *Namn och bygd* 101: 212-14.

Eriksen, Anne. 1991. Den Norderhougs mandige qvinde: Noe om heltestatus og kvinnelighet. *Tradisjon* 21: 87-99.

Espeland, Velle, et al. 1997. *Ballader i Norge*. Norsk visearkiv. Accessed June 18, 2014. http://www.visearkivet.no/sider/ballader_i_norge

Etheridge, Christian. 2012. *Understanding Medieval Icelandic Astronomy through the Sources of the Manuscript GKS 1812 4to*. MA Thesis, Aarhus University, Denmark.

Eyrbyggja saga. 1935. Edited by Einar Ól. Sveinsson and Matthías Þórðarson. Íslenzk fornrit 4. Pp. 1-184. Reykjavík: Hið íslenzka fornritafélag.

Fabian, Stephen M. 2001. *Patterns in the Sky: An Introduction to Ethnoastronomy*. Long Grove IL: Waveland Press.

Falk, Hjalmar. 1893. Om Svipdagsmál. *Arkiv för nordisk filologi* 9: 311-62.

Falk, Hjalmar. 1894. Om Svipdagsmál. *Arkiv för nordisk filologi* 10: 26-82.

Falk, Hjalmar. 1924. *Odensheite*. Skrifter, utgitt av Videnskapsselskapet i Kristiania 1924, 10. II. historisk-filologisk klasse. Kristiania: Jacob Dybwad.

Faulkes, Anthony, ed. 1998. *Snorri Sturluson-Edda: Skáldskaparmál*. 2 vols. London: Viking Society for Northern Research.

Faulkes, Anthony, ed. 2005. *Snorri Sturluson-Edda: Prologue and Gylfaginning*. 2nd edition. London: Viking Society for Northern Research.

Faulkes, Anthony, ed. 2007. *Háttatal*. 2nd edition. London: Viking Society for Northern Research.

Faulkes, Anthony, transl. 1987. *Snorri Sturluson-Edda*. The Everyman Library. London: J. M. Dent, 1995.

Faulkes, Anthony, transl. 2012. See Heimir Pálsson, ed. 2012.

Feilberg, Henning F. 1901. Der böser Blick in nordischer Überlieferung. *Zeitschrift des Vereins für Volkskunde* 11: 304-30.

Feist, Sigmund. 1939. *Vergleichendes Wörterbuch der Gotishen Sprache*. 3rd edition. Leiden: Brill.

Fidjestøl, Bjarne. 1999. *The Dating of Eddic Poetry: A Historical Survey and Methodological Investigation*. Edited by Odd Einar Haugen. Bibliotheca Arnamagnæana 41. Copenhagen: Reitzel.

Fjellner, Anders. 2003. *Biejjien baernie. Beaivvi bárdni. Sámi Son of the Sun.* Karasjok: Davvi Girji.

Flateyjarbók: En samling af norske konge-sagaer med indskudte mindre fortællinger om begivenheder i og udenfor Norge samt annaler 1860-8. Edited by Guðbrandur Vigfússon and Carl R. Unger. 3 vols. Christiania: Malling.

Fljótsdæla saga. 1950. In *Austfirðinga sögur.* Edited by Jón Jóhannesson. Pp. 215-296. Íslenzk fornrit 11. Reykjavík: Hið íslenzka bókmenntafélag.

Fornaldar sögur Norðurlanda. 1954. Edited by Guðni Jónsson. 4 vols. Akureyri: Íslendingasagnaútgáfan.

Fóstbræðra saga. 1943. In *Vestfirðinga sögur.* Edited by Björn K. Þorólfsson and Guðni Jónsson. Pp. 121-288. Íslenzk fornrit 6. Reykjavík: Hið íslenzka fornritafélag.

Fredengren, Christina. 2011. Where Wandering Water Gushes: The Depositional Landscape of the Mälaren Valley in the Late Bronze Age and Earliest Iron Age of Scandinavia. *Journal of Wetland Archaeology* 10: 109-35.

Freidel, David, Linda Schele, and Joy Parker. 1993. *Maya Cosmos: Three Thousand Years on the Shaman's Path.* New York: William Morrow and Company, Inc.

Freitag, Barbara. 2004. *Sheela-na-Gigs: Unravelling an Enigma.* London and New York. Routledge.

Friðþjófs saga in frækna. 1954. In *Fornaldar sögur Norðurlanda.* Edited by Guðni Jónsson. 3: 75-104. Akureyri: Íslendingasagnaútgáfa.

Friðþjófs saga. 1893. In *Sagan ock rimorna om Friðþjófr hinn frækni.* Edited by Ludvig Larsson. Pp. 1-61. Samfund til udgivelse af gammel nordisk litteratur 22. Lund: Malmström.

Frog and Jonathan Roper. 2011. Verses *versus* the 'Vanir': Response to Simek's 'Vanir Obituary'. *Retrospective Methods Network Newsletter* 2: 29-37.

Fuglesang, Signe Horn. 2007. Ekphrasis and Surviving Imagery in Viking Scandinavia. *Viking and Medieval Scandinavia* 3: 193-224.

Gibbon, William B. 1972. Asiatic Parallels in North American Star Lore: Milky Way, Pleiades, Orion. *Journal of American Folklore* 85(337): 236-47.

Gísla saga Súrssonar. 1943. Edited by Björn K. Þórólfsson and Guðni Jónsson. Íslenzk fornrit 6. Pp. 1-118. Reykjavík: Hið íslenzka fornritafélag.

Gísli Sigurðsson, ed. 1998. *Eddukvæði.* Reykjavík: Mál og menning.

Giunta, Francesco, and Antonino Grillone, eds. 1991. *Iordanis De Origine actibusque getarum.* Roma: Istituto Palazzo Borromini.

Gjessing, Gutorm. 1943. Hesten i førhistorisk kunst og kultus. *Viking* 7: 5-143.

Glasyrina, Galina, 2003. On Heliopolis in *Yngvars saga víðförla*, Scandinavia and Christian Europe in the Middle Ages. In *Papers of the 12th International Saga Conference*. Edited by Rudolf Simek and Judith Meurer. Pp. 175-78. Bonn.

Glasyrina, Galina. 2002. *Сага об Ингваре Путешественнике.Текст. Перевод. Комментарий. Moscow: Восточная литература.*

Göngu-Hrolfs saga. 1954. In *Fornaldar sögur Norðurlanda*. Edited by Guðni Jónsson. 3: 161-280. Akureyri: Íslendingasagnaútgáfa.

Gößwein, Michael, ed. 2009. *Þorsteins þáttr bæjarmagns: Textausgabe nach der Handschrift AM 510, 4to*. Diss. Erlangen-Nürnberg.

Gräslund, Anne-Sofie. 2004. Dogs in Graves: A Question of Symbolism? In *PECUS: Man and Animal in Antiquity; Proceedings of the Conference at the Swedish Institute in Rome, September 9-12, 2002*. Edited by Barbro Santillo Frizell. Pp. 171-80. Rome: The Swedish Institute in Rome, Projects and Seminars 1.

Gräslund, Bo. 2007. Fimbulvintern, Ragnarök, och klimatkrisen år 536-537 e. Kr. *Saga och Sed* 2007: 93-123.

Grettis saga Ásmundssonar. 1936. Edited by Guðni Jónsson. Íslenzk fornrit 7. Pp. 1-290. Reykjavík: Hið íslenzka fornritafélag.

Grimm, Jacob. 1882. *Teutonic Mythology*. London: George Bell and Sons.

Grímnir: Rit um nafnfræði. 1980-1997. Reykjavík: Örnefnastofnun þjóðminjasafns.

Grímnismál. In *Eddukvæði*. Edited by Gísli Sigurðsson. Pp. 70-83. Reykjavík: Mál og menning.

Grimstad, Kaaren. 1988. Svipdagsmál. In *Dictionary of the Middle Ages*. 11: 524-25. New York: Scribner.

Grundtvig, Svend. 1854. *Danmarks gamle Folkeviser* [=*DgF*]. 2: 238-39 [headnote to *DgF* 70], 2: 239-54 [texts and notes]. Copenhagen: Universitets-Jubilæets Danske Samfund (1966).

Grundtvig, Svend. 1856. *DgF*. 2: 667-73 [Tillæg og Rettelser to Nr. 70].

Grundtvig, Svend. 1858-63. *DgF*. 3: 841-43 [texts F-G and notes].

Grundtvig, Svend, et al. 1933-65. *DgF*. 10: 82-91 [texts Fb-P]. Copenhagen: Universitets-Jubilæets Danske Samfund, 1967.

Gudbrand Vigfusson, and Carl Richard Unger, eds. 1860-8. *Flateyjarbók. En samling af norske konge-sagaer med indskudte mindre fortællinger om begivenheder i og udenfor Norge samt annaler.* 3 vols. Det norske historiske kildeskriftfond skrifter 4. Christiania (Oslo): Malling.

Guðni Jónsson, ed. 1954. *Fornaldar sögur Norðurlanda.* 4 vols. Akureyri: Íslendingasagnaútgáfan.

Guðni Jónsson and Bjarni Vilhjálmsson, ed. 1943-44. *Fornaldar sögur Norðurlanda.* 3 vols. Reykjavík: Bókaútgáfan Forni.

Gunnell, Terry, ed. 2005. *Masks and Mumming in the Nordic Area.* Uppsala: Kungl. Gustav Adolfs Akademien för svensk folkkultur.

Gurshstein, Alexande A. 2005. Did the Pre-Indo-Europeams Influence the Formation of the Western Zodiac? *Journal of Indo-European Studies* 33(1/2): 103-50.

Gylfaginning. See Faulkes 2005.

Haavio, Martti. 1952. *Väinämöinen: Eternal Sage*. Helsinki: Suomalainen Tiedeakatemia, 1991.

Haki Antonsson. 2012. Salvation and Early Saga Writing in Iceland: Aspects of the Works of the Þingeyrar Monks and Their Associates. *Viking and Medieval Scandinavia* 8: 71-140.

Haraway, Donna J. 1991. A Cyborg Manifesto: Science, Technology and Socialist-Feminism in the Late Twentieth Century. In *Simians, Cyborgs and Women: The Reinvention of Nature*. Pp. 149-181. New York: Routledge.

Harðar Saga Grímkelssonar eða Hólmverja saga. 1991. Edited by Þórhallur Vilmundarson og Bjarni Vilhjálmsson. Íslenzk fornrit 13. Pp. 1-97. Reykjavík: Hið íslenzka fornritafélag.

Harris, Joseph. 1985. Eddic Poetry. In *Old Norse-Icelandic Literature: A Critical Guide*. Edited by Carol J. Clover and John Lindow. Pp. 68-156. Islandica 45. Ithaca: Cornell University Press.

Harris, Joseph. 2000. Review of *The Dating of Eddic Poetry* by Bjarne Fidjestøl (1999). *Maal og minne* 2: 213-23.

Harris, Joseph. 2012. Eddische Dichtung und die Ballade. Stimme, Vokalität und Performanz unter besonderer Berücksichtigung von *DgF* 1. In *Balladen-Stimmen: Vokalität als theoretisches und historisches Phänomen*. Edited by Jürg Glauser. Pp. 39-57. Tübingen/Basel: Francke. (= Eddic Poetry and the Ballad: Voice, Vocality, and Performance, with Special Reference to *DgF* 1. In *Child's Children: Ballad Study and its Legacies*. Edited by Joseph Harris and Barbara Hillers. Pp. 155-70. BASIS 7. Trier: WVT, 2012.)

Harris, Joseph. 2013. *Svipdagsmál*: Gender, Genre, and Reconstruction. In *Narration and Hero: Recounting the Deeds of Heroes in Literature and Art of the Early Medieval Period*. Edited by Victor Millet and Heike Sahm. Pp. 403-45. Ergänzungsbände zum Reallexikon der Germanischen Altertumskunde 87. Berlin: de Gruyter.

Hastrup, Kirsten. 1981. Cosmology and Society in Medieval Iceland. *Ethnologia Scandinavica* 1981: 63-78.

Hastrup, Kirsten. 1985. *Culture and History in Medieval Iceland: An Anthropological Analysis of Structure and Change*. Oxford: Oxford University Press.

Hastrup, Kirsten. 1990. *Nature and Policy in Iceland 1400-1800: An Anthropological Analysis of History and Mentality*. Oxford: Oxford University Press.

Háttatal. See Faulkes 2007.

Hautala, Jouko. 1954. Kansanperinteen tähtitaivas. *Tähtitiedettä harrastajille* 3: 95-111.

Hávarðar saga Ísfirðings. 1943. Edited by Björn K. Þórólfsson and Guðni Jónsson. Íslenzk fornrit 6. Pp. 289-358. Reykjavík: Hið íslenzka fornritafélag.

Hedeager, Lotte. 2011. *Iron Age Myth and Materiality: An Archaeology of Scandinavia AD 400-1000*. London: Routledge.

Heide, Eldar. 1997. Fjølsvinnsmål. Ei oversett nøkkelkjelde til nordisk mytologi. MA thesis, Norrøn filologi, Universitetet i Oslo, Norway.

Heimir Pálsson, ed. 1988. *Edda Snorra Sturlusonar*. Reykjavík: Mál og menning.

Heimir Pálsson, ed. 2012. *Snorri Sturluson: The Uppsala Edda: DG 11 4to*. Translated by Anthony Faulkes. London: Viking Society for Northern Research.

Heimskringla 1-3. 1941-1951. Edited by Bjarni Aðalbjarnarson. Íslenzk fornrit 26-28. Reykjavík: Hið íslenzka fornritafélag, 1979.

Heinzle, Joachim. 2003. Von Sage zum Epos. In *'Uns ist alten Mären…': Das Nibelungenlied und seine Welt*. Pp. 20-29. Darmstadt: Wissenschaftliche Buchgesellschaft.

Heizmann, Wilhelm. 1993. Flóamanna saga. In *Medieval Scandinavia: An Encyclopedia*. Edited by Phillip Pulsiano et al. Pp. 199-200. New York: Garland Publishing.

Hellberg, Lars. 1975. Ortnamnen och den forntida sveastaten. In *Inledningar till NORNAs fjärde symposium Ortnamn och samhälle på Hanaholmen den 25.-27.4.1975* [dupl.].

Hellberg, Lars. 1979. Forn-Kalmar. Ortnamnen och stadens förhistoria. In *Kalmar stads historia, 1: Kalmarområdets forntid och stadens äldsta utveckling. Tiden intill 1300-talets mitt*. Edited by Ingrid Hammarström. Pp. 119-66. Kalmar: Kulturnämnden i Kalmar.

Hellberg, Lars. 1984. De finländska Karlabyarna och deras svenska bakgrund. *Svenska Literatursällskapet* 65: 85-106.

Hellberg, Lars. 1986. Hedendomens spår i uppländska ortnamn. *Ortnamnssällskapets i Uppsala årsskrift*: 40-71.

Hellquist, Elof, 1949. *Svensk etymologisk ordbok*. 3rd edition. Lund: Gleerups.

Helm, Karl. 1953. *Altgermanische Religionsgeschichte*. Vol. 2. Heidelberg: C. Winter.

Helm, Karl. 1955. Mythologie auf alten und neuen Wegen. *Beiträge zur geschichte der deutschen Sprache und Literatur* 77: 333-65.

Helskog, Knut. 1988. *Helleristningene i Alta: Spor etter ritualer og dagligliv i Finnmarks forhistorie*. Alta: Alta Museum.

Hermann Pálsson, and Paul Edwards, transl. 1968. *Gautreks Saga and Other Medieval Tales*. New York: New York University Press.

Heusler, Andreas. 1908. *Die gelehrte Urgeschichte im altisländischen Schrifttum.* Abhandlungen der kön. preuss. Akademie der Wissenschaften. Phil.-hist. Klasse Abh. III. Berlin: Verlag der Akademie.

Hildebrand, Hans. 1898-1903. *Sveriges medeltid.* Kulturhistorisk skildring 3. Stockholm : P.A. Norstedt.

Hildebrand, Karl, ed. 1904. *Die Lieder der älteren Edda (Sæmundar Edda).* 2nd revised edition. Edited by Hugo Gering. Paderborn: Ferdinand Schöning.

Höfler, Otto. 1952. Das Opfer im Semnonenhain und die Edda. In *Edda, Skalden, Saga: Festschrift zum 70. Geburtstag von Felix Genzmer.* Edited by Hermann Schneider. Pp. 1-67. Heidelberg: Winter.

Hofmann, Dietrich, 1981. Die *Yngvars saga víðförla* und Oddr munkr inn fróði. *Speculum Norroenum: Norse Studies in Memory of Gabriel Turville-Petre.* Pp. 188-222. Odense: Odense University Press.

Hollander, Lee M., transl. 1962. *The Poetic Edda, with Introduction and Expanatory Notes.* 2nd revised edition. Austin: University of Texas Press.

Holm-Olsen, Ludvig. 1981. *Lys over norrøn kultur: Norrøne studier i Norge.* Oslo: J. W. Cappelens forlag.

Holmbäck, Åke, and Elias Wessén, eds. 1943. *Svenska landskapslagar* 4. *Skånelagen och Gutalagen.* Stockholm: Geber.

Holmberg, Bente. 1986. Den hedenske gud Tyr i danske stednavne. In *Mange bække små: Til John Kousgård Sørensen på tresårsdagen 6.12.1985.* Edited by Vibeke Dalberg and Gillian Fellows-Jensen. Pp. 109-27. Navnestudier udg. af Institut for Navneforskning 27. Copenhagen: Reitzel.

Holtsmark, Anne, and Jón Helgason, eds. 1950. *Snorri Sturluson: Edda; Gylfaginning og Prosafortellingene av Skáldskaparmál.* Copenhagen: Ejnar Munksgaard.

Holtsmark, Anne. 1972. Svipdagsmál. In *Kulturhistorisk leksikon for nordisk middelalder fra vikingetid til reformationstid.* Edited by Johannes Brøndsted, John Danstrup, and Lis Jacobsen. 17: 585-87. Copenhagen: Rosenkilde og Bagger.

Hoskin, Michael, ed. 1997. *The Cambridge Illustrated History of Astronomy.* Cambridge: Cambridge University Press.

Hrólfs saga kraka. 1954. In *Fornaldar sögur Norðurlanda.* Edited by Guðni Jónsson. 1: 1-105. Akureyri: Íslendingasagnaútgáfa.

Íslenzkar þjóðsögur og Æfintýri. 1862. Fyrsta bindi. Safnað hefir Jón Árnason. Leipzig: Að forlagi J. C. Hinrichs's bókaverzlunar.

Jacoby, Carolus. 1885. *Dionysii Halicarnasei Antiquitates Romanorum* I. Leipzig: Teubner.

Jakob Benediktsson, ed. 1968. *Íslendingabók. Landnámabók.* Íslenzk fornrit 1, Parts 1 and 2. Reykjavík: Hið íslenzka fornritafélag, 1986.

Jensen, Hans Jørgen Lundager, and Jens Peter Schjødt. 1994. *Suveræniteten, kampen of frugtbarheden: Georges Dumézil og den indoeuropæiske ideology*. Aarhus: Aarhus Universitetsforlag.

Jesch, Judith. 2009. The Threatening Wave: Norse Poetry and the Scottish Isles. (Unpublished conference paper).

Jón Helgason, ed. 1964 and 1971. *Eddadigte*. 2 vols. Nordisk filologi, serie A: tekster: I: Völuspá. Hávamál, 2nd edition (1964); II: Gudedigte, 3rd edition (1971). Copenhagen: Munksgaard.

Jón Hnefill Aðalsteinsson. 1992. A Piece of Horse-Liver and the Ratification of Law. In *Snorrastefna 25-27 júli 1990*. Edited by Úlfar Bragason. Pp. 81-98. Reykjavík: Stofnun Sigurðar Nordals.

Jón Þorkelsson. 1956. *Þjóðsögur og munnmæli*. 2nd edition. Reykjavík: Bókfellsútgáfan.

Jónas Kristjánsson. 1956. *Eyfirðinga sögur: Víga-Glums saga: Qgmundar þáttr dytts: Þorvalds þáttr tasalda: Svarfdoela saga: Þorleifs þáttr Jarlsskalds: Valla-Ljóts saga: Sneglu-Halla þáttr: Þorgrims þáttr Hallasonar*. Íslenzk fornrit 9. Reykjavík: Hið íslenzka fornritafélag.

Jónas Kristjánsson. 1987. Um Grógaldur og Fjölsvinnsmál. In *Grímsævintýri sögð Grími M. Helgasyni sextugum 2 September 1987*. 2: 13-15. Reykjavík: Stofnun Árnamagnússonar á Islandi.

Jónas Kristjánsson. 1993. *Handritaspegill*. Reykjavík: Hið íslenska bókmenntafélag.

Jóns saga ins Helga. 2003. In *Biskupa sögur* I, part 2. Edited by Sigurgeir Steingrímsson, Ólafur Halldórsson and Peter Foote. Íslenzk fornrit 15. Pp. 173-316. Reykjavík: Hið íslenzka fornritafélag.

Jonsson, Bengt R. 1991a. Oral Literature, Written Literature: The Ballad and Old Norse Genres. In *The Ballad and Oral Literature*. Edited by Joseph Harris. Harvard English Studies 17. Pp. 139-70. Cambridge MA: Harvard University Press.

Jonsson, Bengt R. 1991b. Bråvalla och Lena: Kring balladen SMB 56. *Sumlen 1989*: 49-166. Stockholm: Svensk visarkiv.

Jonsson, Bengt R. 1993a. Bråvalla och Lena: Kring balladen SMB 56: II. *Sumlen 1990-91*: 163-458. Stockholm: Svensk visarkiv.

Jonsson, Bengt R. 1993b. Sir Olav and the Elves: The Position of the Scandinavian Version. In *The Stockholm Ballad Conference 1991*. Edited by Bengt R. Jonsson. Pp. 65-90. Stockholm: Svensk visarkiv, 1993. First published in Arv 48 (1992): 65-90.

Jonsson, Bengt R. 1999. Bråvalla och Lena: Kring balladen SMB 56: III. *Sumlen 1992-1993*: 49-166. Stockholm: Svensk visarkiv.

Jonsson, Bengt R., Svale Solheim, and Eva Danielson. 1978. *The Types of the Scandinavian Medieval Ballad: A Descriptive Catalogue*. In collaboration with Mortan Nolsøe and W. Edson Richmond. Oslo: Universitetsforlaget.

Jonsson, Bengt R., Sven-Bertil Jansson, and Margareta Jersild, eds. 1983. *Sveriges medeltida ballader.* Vol. 1, *Naturmytiska visor (nr 1-36).* Stockholm: Almqvist & Wiksell.

Jungner, Hugo. 1922. *Gudinnan Frigg och Als härad: En studie i Västergötlands religions-, språk- och bebyggelsehistoria.* Dissertation, University of Uppsala.

Justi, Ferdinand. 1864. Ueber das eddische Lied von Fiölsvidr. *Orient und Occident, insbesondere in ihren gegenseitigen Beziehungen: Forschungen und Mitteilungen* 2: 45-74.

Kaalund, Kristian, ed. 1920. *Arne Magnussons private brevveksling.* Copenhagen: Gyldendal.

Kirk, Robert. 1893. *The Secret Commonwealth of Elves, Fauns and Fairies: A Study in Folk-Lore and Psychical Research.* London: David Nutt.

Klingenberg, Heinz. 1999. *Heidnisches Altertum und nordisches Mittelalter: Strukturbildende Perspektiven des Snorri Sturluson.* Freiburg(Breisgau): HochschulVerlag.

Klintberg, Bengt af. 1972. *Svensk folksägner.* Stockholm: Norstedt.

Klintberg, Bengt af. 2010. *The Types of the Swedish Legend.* FF Communications 300. Helsinki: Academica Scientiarum Fennica.

Kock, Ernst A. 1923-44. *Notationes Norrœnæ: anteckningar till Edda och skaldediktning.* Lunds universitets årsskrift, n. s., sec. 1. Lund: Gleerup.

Koeppen, Carl Friedrich. 1837. *Literarische Einleitung in die Nordische Mythologie.* Berlin: Bechtold and Hartje.

Konungs skuggsiá. 1983. Edited by Ludvig Holm-Olsen. 2nd edition. Oslo: Norsk historisk kjeldeskrift-institut.

Kormáks saga. 1939. Edited by Einar Ól. Sveinsson. Íslenzk fornrit 8. Pp. 201-302. Reykjavík: Hið íslenzka fornritafélag.

Kousgård Sørensen, John. 1992. Haupttypen sakraler Ortsnamen Südskandinaviens. In *Der historisch Horizont der Götterbild-Amulette aus der Übergangsepoche von der Spätantike zum Frühmittelalter.* Edited by Karl Hauck. Abhandlungen der Akademie der Wissenschaften in Göttingen. Philol.-Hist. Klasse 3:200. Göttingen: Vandenhoeck und Ruprecht.

Kristni saga. 2003. In *Biskupa sögur.* Edited by Sigurgeir Steingrímsson, Ólafur Halldórsson and Peter Foote. Íslenzk fornrit 15a. Pp. 1-48. Reykjavík: Hið íslenzka fornritafélag.

Kroll, Katrin, and Hugo Steger, eds. 1994. *Mein ganzer Körper ist Gesicht.* Freiburg: Rombach Verlag KG.

Kuhn, Hans. 1978. Philologisches zur altgermanischen Religionsgeschichte. In *Kleine Schriften* IV. Edited by Dietrich Hoffmann. Pp. 223-321. Berlin: De Gruyter.

Kuperjanov, Andres. 2006. Pseudomythological Constellation Maps. *Folklore: Electronic Journal of Folklore* 32: 37-62.

Kusmenko, Jurij. 2006. Jätten Thazi och det samiska elementet i nordisk mytologi. In *Sápmi Y1K: Livet i samernas bosättningsområden för ett tusen år sedan*. Edtied by Andrea Amft and Mikael Svonni. Pp. 11-28. Umeå: Umeå universitet, Sámi dutkan.

Kuusi, Matti, and Pertti Anttonen. 1999. *Kalevalalipas*. Helsinki: Suomalaisen Kirjallisuuden Seura.

Kuusi, Matti, Keith Bosley, and Michael Branch, eds. 1977. *Finnish Folk Poetry: Epic*. Helsinki: Finnish Literature Society.

Kuusi, Matti. 1963. *Suomen kirjallisuus I: Kirjoittamaton kirjallisuus*. Helsinki: Suomalaisen Kirjallisuuden Seura + WSOY.

Kvideland, Reimund, and Sehmsdorf, Henning K., eds. 1988. *Scandinavian Folk Belief and Legend*. Minneapolis: University of Minnesota Press.

Kværndrup, Sigurd. 2006. *Den østnordiske ballade: oral teori og tekstanalyse; Studier i Danmarks gamle Folkeviser*. Copenhagen: Museum Tusculanum.

Læstadius, Lars L. 2002. *Fragments of Lappish Mythology*. Beaverton, Ontario: Aspasia Books.

Landnámabók. 1968. Edited by Jakob Benediktsson. Íslenzk fornrit 1. Pp. 29-397. Reykjavík: Hið íslenzka fornritafélag.

Lange, Wolfgang. 1964. Review of *Edda*... Edited by Gustav Neckel. I: text. 4th edition. Revised by Hans Kuhn, 1962. *Göttingsche Gelehrte Anzeigen* 216 (3-4): 195-211.

Larrington, Carolyne. 2004. 'Undruðusk þá, sem fyrir var': Wonder, Vínland and Mediaeval Travel Narratives. *Medieval Scandinavia* 14: 91-114.

Larsson, Mats G. 1987. Yngvarr's Expedition and the Georgian Chronicle. In *Saga-Book of the Viking Society*: 98-108.

Larsson, Mats G. 1990. *Ett ödesdigert vikingatåg: Ingvar den vittfarnes resa 1036-1041*. Stockholm: Atlantis.

Lassen, Annette. 2011. *Odin på kristent pergament: En teksthistorisk studie*. Copenhagen: Museum Tusculanums Forlag.

Laxdæla saga. 1934. Edited by Einar Ól. Sveinsson. Íslenzk fornrit 5. Pp. 1-248. Reykjavík: Hið íslenzka fornritafélag.

Leach, Edmund. 1972. Anthropological Aspects of Language: Animal Categories and Verbal Abuse. In *Mythology*. Edited by Pierre Maranda. Penguin Modern Sociology Readings. Pp. 39-67. Harmondsworth: Penguin Books Ltd. Reprinted from, *New Directions in the Study of Language*. Edited by E. H. Lenneberg. Pp. 23-63: MIT Press, 1964.

Leach, Edmund. 1976. *Culture and Communication: The Logic by which Symbols are Connected: An Introduction to the Use of Structuralist Analysis in Social Anthropology*. Cambridge: Cambridge University Press.

Leach, Edmund. 1996. *Lévi-Strauss*. Revised and updated by James Laidlaw. 4th edition. London: Fontana.

Lerbom, Jens. 2003. *Mellan två riken: Integration, politisk kultur och förnationella identiteter på Gotland 1500-1700.* Studia historica Lundensia 11. Lund: Nordic Academic Press.

Lévi-Strauss, Claude. 1977-8. *Structural Anthropology.* Translated by Claire Jacobson and Brooke Grundfest Schoepf. Harmondsworth: Penguin.

Liebenberg, Frederik L., ed. 1857-1862. *Oehlenschlägers poetiske Skrifter.* 32 vols. Copenhagen: Selskabet til Udgivelse af Oehlenschlägers skrifter.

Liestøl, Knut. 1915. *Norske trollvisor og Norrøne sogor.* Kristiania: Norlis forlag.

Lindow, John. 1988. Addressing Thor. *Scandinavian Studies* 60: 119-36.

Lindow, John. 1997. *Murder and Vengeance among the Gods: Baldr in Scandinavian Mythology.* FF Communications 262. Helsinki: Suomalainen Tiedeakatemia.

Lindow, John. 2001. *Norse Mythology: A Guide to the Gods, Heroes, Rituals, and Beliefs.* Oxford: Oxford University Press.

Lindow, John. 2012. Stability and Variation in the Myth(s) of Þórr's Battle with Geirrøðr (and his Daughters). Paper presented at the Norse mythology conference at UCLA, April 2012.

Lindow, John. Forthcoming. Euhemerism. In *Vocabulary for the Study of Religion.* Edited by Kocku von Stuckrad and Robert A. Segal. Leiden: Brill.

Lönnrot, Elias. 1963. *The Kalevala or Poems of the Kaleva District.* Cambridge MA: Harvard University Press.

Lönnrot, Elias. 1993. *Valitut teokset 5. Muinaisrunoutta.* Helsinki: Suomalaisen Kirjallisuuden Seura.

Lönnroth, Lars. 1963. Studier i Olaf Tryggvasons saga. *Samlaren* 84: 54-94.

Lönnroth, Lars. 2000. The Baptist and the Saint: Oddr Snorrason's View of the Two King Olavs. In *International Scandinavian and Medieval Studies in Memory of Gerd Wolfgang Weber.* Edited by Michael Dallapiazza et al. Pp. 257-64. Trieste: Edizioni Parnasso

Lönnroth, Lars. 2013. En medeltida fantasyroman. *Axess* # 4(May): 65-66.

Loth, Agnete. 1977. *Fornaldarsagas and Late Medieval Icelandic Romances: AM 586 4to and AM 589 a-f 4to.* Early Icelandic Manuscripts in Facsimile 11. Copenhagen: Rosenkilde and Bagger.

Loumand, Ulla. 2006. The Horse and its Role in Icelandic Burial Practices, Mythology, and Society. In *Old Norse Religion in Long-term Perspectives: Origins, Changes, and Interactions. An International Conference in Lund, Sweden, June 3-7, 2004.* Edited by Anders Andrén, Kristina Jennbert and Catharina Raudvere. Pp. 130-134. Lund: Nordic Academic Press.

Lundberg, Oskar. 1913. Den heliga murgrönan: Till ortnamnet Vrindavi. *Namn och bygd* 1: 49-58.

Lundgreen-Nielsen, Flemming, and Hanne Ruus, eds. 1999. *Svøbt i mår: Dansk Folkevisekultur 1550-1700.* Vol. 1, *Adelskultur og visebøger.* Copenhagen: Reitzel.

Lundgren, Magnus Fredrik. 1878. *Språkliga intyg om hednisk gudatro i Sverige.* Göteborg: Bonniers.

Lundmark, Bo. 1979. *Anders Fjellner: Samernas Homeros och diktningen om Solsönerna.* Umeå: Västerbottens läns hembygdsföreningen.

Lundmark, Bo. 1982. *Bæi'vi Mánno Nástit: Sol- och månkult samt astrala och celesta föreställingar bland samerna.* Umeå: Västerbottens läns hembygdsförening and Västerbottens Museum.

Lundmark, Efraim. 1929. *Kyrkor i Bro ting, Gotland: Konsthistorisk inventarium.* Sveriges kyrkor 31. Stockholm: Svenska Bokhandelscentralen.

Lüning, Hermann, ed. 1859. *Die Edda: Eine sammlung altnordischer götter- und heldenlieder.* Zurich: Meyer & Zeller.

Luuko, Armas. 1964. Kväner. In *Kulturhistoriskt lexikon för nordisk medeltid från vikingatid till reformationstid.* Edited by Ingvar Andersson and John Granlund. 9: 599-602. Malmö: Allhem.

Malkin, Irad. 1998. *The Returns of Odysseus: Colonization and Ethnicity.* Berkeley: University of California Press.

Manovich, Lev 2001. *The Language of New Media.* Cambridge MA: MIT Press.

Marold, Edith. 1988. Skaldendichtung und Mythologie. In *The Seventh International Saga Conference, Spoleto 4-10 sept 1988: Poetry in the Scandinavian Middle Ages.* Pp. 201-213. Spoleto: Reprints Spoleto.

Marold, Edith. 2007. Þórsdrápa. *Reallexikon der germanischen Altertumskunde* Edited by Johannes Hoops, Heinrich Beck, Dieter Geuenich, and Heiko Steuer. 35: 127-34. Berlin: W. de Gruyter.

Marold, Edith. 2008. Uddr und das Pferd: Ein neuer Versuch den Stein von Roes zu deuten. In *Rund um die Meere des Nordens: Festschrift für Hain Rebas.* Edited by Michael Engelbrecht, Ulrike Hanssen-Decker and Daniel Höffker. Pp.189-202. Heide: n. p.

Maurer, Konrad von. 1856. *Die Bekehrung des norwegischen Stammes zum Christenthume, in ihrem geschichtlichen Verlaufe quellenmässig geschildert.* Vol. 2. München: Christian Kaiser.

Mayr-Harting, Henry. 1991. *The Coming of Christianity to Anglo-Saxon England.* 3rd edition. London: Batsford.

McDonald, Marianne. 1996. *Star Myths: Tales of the Constellations.* New York: Michael Friedman Publishing Group, Inc.

McKinnell, John. 1993. Vatnshyrna. In *Medieval Scandinavia: An Encyclopedia.* Edited by Phillip Pulsiano et al. Pp. 689-90. New York: Garland Publishing.

McKinnell, John. 2005. *Meeting the Other in Norse Myth and Legend*. Cambridge: Brewer.

Meineke, Augustus. 1909. *Strabonis Geographica* I. Leipzig: Teubner.

Meissner, Rudolf. 1921. *Die Kenningar der Skalden: Ein Beitrag zur skaldischen Poetik*. Bonn: Schroeder. Reprinted 1984, Hildesheim: Olms.

Meister, Ferdinandus, ed. 1873. *Daretis Phrygii de excidio Troiae historia*. Leipzig: Teubner.

Meller, Harald. 2004. Star Search. *National Geographic* 205(1): 77-87.

Melnikova, Elena. 1976. Ingvar den vittfarnes härfärd till öst och ryssarnas fälttåg mot Bysantion 1043. *Скандинавский сборник* 21: 74-88.

Meulengracht Sørensen, Preben. 1983. *The Unmanly Man: Concepts of Sexual Defamation in Early Northern Society*. Translated by Joan Turville-Petre. The Viking Collection 1. Odense: Odense University Press.

Miettinen, Timo. 2006. Karhukultin juuret uskontoarkeologisen tutkimuksen valossa. In *Karhun kannoilla: In the Footsteps of the Bear*. Edited by Clive Tolley. Pp. 117-26. Turku: Turun yliopisto ja Satakunnan Museo.

Miller, Kiri. 2008. Grove Street Grimm: Grand Theft Auto and Digital Folklore. *Journal of American Folklore* 121(481): 255-285.

Mitchell, Stephen A. 1991. *Heroic Sagas and Ballads*. Ithaca: Cornell University Press.

Mitchell, Stephen A. 2009. Odin, Magic, and a Swedish Trial from 1484. *Scandinavian Studies* 81(3): 263-86.

Mitchell, Stephen A. 2011. *Witchcraft and Magic in the Nordic Middle Ages*. Philadelphia: University of Philadelphia Press.

Moberg, Lennart. 1965. Norrköpingstraktens ortnamn. In *Norrköpings historia* 1. Edited by Björn Helmfrid and Salomon Kraft. Pp. 172-251. Norrköping: Norrköpings stad.

Mogk, Eugen. 1924. Die Überlieferungen von Thors Kampf mit dem Riesen Geirröð. In *Festskrift tillägnad Hugo Pipping på hans sextioårsdag den 5 november 1924*. Pp. 379-88. Skrifter utg. av Svenska litteratursällskapet i Finland 175. Helsinki: Mercators tryckeri.

Mohr, Wolfgang. 1938-39. Entstehungsgeschichte und Heimat der jüngeren Eddalieder südgermanischen Stoffes. *Zeitschrift für deutsches Altertum* 75: 217-80.

Mohr, Wolfgang. 1939-40. Wortschtaz und Motive der jüngeren Eddalieder mit südgermanischem Stoff. *Zeitschrift für deutsches Altertum* 76: 149-217.

Monikander, Anna. 2010. *Våld och vatten: Våtmarkskult vid Skedemosse under järnåldern*. PhD diss., Institutionen för arkeologi och antikens kultur, Stockholms Universitet, Sweden.

Montgomery, James. 2000. Ibn Fādlan and the Rūsiyyah. *Journal of Arabic and Islamic Studies* 3: 1-25. http://www.uib.no/jais/v003ht/03-001-025Montgom1.htm. Last accessed October 9, 2014.

Motz, Lotte. 1975. The King and the Goddess: An Interpretation of the Svipdagsmál. *Arkiv för nordisk filologi* 90: 133-50.

Motz, Lotte. 1993. Svipdagsmál. In *Medieval Scandinavia: An Encyclopedia.* Edited by Phillip Pulsiano et al. Pp. 629. New York: Garland.

Motz, Lotte. 1996. *The King, the Champion, and the Sorcerer: A Study in Germanic Myth.* Studia Medievalia Septentrionalia 1. Vienna: Verlag Fassbaender.

Munch, Peter Andreas. 1840. *Nordens gamle Gude- og Helte-Sagn.* Christiania: Guldberg & Dzwonkowski.

Munch, Peter Andreas. 1852-63. *Det norske folks historie.* 8 vols. Christiania: Chr. Tønsbergs Forlag.

Munch, Peter Andreas. 1922. *Nordens gamle Gude- og Helte-Sagn, efter A. Kjær's bearbeidelse ved Magnus Olsen.* Kristiania: Steensballes boghandel.

Munch, Peter Andreas. 1926. *Norse Mythology: Legends of Gods and Heroes; In the Revision of Magnus Olsen, trans. from the Norwegian by Sigurd Bernhard Hustvedt.* Scandinavian Classics 27. New York: The American-Scandinavian Foundation.

Mundal, Else, ed. 2013. *Dating the Saga: Reviews and Revisions.* Copenhagen: Museum Tusculanum Press.

Myrberg, Nanouschka. 2005. Burning Down the House: Mythological Chaos and World Order on Gotlandic Picture Stones. *Current Swedish Archaeology* 13: 99-119.

Myrberg, Nanouschka. 2008. *Ett eget värde: Gotlands tidigaste myntning, ca 1140-1220.* Stockholm Studies in Archaeology 45. Stockholm: Stockholm University.

Neckel, Gustav, ed. 1914. *Edda: Die Lieder des Codex Regius nebst verwandten Denkmälern. I. Text.* Heidelberg: Winter.

Neckel, Gustav, ed. 1983. *Edda: Die Lieder des Codex Regius.* Revised Hans Kuhn. 5th edition. Heidelberg: Winter.

Nilsson, Catharina. 1995. Fången på fortet? *Gotländskt arkiv* 1995: 253-254.

Noreen, Erik. 1914. Quadhowi, nuvarande Kåvö i Närke. *Namn och bygd* 2: 121-26.

Ogier, James. 2002. Eddic Constellations. Paper presented at the International Medieval Congress, Western Michigan University, Kalamazoo, Michigan, May 3.

Ogier, James. Eddic Constellations. Accessed June 18, 2014. http://www.roanoke.edu/forlang/ogier/EddicConstellations.htm.

Ogier, James. 2011. Islands and Skylands: An Eddic Geography. In *Islands and Cities in Medieval Myth, Literature, and History.* Edited by Andrea

Grafetstätter, Sieglinde Hartmann, and James Ogier. Pp. 9-19. Beihefte zur Mediaevistik 14. Frankfurt: Peter Lang.

Ogier, James. Misinterpretatio Romana et Interpretatio Germanica Planetaria. Unpublished paper from SASS-conference April 30, 2011.

Ohmae, Kenichi 1995. Letter from Japan. *Harvard Business Review* 73(3): 154-163.

Öhrman, Roger. 1983. *Slite förr i tiden.* Karlstad: Press Grafica/Press förlag.

Olrik, Axel. 1939. *A Book of Danish Ballads.* Translated by E. M. Smith-Dampier. Princeton: Princeton University Press; New York: American-Scandinavian Foundation. [= *Danske folkeviser i udvalg ved A.O. under medvirkning af Ida Falbe-Hansen. Første samling.* 2nd edition. Copenhagen and Kristiania: Gyldendal, 1908]

Olsen, Magnus. 1905. *Det gamle norske ønavn Njarðarlǫg.* Christiania videnskabs-selskabs forhandlinger for 1905:5. Christiania: J. Dybwad.

Olsen, Magnus. 1908. *Hærnavi: En gammel svensk og norsk gudinde.* Christiania videnskabs-selskabs forhandlinger for 1908. Christiania.

Olsen, Magnus. 1915. *Hedenske kultminder i norske stedsnavne* 1. Videnskapsselskapets Skrifter II. Hist.-Filos. Klasse 1914:4. Kristiania.

Olsen, Magnus. 1926. *Ættegård og helligdom: Norske stedsnavne sosialt og religionshistorisk belyst.* Institutt for sammenlignende kulturforskning A:9a. Oslo: Aschehoug.

Olsen, Magnus. 1928. *Farms and Fanes of Ancient Norway: The Place-names of a Country Discussed in Their Bearings on Social and Religious History.* Instituttet for sammenlignende kulturforskning. Serie A: Forelesninger 9. Oslo: Aschehoug.

Peel, Christine, ed. 1999. *Guta saga: The History of the Gotlanders.* London: Viking Society for Northern Research.

Pentikäinen, Juha. 1989. *Kalevala Mythology.* Bloomington: Indiana University Press.

Pentikäinen, Juha. 1995. *Saamelaiset: Pohjoisen kansan mytologia.* Helsinki: Suomalaisen Kirjallisuuden Seura.

Pentikäinen, Juha. 2005. *Karhun kannoilla: Metsänpitäjä ja mies.* Helsinki: Etnika.

Pentikäinen, Juha. 2007. *Golden King of the Forest: The Lore of the Northern Bear.* Helsinki: Etnika.

Perkins, Richard. 2001. *Thor the Wind-Raiser and the Eyrarland Image.* London: Viking Society for Northern Research.

Petersen, Henry. 1876. *Om nordboernes gudedyrkelse og gudetro i hedenold: En antikvarisk undersøgelse.* Copenhagen: Reitzel.

Philippson, Ernst A. 1953. *Die Genealogie der Götter in germanischer Religion, Mythologie und Theologie.* Urbana: University of Illinois Press.

Piludu, Vesa M. 2006. Songs and Rituals of the Bear Hunt in Karelia and Savo. In *Karhun kannoilla: In the Footsteps of the Bear.* Edited by Clive Tolley. Pp. 231-42. Turku: Turun yliopisto ja Satakunnan Museo.

Price, Neil S. 2002. *The Viking Way: Religion and War in Iron Age Scandinavia.* Aun 31 Uppsala: Department of Archaeology and Ancient History.

Price, Neil S. 2008. Dying and the Dead: Viking Age Mortuary Behaviour. In *The Viking World.* Edited by Stefan Brink in collaboration with Neil S. Price. Pp. 257-73. London: Routledge.

Puhvel, Jaan. 1955. Vedic á's'vamedha- and Gaulish IIPOMIIDVOS. *Language* 31: 353-4.

Puhvel, Jaan. 1987. Baltic and Slavic Myth. In *Comparative Mythology.* Pp. 222-40. Baltimore: The Johns Hopkins University Press.

Quinn, Judy. 2006. The Gendering of Death in Eddic Cosmology. In *Old Norse Religion in Long-term Perspectives: Origins, Changes, Interactions.* Edited by Anders Andrén, Kristina Jennbert, and Catherina Raudvere. Pp. 54-57. Vägar till Midgård 8. Lund: Nordic Academic Press.

Qviström, Linda, 1995. *Medeltida stenhus på Gotlands landsbygd.* Lund: Seminar paper, Department of Archaeology, University of Lund.

Rafn, Carl Christian, Þorgeir Guðmundsson and Rasmus Rask, ed. 1827. *Saga Ólafs konungs Tryggvasonar.* Vol. 3, *Niðrlag sögunnar með tilheyrandi þáttum.* Copenhagen: Det nordiske oldskriftsselskab.

Ramus, Jonas. 1693. *Nori Regnum: Hoc est Norvegia antiqva et ethnica, sive historiae Norvegicae prima initia, a primo Norvegiae Rege, Noro, usqve ad Haraldum Harfagerum.* Christiania: Wilhelm Wedemann.

Ramus, Jonas. 1702. *Ulysses et Otinus Unus & idem Sive Disqvisitio Historica & Geographica, qvâ, ex collatis inter se Odyssea Homeri, & Edda Island. Homerizante, Othini fraudes deteguntur, ac detractâ larva in lucem protrahitur Ulysses.* Copenhagen: Johan Jacob Bornheinrich.

Rebourcet, Gabriel. 2006. The Bear Cult in Finno-Ugrian Folk Poetry and in the *Kalevala.* In *Karhun kannoilla: In the Footsteps of the Bear.* Edited by Clive Tolley. Pp. 203-18. Turku: Turun yliopisto ja Satakunnan Museo.

Reykdæla saga ok Víga-Skúta. 1940. Edited by Björn Sigfússon. Íslenzk fornrit 1. Pp. 149-243. Reykjavík: Hið íslenzka fornritafélag.

Rives, James B. 1999. *Tacitus: Germania, translated with introduction and commentary.* Oxford: Clarendon.

Robinson, Peter M. W. 1989a. The Collation and Textual Criticism of Icelandic Manuscripts (1): Collation. *Literary and Linguistic Computing* 4(2): 99-105.

Robinson, Peter M. W. 1989b. The Collation and Textual Criticism of Icelandic Manuscripts (2): Textual Criticism. *Literary and Linguistic Computing* 4(3): 174-81

Robinson, Peter M. W. 1991. *An Edition of Svipdagsmál*. PhD diss., Oxford University.

Robinson, Peter M. W. 1994. Collate: A Program for Interactive Collation of Large Textual Traditions. In *Research in Humanities Computing* 3. Edited by Susan Hockey and Nancy Ide. Oxford: Oxford University Press.

Robinson, Peter M. W. and Robert J. O'Hara. 1996. Cladistic Analysis of an Old Norse Manuscript Tradition. *Research in Humanities Computing* 4: 115-37.

Roesdahl, Else. 1978. Vognen og vikingerne. *Skalk* 4: 9-14.

Rupp, Theophil. 1871. Zur deutung von Fiölsvinnsmâl. *Germania* 16: 50-54.

Rydving, Håkan. 1992. The Names of the Saami Thunder-God in the Light of Dialect Geography. *Readings in Saami History, Culture and Language III*. Edited by Roger Kvist. Pp: 25-40. Umeå: University of Umeå.

Sahlgren, Jöran. 1923a. Är mytosofien en vetenskap? *Vetenskaps-societeten i Lund Årsbok*: 27-36.

Sahlgren, Jöran. 1923b. Nordiska ortnamn i språklig och saklig belysning 6: Oäkta vi-namn. *Namn och bygd* 11: 110-34.

Sahlgren, Jöran. 1950. Hednisk gudalära och nordiska ortnamn: Kritiska inlägg. *Namn och bygd* 38: 1-37.

Sakrale navne. 1992. In *Rapport fra NORNAs sekstende symposium i Gilleleje 30.11.-2.12.1990*. Edited by Gillian Fellows-Jensen and Bente Holmberg. Norna-rapporter 48. Uppsala: Nornaförlaget.

Salen, Katie and Eric Zimmerman. 2004. *Rules of Play: Game Design Fundamentals*. Cambridge MA: MIT Press.

Sammallahti, Pekka. 2012. Nástegovat. *Sámis* 11: 24-28.

Sandnes, Jørn. 1992. Haupttypen sakraler Ortsnamen Südskandinaviens. In *Der historisch Horizont der Götterbild-Amulette aus der Übergangsepoche von der Spätantike zum Frühmittelalter*. Pp. 228-40. Edited by Karl Hauck. Abhandlungen der Akademie der Wissenschaften in Göttingen. Philol.-Hist. Klasse 3:200. Göttingen: Vandenhoeck und Ruprecht.

Santillana, Giorgio de, and Hertha von Dechend. 1994. *Die Mühle des Hamlet: ein Essay über Mythos und das Gerüst der Zeit*. 2nd exp. edition. Wien: Springer-Verlag.

Sauvé, James L. 1970. The Divine Victim: Aspects of Human Sacrifice in Viking Scandinavia and Vedic India. In *Myth and Law among the Indo-Europeans: Studies in Indo-European Comparative Mythology*. Edited by Jaan Puhvel. Pp. 173-192. Berkeley: University of California Press.

Schjødt, Jens Peter. 1991. Relationen mellem aser og vaner og dens ideologiske funktioner. In *Nordisk Hedendom: Et Symposium*. Edited by Gro Steinsland et al. Pp. 303-19. Odense: Odense Universitetsforlag.

Schjødt, Jens Peter. 2003. *Initiation, liminalitet og tilegnelse af numinøs viden. En undersøgelse af strukutr og symbolik i førkristen nordisk religion*. Århus: Det Teologiske Fakultet.

Schjødt, Jens Peter. 2007. Ibn Fadlan's Account of a Rus Funeral: To What Degree Does It Reflect Nordic Myths? In *Reflections on Old Norse Myths*. Edited by Pernille Herrmann et al. Pp. 133-48. Turnhout: Brepols.

Schjødt, Jens Peter. 2008. *Initiation Between Two Worlds: Structure and Symbolism in Pre-Christian Scandinavian Religion*. Translated by Victor Hansen. The Viking Collection 17. Odense: University Press of Southern Denmark.

Schjødt, Jens Peter. 2009. Diversity and Its Consequences for the Study of Old Norse Religion: What Is It We Are Trying to Reconstruct? In *Between Paganism and Christianity in the North*. Edited by Leszek P. Slupecki and Jakup Morawiec. Pp. 9-22. Rzeszow: Wydawnichtwo Universytetu Rzeszowskiego.

Schjødt, Jens Peter. 2012a. Wilderness, Liminality, and the Other in Old Norse Myth and Cosmology. In *Wilderness in Mythology and Religion: Approaching Religious Spatialities, Cosmologies, and Ideas of Wild Nature*. Edited by Laura Feldt. Pp. 183-204. Berlin: Walter de Gruyter.

Schjødt, Jens Peter. 2012b. Reflections on Aims and Methods in the Study of Old Norse Religion. In *More than Mythology: Narratives, Ritual Practices and Regional Distribution in Pre-Christian Scandinavian Religions*. Edited by Catharina Raudvere and Jens Peter Schjødt. Pp. 263-287. Lund: Nordic Academic Press.

Schjødt, Jens Peter. 2012c. Óðinn, Þórr, and Freyr: Functions and Relations. In *News from Other Worlds: Studies in Nordic Folklore, Mythology and Culture in Honor of John F. Lindow*. Edited by Merrill Kaplan and Timothy R. Tangherlini. Pp. 61-91. Berkeley: North Pinehurst Press.

Schjødt, Jens Peter. 2013. The Notions of Model, Discourse, and Semantic Center as Tools for the (Re)Construction of Old Norse Religion. *Retrospective Methods Network Newsletter* 6: 6-15.

Schmeidler, Bernhard, ed. 1917. *Gesta Hammaburgensis ecclesiæ pontificum*. Scriptores rerum Germanicarum, 3rd edition. Hanover: Hahnsche.

Schmidt, Leopold. 1953. Die volkstümlichen Grundlagen der Gebärdensprache. In *Beiträge zur sprachlichen Volksüberlieferung*. Pp. 233-49. Veröffentlichungen der Kommission für Volkskunde 2. Berlin: Deutsche Akademie der Wissenschaften zu Berlin.

Schmitt, Rüdiger. 1967. *Dichtung und Dichtersprache in indogermanischer Zeit*. Wiesbaden: Harrassowitz.

Schröder, Franz Rolf. 1954. Eine indogermanische Liedform: Das Aufreihlied. *Germanisch-Romanische Monatsschrift* 35: 179-85.

Schröder, Franz Rolf. 1966. Svipdagsmál. *Germanisch-Romanische Monatsschrift* 47, N.F. 16: 113-19.

Selin, Helaine, ed. 2000. *Astronomy across Cultures: The History of Non-Western Astronomy*. Dordrecht: Kluwer Academic Publishers.

Shaw, Philip A. 2007. The Origins of the Theophoric Week in the Germanic Languages. *Early Medieval Europe* 15(4): 386-401.

Shepard, Jonathan. 1984-85. Yngvarr's Expedition East and a Russian Inscribed Stone Cross. *Saga-Book of the Viking Society* 21: 222-92.

Siikala, Anna-Leena. 2002. *Mythic Images and Shamanism: A Perspective on Kalevala Poetry*. Helsinki: Suomalainen Tiedeakatemia.

Sijmons, Barend and Hugo Gering. 1903-31. *Die Lieder der Edda*. 3 vols. Halle: Waisenhaus.

Simek, Rudolf. 2010. The Vanir: An Obituary. *Retrospective Methods Network Newsletter* 1: 10-19.

Simpson, Jacqueline. 1966. Otherworld Adventures in an Icelandic Saga. *Folklore* 77: 1-20.

Skáldskaparmál. See Faulkes 1998.

Skj = Finnur Jónsson, ed. 1908-15. *Den norsk-islandske skjaldedigtning*. Vols. A 1-2 and B 1-2. Copenhagen: Rosenkilde & Bagger, 1967 (A) and 1973 (B).

SkP I = Whaley, Diana, ed. 2012. *Poetry from the Kings' Sagas 1*. 2 vols. Skaldic Poetry of the Scandinavian Middle Ages 1. Turnhout: Brepols

SkP II = Gade, Kari Ellen, ed. 2009. *Poetry from the Kings' Sagas 2*. 2 vols. Skaldic Poetry of the Scandinavian Middle Ages 2. Turnhout: Brepols.

Snædal, Thorgunn. 2002. *Medan världen vakar: Studier i de gotländska runinskrifternas språk och kronologi*. Runrön 16. Uppsala: Institutionen för nordiska språk.

Sneglu-Halla þáttr. 1956. Edited by Jónas Kristjánsson. Íslenzk fornrit 9. Pp. 263-295. Reykjavík: Hið íslenzka fornritafélag.

Snyder, George Sergeant. 1984. *Maps of the Heavens*. New York: Abbeville Press.

Solheim, Svale. 1956. Horse-fight and Horse-race in Norse Tradition. *Studia Norvegica* 3: 1-173.

Solmsen, Friedrich, Reinhold Merkelbach, and Martin L. West, eds. 1983. *Hesiodi Theogonia: Opera et dies; Scutum; Editio altera cum appendice nova fragmentorum*. Oxford: Clarendon.

Solmsen, Friedrich. 1986. Aeneas founded Rome with Odysseus. *Harvard Studies in Classical Philology* 90: 93-110.

Sommarström, Bo. 1991. The Saami Shaman's Drum and the Star Horizons. In *The Saami Shaman Drum: Based on Papers Read at the Symposium on the Saami Shaman Drum, Held at Åbo, Finland, on the 19th-20th of August 1988*. Edited by Tore Ahlbäck and Jan Bergman. Pp. 136-68. Stockholm: Almqvist & Wiksell.

Steenstrup, Johannes C. H. R. 1891. *The Medieval Popular Ballad*. Translated by Edward G. Cox. Seattle: University of Washington Press, 1968.

Steenstrup, Johannes C. H. R. 1896. Nogle Undersøgelser om Guders Navne i de nordiske Stedsnavne. *Historisk Tidsskrift* 6 (Række 6): 353-87.

Sten, Sabine, and Maria Vretemark. 1988. Storgravsprojektet: osteologiska analyser av yngre järnålderns benrika brandgraver. *Fornvännen* 83: 145-156.

Steuer, Heiko. 2003. Pferdegräber. In *Reallexikon der germanischen Altertumskunde*. 2nd revised edition. Edited by Kurt Ranke et al. 23: 50-96.

Stoppa, Felice. Atlas Coelistis. Accessed August 15, 2013. http://www.atlascoelestis.com/

Ström, Folke. 1974. *Níð, ergi and Old Norse Moral Attitudes*. Dorothea Coke Memorial Lecture in Northern Studies 6. London: Viking Society for Northern Research.

Strömbäck, Dag. 2000. *Sejd och andra studier i nordisk själsuppfattning*. Skrifter utgivna av Kungl. Gustav Adolfs akademien 72. Hedemora: Kungl. Gustav Adolfs Akademien för Svensk Folkkultur, Gidlunds förlag. Originally published 1935.

Suhm, Peter Frederik. 1771. *Om Odin og den hedniske gudelære og gudstieneste udi Norden*. Copenhagen: Brødrene Berling.

Sundkvist, Anneli. 2001. *Hästarnas land: Aristokratisk hästhållning och ridkonst i Svealands yngre järnålder*. Uppsala: Societas Archaeologia Upsaliensis.

Sutton-Smith, Brian 2001. *The Ambiguity of Play*. Cambridge MA: Harvard University Press.

Svonni, Mikael. 2006. Legenden om Riihmagállis—Mannen från Rávttasjávri" *Grenzgänger. Festschrift zum 65. Geburtstag von Jurij Kosmenko*. Edited by Antje Hornscheidt, Kristina Kotcheva, Tomas Milosch and Michael Riessler. Pp. 315-29. Berlin: Nord-Europa Institute.

Særheim, Inge. 2012. Sakrale stadnamn. *Namn och bygd* 100: 181-200.

Sævar Helgi Bragason et al. Stjörnufræðivefinn. Accessed September 3, 2009. http://www.stjornufraedi.is/stjornuskodun/naturvaldi.

Sævar Helgi Bragason et al. Stjörnumerkin. Accessed September 3, 2009. http://www.stjornufraedi.is/stjornuskodun/stjornumerkin.

Sørensen, Preben Meulengracht. 1991. Om eddadigtenes alder. In *Nordisk Hedendom: Et Symposium*. Edited by Gro Steinsland et al. Pp. 217-28. Odense: Odense Universitetsforlag.

Thomson, Robert W., transl. 1978. *Moses Khorenats'i: History of the Armenians*: Cambridge MA: Harvard University Press.

Thordeman, Bengt. 1944. *Invasion på Gotland 1361: Dikt eller verklighet*. Stockholm: Gebers.

Tolkien, Christopher, ed. and transl. 1960. *The Saga of King Heidrek the Wise*. London: Nelson.

Tolley, Clive. 2009. *Shamanism in Norse Myth and Magic*. 2 vols. FF Communications, 296-7. Helsinki: Academica Scientiarum Fennica.

Tolley, Clive. 2011. In Defence of the Vanir. *The Retrospective Methods Network Newsletter* 2: 20-8

Tschan, Francis J., ed. and transl. 1959. *The History of the Archbishops of Hamburg-Bremen*. New York: Columbia University Press.

Turi, Johan. 2010. *Muitalus sámiid birra*. Karasjok: ČálliidLágádus.

Turi, Johan. 2012. *An Account of the Sámi*. Chicago: Nordic Studies Press.

Turner, Victor 1982. *From Ritual to Theatre: The Human Seriousness of Play*. New York: Performing Arts Journal Publications.

Turville-Petre, E. O. Gabriel. 1964. *Myth and Religion of the North: The Religion of Ancient Scandinavia*. New York: Holt, Rinehart and Winston.

Valk, Ülo. 2000. *Ex Ovo Omnia:* Where Does the Balto-Finnic Cosmogony Originate? The Etiology of an Etiology. *Oral Tradition* 15(1): 145-58.

Valonen, Niilo. 1984. Ancient Folk Poetry in Eastern Karelian Petroglyphs. *Ethnologia Fennica* 1982/83: 9-48.

van Gennep, Arnold. 1960. *Rites of Passage*. Translated by Monika B. Vizedom. London: Routledge and Kegan Paul.

van Gent, Robert Harry. Historical Celestial Atlases on the World Wide Web. Accessed August 15, 2013. http://www.phys.uu.nl/~vgent/celestia/celestia.htm.

Vatnsdœla saga. 1939. Edited by Einar Ól. Sveinsson. Íslenzk fornrit 8. Pp. 1-131. Reykjavík: Hið íslenzka fornritafélag.

Vésteinn Ólason. 1990. The West-Nordic Hero in Saga and Ballad: Marginal Notes. In *Inte bara visor: Studier kring folklig diktning och musik tillägnade Bengt R. Jonsson den 19 mars 1990*. Edited by Eva Danielson et al. Pp. 275-86. Stockholm: Svenskt visarkiv.

Vésteinn Ólason. 1991. The Literary Backgrounds of the Scandinavian Ballad. In *The Ballad and Oral Literature*. Edited by Joseph Harris. Pp. 116-38. Harvard English Studies 17. Cambridge MA: Harvard University Press.

Viðar Hreinsson, ed. 1997. Star-Oddi's Dream. Translated by Marvin Taylor. In *The Complete Sagas of Icelanders* 2: 448-59. Reykjavík: Leifur Eiríksson Publishing.

Víglunda saga. 1959. Edited by Jóhannes Halldórsson. In Íslenzk fornrit 14. Pp. 61-116. Reykjavík: Hið íslenzka fornritafélag.

Vikstrand, Per. 2001. *Gudarnas platser: Förkristna sakrala ortnamn i Mälarlandskapen*. Acta Academiae Regiae Gustavi Adolphi 77. Uppsala: Kungl. Gustav Adolfs akademi.

Vinci, Felice. 1995. *Omero nel Baltico: Saggio sulla geografia omerica*. Rome: Fratelli Palombi.

Vries, Jan de. 1934. Om Eddaens Visdomsdigtning. *Arkiv för nordisk filologi* 50: 1-59.

Vries, Jan de. 1956-57. *Altgermanische Religionsgeschichte I-II*. Berlin: Walter de Gruyter.

Vries, Jan de. 1964-67. *Altnordische Literaturgeschichte*. 2 vols. Berlin: de Gruyter.

Vågslid, Eivind. 1963-84. *Stadnamntydingar*. 4 vols. Oslo: J.G. Tanum.

Waitz, Georg, ed. 1878. *Scriptores rerum langobardicarum et Italicarum saec. VI-IX*. MGH SS rer. Lang. 1. Hannover: Hahn.

Wallace-Hadrill, John M. 1988. *Bede's Ecclesiastical History of the English People: A Historical Commentary*. Oxford: Clarendon Press.

Wardrip-Fruin, Noah, and Pat Harrigan, eds. 2003. *First Person: New Media as Story, Performance, and Game*. Cambridge MA: MIT Press.

Wellendorf, Jonas. 2013. Zoroaster, Saturn and Óðinn: The Loss of Language and the Rise of Idolatry. In *The Performance of Christian and Pagan Storyworlds: Uncanonical Chapters of the History of Nordic Medieval Literature*. Edited by Tuomas Lehtonen and Lars Boje Mortensen. Pp. 243-270. Turnhout: Brepols.

Wessén, Elias. 1921-22. *Forntida gudsdyrkan i Östergötland*. 2 vols. Meddelanden från Östergötlands fornminnes- och museiförening. Linköping.

Wessén, Elias. 1923. Minnen av forntida gudsdyrkan i Mellan-Sveriges ortnamn. *Studier i nordisk filologi* 14: 1-26.

Wessén, Elias. 1924. *Studier till Sveriges hedna mytologi och fornhistoria*. Uppsala universitets årsskrift 1924. Filosofi, språkvetenskap och historiska vetenskaper 6. Uppsala.

West, Martin L. 2013. *The Epic Cycle: A Commentary on the Lost Troy Epics*. Oxford: Oxford University Press.

Westholm, Gun. 2007. *Visby 1361: Invasionen*. Stockholm: Prisma.

Whaley, Diana, ed. and transl. 2009. Þjóðólfr Árnason. In *SkP II*, part 1. Pp. 177-281. Turnhout: Brepols.

Whitelock, Dorothy, ed. 1979. *English Historical Documents, Volume I, c. 500-1042*. 2nd edition. London: Eyre Methuen.

Winterbottom, Michael, and Robert Maxwell Ogilvie, eds. 1975. De origine et sitv Germanorvm. In *Cornelii Taciti Opera Minora*. Pp. 35-62. Oxford: Clarendon.

Witzel, Michael. 2012. *The Origins of the World's Mythologies*. Oxford: Oxford University Press.

Wolf, Kordula. 2007. *Troja: Metamorphosen eines Mythos. Französische, englische und italienische Überlieferungen des 12. Jahrhunderts im Vergleich*. Berlin: Akademie Verlag.

Yngvars saga víðfǫrla. 1912. Edited by Emil Olsson. Copenhagen: Samfund til Udgivelse af gammel nordisk Litteratur.

Yrwing, Hugo. 1978. *Gotlands medeltid.* Visby: Gotlandskonst.

Þórhallur Vilmundarson. 1992. Kultnavn eller ej? Sakrale navne. In *Rapport fra NORNAs sekstende symposium i Gilleleje 30.11.-2.12.1990.* Edited by Gillian Fellows-Jensen and Bente Holmberg. Pp. 35-53. Norna-rapporter 48. Uppsala: Nornaförlaget 1992.

Þorleifs þáttr jarlsskálds. 1956. Edited by Jónas Kristjánsson. Íslenzk fornrit 9. Pp. 213-29. Reykjavík: Hið íslenzka fornritafélag.

Þorleifur Jónsson. 1904. *Fjörutíu Íslendinga-þættir.* Reykjavík: Kostnaðarmaður Sigurður Kristjánsson.

Þorskfirðinga saga. 1991. Edited by Þórhallur Vilmundarson and Bjarni Vilhjálmsson. Íslenzk fornrit 13. Pp. 173-227. Reykjavík: Hið íslenzka fornritafélag.

Þorsteinn Vilhjálmsson. 1986-87. *Heimsmynd á hverfanda hveli* I-II. Reykjavík: Mál og menning.

Þorsteins saga Víkingssonar. 1954. In *Fornaldar sögur Norðurlanda.* Edited by Guðni Jónsson. 4: 1-73. Akureyri: Íslendingasagnaútgáfa.

Ǫlkofra þáttr. 1950. In *Austfirðinga sögur.* Edited by Jón Jóhannesson. Íslenzk fornrit 11. Pp. 83-94. Reykjavík: Hið íslenzka fornritafélag.

Index

www.ingramcontent.com/pod-product-compliance
Lightning Source LLC
Chambersburg PA
CBHW030414100426
42812CB00028B/2950/J

* 9 7 8 0 6 9 2 3 2 8 8 6 6 *